North American Game Birds and Mammals

North American Game Birds and Mammals

A. Starker Leopold
Ralph J. Gutiérrez
Michael T. Bronson

Illustrated by Gene M. Christman

CHARLES SCRIBNER'S SONS NEW YORK

The authors wish to thank the Museum of Vertebrate Zoology and the Department of Forestry and Resource Management at the University of California, Berkeley, and the Department of Wildlife Management at Humboldt State University, Arcata, California, who hosted this endeavor.

Library of Congress Cataloging in Publication Data

Leopold, A. Starker (Aldo Starker), 1913–
North American game birds and mammals.

Bibliography: p.
Includes index.
1. Game and game-birds—North America.
2. Birds—North America. 3. Mammals—North America.
I. Gutiérrez, Ralph J. II. Bronson, Michael T.
III. Christman, Gene M. IV. Title.
QL151.L46 599.097 81.9268
ISBN 0-684-17270-4 AACR2

This book published simultaneously in the United States of America and in Canada—Copyright under the Berne Convention.

1 3 5 7 9 11 13 15 17 19 Q/C 20 18 16 14 12 10 8 6 4 2

Printed in the United States of America

Contents

Introduction

When ancient peoples entered North America via the Bering land bridge, they found a rich variety of animal life that offered them the necessities of survival—food, clothing, tools, and shelter. Subsequently, many species—such as mammoths, saber-toothed tigers, giant bison, and others—disappeared from North America. The cause of their extinction might have been climatic change or perhaps hunting pressure from the expanding human population.

There still persisted, however, a considerable variety of birds and mammals that provided continuing sustenance for the aborigines and later for settlers who came from Europe. As modern society on this continent developed, some groups of animals remained important as game, although the emphasis shifted from subsistence values to recreational values.

The purpose of this book is to present—in concise, summarized form—the latest information available on the habits, distribution, and status of important North American game species. The species here considered are those *currently* or *formerly* exploited for food, sport, or profit, as game animals or fur bearers. It is hoped that the book will prove useful to anyone interested in wild game, whether he or she is a sportsman, birder, naturalist, scientist, wildlife biologist, or wildlife-management student.

Species are grouped by families and orders, but the sequence of listing the orders is different from standard taxonomic arrangement. The sequence used in this book has been arrived at by thorough testing over a period of 35 years as the most effective order of presenting this material to interested but inexperienced people. This arrangement, incidentally, is the one actually used in the laboratory of a course offered at the University of California, Berkeley, and entitled "American Game Birds and Mammals."

In conventional taxonomic sequence, for instance, waterfowl would be listed first among the birds. Experience in the laboratory has shown, though, that students have considerable difficulty identifying ducks. The same difficulty has been experienced by many wildlife agencies when teaching waterfowl identification to hunters. So in this book the coverage of waterfowl is deferred until more readily identifiable groups such as rails, doves, and galliforms have been covered. Similarly, the sequence of mammals is somewhat varied from traditional taxonomic arrangement in order to stimulate interest and facilitate learning.

The illustrations by Gene Christman were drawn to emphasize those diagnostic characters that are most useful in differentiating species. Among the mammals, for example, skulls are illustrated for one species in each family.

Philosophical Perspectives

Against a background of brilliant autumn colors, a pointing dog eagerly quarters a wooded hillside. Suddenly, the dog skids into a solid point. The hunter moves in from above and behind the dog, thoughts of "Woodcock? Grouse?" racing through his mind as he relives past experiences in this same covert. With roaring wings, a grouse bursts from behind a log and flies low and downhill. Instantly, the gun is moving and almost to the shoulder. Then, just as quickly, it stops and slowly descends. This wily old bird's maneuvering has kept the dog in the hunter's line of fire. Such are the vagaries of grouse hunting. Perhaps the next bird will offer a shot.

This type of outdoor experience involving a hunter, fine dogs, and a fall day provides the basis for the feelings about which sportsmen talk and write. But never can the true emotional tie of love for the wildlife be fully portrayed. Indeed, expressions of affection and respect for game by hunters can sound like hypocrisy to some nonhunters. It is clear, however, that as society evolves away from a dependence on game species for survival, the bond with game will become more psychological than biological. It is not our intention to discuss hunting except to acknowledge that a great many men and women in the United States and Canada hunt, and to observe that as society changes, more will be demanded of hunters to demonstrate high ethical standards in hunting. The development of respect for wildlife often follows close contact with and knowledge of wildlife. The authors hope this book will introduce a great many hunters and nonhunters alike to the lives of game animals.

The rewards of a beautiful fall day afield are by no means the exclusive prerogative of hunters. As many or more people appreciate watching wildlife, with no intent of capturing or killing it. Birders derive enormous pleasure from visiting a waterfowl refuge during a peak period of migration, seeing and hearing the hordes of ducks, geese, shorebirds, and marsh birds there assembled. On a typical Sunday in late October, thousands of people park along the roads through Horicon Marsh in Wisconsin to watch the ebb and flow of Canada geese. On Gray Lodge Waterfowl Area in California, birders greatly outnumber the men and women who come to participate in the hunting. Yet both groups profit from the ongoing program of wildlife habitat preservation, which is paid for largely from fees levied on sportsmen. Hunting licenses, duck-stamp revenues, and excise taxes on sporting arms and ammunition support most aspects of wildlife conservation in the United States and Canada. The interest in game birds and mammals thus has provided the backbone for wildlife protection and habitat restoration.

Identification

This book is not designed primarily as a guide to identification of game species. A number of good field guides are available to help the observer identify game birds and mammals. The emphasis in this book is on the salient facts of natural history, geographic distribution, and ecological status of the game birds and mammals. Our aim is for this book to serve as a companion to your favorite field guide. The materials in this volume augment and amplify the field-guide information. If you are fortunate enough to have access to a good collection of preserved specimens at a museum or university, you can learn a great deal of identification directly from them.

In the identification of birds, the best criteria are usually in the plumage, bills, and feet or in size and body proportions. Some birds have diagnostic bare areas, devoid of plumage, such as the air sacs of the male prairie chicken or the forehead of the sandhill crane. Others have special appendages or accessories, like the spurs on the legs of male ring-necked pheasants or the "beard" on the wild turkey gobbler. Most birds, however, lack such obvious markers and must be identified by details of plumage coloration or other characters that differ only slightly between related species.

In the identification of mammals, the color and texture of pelage, relative size and proportions of body and appendages, and certain characters of the skull are all possibly diagnostic. Some mammal species have special identifying structures, such as the antlers of members of the deer family. Ears and tails frequently are of identification value. The proportions of the skull and number and shape of teeth may be very characteristic.

Range and Habitat

No living species is universal in its distribution or uniform in its local abundance. Each wild bird or mammal is best adapted to one or more specific types of habitat, and the geographic distribution of habitat types in turn dictates the distribution or range of animal species. Habitat also dictates local abundance, since nearly all species attain higher densities in some habitat types than in others. The study of animal distribution is much more meaningful if you approach it from the point of view of habitat adaptation than if you view distribution maps merely as something static, to be memorized.

The ability of a species to exist in more than one zone or habitat type may relate to (1) the *adaptability* of the individual animal; (2) the ability and inclination of species members to *migrate* seasonally, utilizing different habitats at different times of year; or (3) *genetic adaptation* of segments of the population to different habitats.

Individual coyotes, for example, are quite at home in a wide variety of habitats ranging from extreme deserts to high mountains. So coyotes are more widespread and are abundant in more types of country than are kit foxes, which have a narrow range of tolerance and are confined largely to desert country. Mourning doves are more adaptable than band-tailed pigeons, bobwhites more so than sage grouse, elk more so than mountain sheep, and so on.

A great many species utilize more than one habitat by migrating seasonally. Waterfowl, for instance, breed mostly in the boreal zones of northern North America and migrate south to winter in more moderate climates that are relatively ice-free. On a more local scale, mountain quail breed commonly in high conifer forests and migrate (mostly afoot) to foothill zones in winter. In contrast, blue grouse live year-round in the higher mountain zones without migrating. This grouse is adapted to eat fir needles in winter and so is not forced to leave with the mountain quail, whose more exacting nutritional needs (seeds, fruits, tender greens) cannot be met in time of deep snow.

Some species, by virtue of genetic adaptation of local races to different habitat types, are distributed in more than one community. Thus the Rocky Mountain mule deer occurs throughout Great Basin ranges, the California mule deer lives on the more humid west slope of the Sierra Nevada, the black-tailed deer is found in the coastal ranges and foothills from California to Alaska, and the burro deer inhabits the desert. All of these are forms of the species *Odocoileus hemionus*, and collectively they occupy every plant community in the western United States. Some local deer populations that summer in high mountains migrate in winter to foothill ranges of mild climate. Others, such as the blacktails in the Pacific coastal ranges, are strictly resident. Considerable evidence indicates genetic adaptation in the deer to meet local habitat conditions. To name only one example, blacktails in California breed more than a full month earlier than races that occupy the mountains. This early breeding allows fawns to be weaned prior to the summer drought. Rocky Mountain mule deer transplanted into blacktail range do very poorly and soon die out. It may be that their fawns are born too late to be weaned on succulent and nutritious foods. Studies of subspeciation in animals have progressed far enough to demonstrate in a few species the nature of genetic adaptation to local environments.

Wild species—which, of course, evolved in natural habitats—react in various ways to changes that mankind makes in the natural environment. Some species like the wolverine, bighorn sheep, or condor seem to disappear with encroachment of the wilderness. These "wilderness species" are of intense interest and esthetic value. But they probably will always remain scarce, if they survive at all. Other species like the mule deer and white-tailed deer, California quail, ruffed grouse, and coyote may actually increase in numbers and expand their range as a result of human changes in natural vegetation. Grazed grasslands, for instance, support more rodents than did the original grasslands and so may support more coyotes. Cutover forests tend to grow up in brush that carries more deer and grouse than the original timber did. Introduced ring-necked pheasants thrive on cultivated farmlands but probably could not have survived in primitive America. The species that adapt most successfully to our current pattern of land use are, as you would expect, most abundant and most important economically today.

Natural History

In everyday usage, the term "natural history" refers to all the habits and actions of a species that constitute its normal way of living. Choice of cover and food, water requirements, breeding cycle, social behavior, and predator relations are among the important aspects of natural history. In this concise text, we focus on a few principal items of natural history of each species. These are presented under the subheading "Remarks."

Related species often are similar in many aspects of natural history. Once this information is presented for one species, it is not repeated in subsequent accounts. The breeding cycle of the mallard, for example, which is described in detail, is meant to apply to river and pond ducks generally, except as otherwise noted. The natural enemies listed for bobwhite quail are essentially the same ones that prey on other quails.

Individual requirements for specific types of food and cover often determine both the total range and the local abundance of a species. In other words, natural history cannot be dissociated from range and habitat. For instance, jackrabbits live in open country, where they escape their predators mostly by sheer speed. Jackrabbits can live satisfactorily on various forbs and grasses that grow in such regions, and these foods may be utilized even after they are completely desiccated. On the other extreme, brush rabbits rarely venture more than a few feet from their protective brush cover. They survive by dodging their enemies in the thicket. Like jackrabbits, they are forb and grass feeders but do best where such foods remain green and succulent even in summer. These predilections and adaptations explain why jackrabbits range in the desert and arid valleys but brush rabbits are found mostly in coastal chaparral that does not desiccate in summer. In a similar vein, brant—which eat almost exclusively a marine plant called eelgrass and favor open water for safety—are confined to coastal bays, but mallards—which eat grain and freshwater weeds and prefer tule cover—are most abundant in interior freshwater marshes.

Knowledge of reproduction is basic in understanding the status of wild populations. In general, species with the highest reproductive rates (California quail, for example) are vulnerable to the highest natural losses. Comparatively low birth rates, as in elk, indicate a lower normal rate of loss. In a stable population of any species, the birth and death rates are, of course, in balance. The annual "turnover" in a quail population (meaning rate of death and replacement in a year's time) may be as high as 70 to 80 percent, but in elk the turnover is usually only 10 to 20 percent.

Reproductive rate is determined principally by (1) the size of normal clutch or litter, (2) the number of clutches or litters produced each year, and (3) the minimum breeding age. Quail breed when they are a year old and hatch one clutch of 7 to 15 eggs. Elk do not bear young until they are three years old, and each breeding female produces only one calf, hence the difference in productivity. The mourning dove, although it lays only two eggs per clutch, may successfully fledge several broods a year, so its breeding potential is almost as high as the quail's. As a result of their high breeding rate, quail and mourning doves are preyed upon by a host of enemies and they may die of disease, starvation, or accident. Relatively few fatal incidents can happen to an elk. It follows that the quail, of high reproductive capacity, can yield a higher annual hunting kill than the elk. Hunting substitutes for part of the natural loss in the life equation (Leopold 1933).

To understand the processes of population dynamics, it is essential to recognize the sex and age of individuals constituting the population. We include mention of only a few of the many characters used by wildlife biologists to classify animals of various species into sex and age categories. For a full discussion we recommend the chapter devoted to this subject in the *Wildlife Management Techniques Manual* (Larson and Taber 1980).

It has long been a matter of wonderment that the factors of attrition and those of production so exactly balance in wild populations. How is it in the life cycle of a quail, for example, that almost exactly as many young are raised as there were adults lost during the preceding year? Recent studies have shown that both birth and death rates are regulated to a considerable extent by the environment (food quality as well as quantity, amount and distribution of cover, and so on). In other words, the surprising consistency of local population levels is no happenstance.

Life history study, therefore, must consider not only the *inherent adaptations of species* to survive the hazards of a given habitat but also the *countereffect of the habitat* on the functioning of these adaptive processes in the species. To take another example: a female deer may produce one or two fawns, a rate of reproduction that, over the period of geologic ages, has proven to be adequate to maintain the population level. In an uncrowded environment where the doe is well fed, she probably will produce twins. Both of these young stand a good chance of surviving. On a crowded range, where the doe gets less high-quality food because of competition, she will likely produce only one fawn. It may be weak and die. The habitat thus tends to regulate the size of the deer population by its effect on birth rate, as well as by the more obvious effect on death rate.

Over and beyond the physical competition for food and living space, there seem to be adverse effects upon the health and productivity of animals from the very fact of crowding. Excessive contact with fellow creatures leads to bickering and "stress" that may actually affect the nervous and endocrine systems, retarding sexual maturity and inhibiting reproductive success. To put it another way, competition can be social as well as physical.

All in all, this means that the welfare of the individual animal is often enhanced by elimination of other individuals from the population. Predation or hunting, for example, will leave the survivors in good health for effective reproduction.

The spatial distribution of animals in a population has been studied in some detail, and two basic types of arrangements now are recognized. A *territory* is an area occupied by an individual or group of individuals and defended from others of the same species. A crowing cock pheasant, a pair of nesting mallards, or a covey of bobwhite quail will all have specific territories from which they exclude others of their kind by threat or actual attack. Most birds defend territories during the breeding season, and some do so even in winter.

Mammals are less obviously territorial. All individual mammals live in their own *home ranges*, but usually these are only weakly defended and tend to overlap. Still, there is recent evidence of a degree of territoriality (defense of area) among female mammals such as tree squirrels, brush rabbits, and black-tailed deer, although males of the same species show less tendency toward area defense. There may be more territorial behavior among mammals than has been suspected.

Social Importance

Wild birds and mammals have many values to human society. Easiest to measure are the direct returns in hunting or trapping—the healthy recreation supplied, the meat and trophies taken home, the pelts marketed. Recent studies have shown that some 16 million persons in the United States hunt and trap. The monetary expenditure by this army of sportsmen is huge. But these values and the industries they support may be of less importance than the purely esthetic values of wildlife, which are impossible to measure. A summer tourist watching deer in a mountain meadow may derive as much pleasure as the hunter that stalks and shoots one of the same deer in October. Practically every American derives some pleasure and profit from wildlife or at least should have the chance to do so (Leopold 1949).

Not all aspects of human contact with wild things are equally pleasant. Predators kill livestock and poultry, rodents destroy food crops and range forage, and even some game species like ducks and deer can do great damage to crops. Wildlife management cannot ignore these losses but rather must attempt to prevent them as a part of good conservation. In our accounts of various game species, some mention will be made of the most obvious and difficult damage cases. Minor ones, such as cottontails consuming backyard radish patches or raccoons tipping over garbage cans, are too numerous and too insignificant to incorporate in a concise text.

The complex problem of interrelationships between predator and prey species is only partially understood, but it is safe to state that the ecologic balance normally maintained among vertebrates may be of great economic significance. Also important is the balance between vertebrates and lower forms (birds versus insects, for instance). It is becoming increasingly evident that the highest yields from agricultural and grazing lands, with minimum damage from wild animals, is derived when a reasonably balanced fauna is retained. Thus, retaining some coyotes, foxes, hawks, and owls may help hold in check rodent populations that could cause far greater loss than that caused by predators. Field borders well stocked with birds have been shown to keep an insect population lower than it is in birdless fields. In our comments on a good many of the species, we mention their ecologic significance.

To sum up, the game birds and mammals that played so important a part in supporting aboriginal North Americans and the subsequent frontier societies have now assumed a new role. Esthetic, recreational, and ecologic values supersede the subsistence values of the past. We hope that this volume will serve to update the status and role of these animals in contemporary North America.

Part One

BIRDS

Game birds are by definition those species that have traditionally been hunted for the table. Some kinds are more savory than others, but all are eaten. Additionally, game birds offer a challenge in the hunting or shooting. Some species, such as ducks and doves, are fast flyers. Others, like woodcock or grouse, offer a dodging, twisting target in dense cover. Still others try the hunter's skill and patience by being exceedingly wary: the wild turkey is a classic example. But when the hunting is over, the game bird is prepared for cooking.

Of the game bird species covered in this book, most are migratory ducks and geese of the Order Anseriformes. Two swans, 6 geese, and 28 kinds of ducks dominate the list of American game birds. Yet of this considerable array, about a dozen species of ducks and three kinds of geese supply most of the waterfowl sport hunting. Another dozen species contribute significantly to the subsistence of Eskimos, Aleuts, and Indians in Alaska and Canada. All waterfowl, however, are objects of great interest to naturalists and birders.

To the average North American hunter, the upland game birds, because they are much more widely available, are of more importance than waterfowl. Doves, grouse, quails, and the introduced ring-necked pheasant supply most of the sport bird shooting in the contiguous United States and Prairie Provinces of Canada. Most of these species thrive in agricultural communities and utilize crop residues for food.

The rest of the game birds discussed in this book are marsh-dwelling members of the Orders that include cranes, rails, and shorebirds. Only the coot, snipe, and woodcock are widely hunted.

A scientific specimen of a bird is represented by the preserved skin and an attached label indicating the date and place of capture and the name of the collector. When available, body weight of the fresh specimen is included on the tag, but measurements are not usually recorded since they can readily be taken directly from the specimen. Length of wing, length of tail, tarsus, and bill are the four measurements of primary interest to bird taxonomists. The accompanying illustration shows how these measures are taken.

The scientific bird names used in this book are derived from the 1957 *Check-list of North American Birds* (and subsequent supplements) published by the American Ornithologists' Union. In compiling our accounts of distribution and natural history of game birds we drew on our own experience but also on the scientific literature. Particularly helpful were publications by Aldrich and Duvall (1955), Bellrose (1976), Johnsgard (1973 and 1975), and Sanderson (1977).

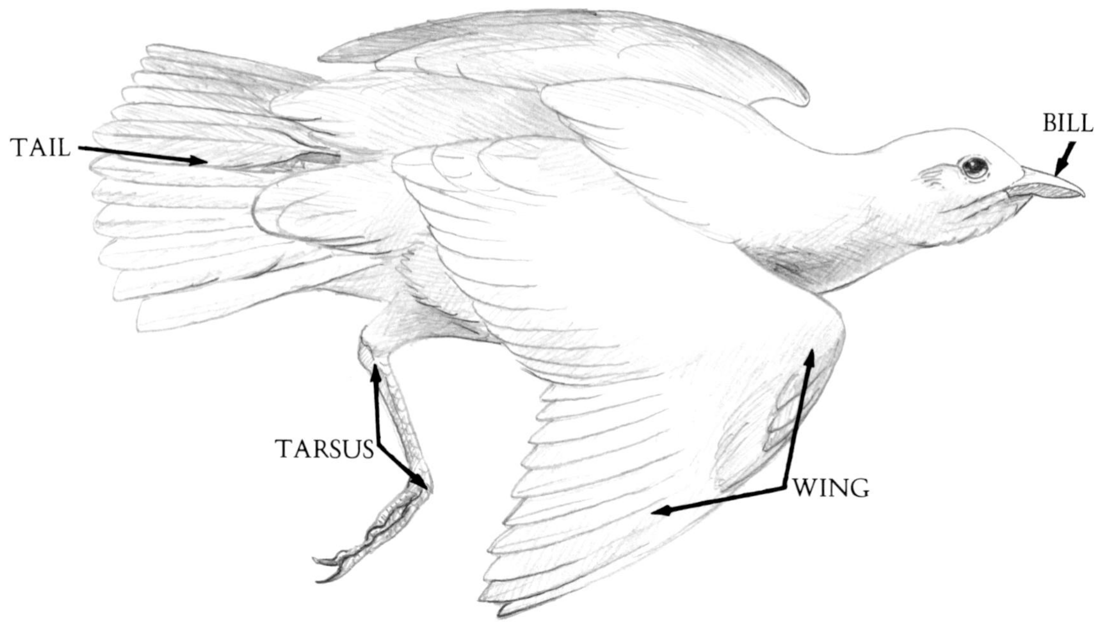

STANDARD MEASUREMENTS OF A BIRD

Order Gruiformes

CRANES, RAILS, GALLINULES, THE COOT

Two species of cranes occur in North America—the large, white whooping crane; and the smaller, gray sandhill crane. Both were once popular game birds. In the early 1900s, the number of cranes decreased alarmingly as a result of overshooting plus alteration of their natural habitat. With the adoption of the Migratory Bird Treaty with Canada in 1916, both species were given full legal protection. The sandhill crane responded spectacularly and is now a common migrant over much of the continent. The whooping crane has barely persisted. Despite special protective measures, it has shown little capacity to adapt to habitat changes.

Several species of rails are listed as legal game in most states and provinces, but even though these birds are prime table fare, relatively few of them are shot. All rails frequent dense marsh vegetation and are difficult to put to flight. Only the clapper rail in the salt marshes of the Atlantic Coast is hunted with any regularity. Elsewhere, rails are taken incidentally to the hunting of other marsh birds. The California clapper rail has become rare as a result of the filling and drainage of coastal estuaries.

The American coot or "mudhen" is an important game bird in the midwestern United States and in Mexico, but it is little hunted elsewhere. Coots compete with ducks for food. And on the breeding grounds, coots tend to be territorial and pugnacious, driving ducks from potential breeding sites. The closely related gallinules are scarcely hunted.

The best recent account of members of the Gruiformes is found in the book edited by Sanderson (1977).

Family Gruidae (Cranes)

SANDHILL CRANE *(Grus canadensis)*

See also pages 16–17.

RANGE: Siberia and North America, except northeastern United States

HABITAT: Tundra marshes, wet meadows, desert lakes and cultivated valleys

REMARKS: There are three migratory subspecies of this crane, differing mainly in size. The smaller two, *G. c. canadensis* and *G. c. rowani*, breed in Alaska and arctic Canada and are common migrants in the United States. The largest race—*G. c. tabida*, known as the greater sandhill crane—breeds in the northern United States and southern Canada from the Lake States to northeastern California and interior Oregon. Three nonmigratory races live in Florida, Mississippi, and Cuba, respectively, and are rare.

Superficially, cranes resemble the larger herons, but they are only distantly related and are very different in habit. Cranes fly with necks outstretched, but herons crook the neck in flight. Herons eat mostly foods of animal origin (fish, amphibians, insects) while cranes are largely vegetarian, at least in winter. Cultivated grains are staple winter foods; green sprouts of wheat, corn, and succulents are taken as well. Adaptability to man's agriculture accounts for the sandhill crane's successful recovery from past scarcity. The whooping crane, because of its narrow habitat preferences and food habits, remains on the verge of extinction.

Cranes require several years to mature, but once mated they are believed to remain so for life. Both sexes defend a territory, incubate the clutch, and defend the brood. The birds perform elaborate courtship dances prior to pair formation. Although two eggs are the normal clutch, usually only one offspring is raised per pair because the younger of the hatchlings is outcompeted by its larger, older sibling. The young (called colts) are precocial. Sometimes each parent will tend one colt, thus increasing the chances that both young will survive. Sexes are indistinguishable but young are recognizable by the presence of tawny juvenal feathers through their first year of age.

Lesser and Canadian sandhill cranes have increased sufficiently to cause substantial damage to wheat and other crops in the northern prairies. This situation has induced the U.S. Fish and Wildlife Service and the Canadian government to permit limited shooting seasons in a few localities of crane concentration. As many as 15,000 cranes are harvested annually in the United States, Canada, Mexico, and Siberia (Lewis 1977), yet the total population is still increasing. Nevertheless, it is unlikely that the sandhill crane will become an important object of sport hunting. Its greatest value is esthetic, the trumpeting calls and sight of a high-flying wedge in the sky inciting more than average interest and admiration among outdoorsmen.

WHOOPING CRANE *(Grus americana)*

See also pages 16–17.

RANGE: Originally bred throughout much of central Canada, migrating in winter through the Rocky Mountains and Great Plains to southern United States and northern Mexico. In recent years, limited to one breeding colony in Wood Buffalo National Park, Northwest Territories, Canada. Winter range limited to Aransas National Wildlife Refuge in southern Texas.

HABITAT: Boreal muskeg, intermountain valleys, coastal marshes

REMARKS: The whooping crane is one of the largest of North American birds. It stands 5 feet tall (1.5 meters) and has a wing spread of 7 feet or more (2.1 meters). The plumage is white with black wing tips. The naked face area is red. The young are brownish white. The species is also one of the rarest birds on the continent.

Because of its scarcity, the whooping crane has been an object of intensive study and management. Aransas National Wildlife Refuge near Corpus Christi, Texas, was developed in 1937 primarily to protect the whooper's wintering grounds. At that time, the total continental population was 26 birds. Under complete protection and intensive scrutiny, the whoopers increased slowly to 31 in 1950 and 36 in 1960. In 1967, a program of artificial propagation was initiated at Patuxent Wildlife Research Center in Maryland, based on breeding stock reared from eggs taken from wild nests in Canada. Like sandhill cranes, whoopers lay two eggs but normally rear only one colt. Removing one egg from a nest apparently does not lower the number of wild young fledged. The captive Patuxent flock numbered over 30 birds in 1977, and four breeding pairs produced 22 eggs that year.

In 1975, a program was initiated to reintroduce whooping cranes to unoccupied breeding range in Idaho. Eggs from the captive flock at Patuxent, and others removed from nests in Wood Buffalo Park, were slipped into nests of sandhill cranes at Gray's Lake National Wildlife Refuge. In the three years 1975–77, 61 eggs were turned over to foster parents for incubation and rearing. Of these eggs, 40 hatched; 17 young fledged and migrated with their foster parents to the Rio Grande Valley in central New Mexico, where this stock of sandhill cranes regularly winters. It seems that a new and independent population of whooping cranes is in the making. It remains to be seen if the whoopers, as they reach the mating age of 5 years, will pair and nest in their adopted summer range in Idaho (Drewien and Bizeau 1977).

Family Rallidae (Rails, gallinules, coot)

CLAPPER RAIL *(Rallus longirostris)*

See also pages 16–17.

RANGE: Coasts of the United States from Connecticut and northern California south to Brazil and Ecuador, respectively

HABITAT: Salt marshes and tidal flats of pickleweed *(Salicornia)*, cordgrass *(Spartina)*, or needlegrass *(Juncus)*

REMARKS: Clapper rails are highly localized in distribution, living largely in dense vegetation of coastal salt marshes. One race occurs in marshes along the lower Colorado River. Their food consists almost entirely of invertebrates. Nests are built on slightly elevated platforms of marsh vegetation and usually contain 8 to 10 eggs. The following should be noted as characteristic of all rails discussed herein: breeding is monogamous; both sexes incubate, defend the nest, and brood the chicks; the young are precocial; and sexes are the same (monomorphic) in plumage characters. As hatchlings, clapper rails are black. In their first winter plumage, they resemble adults but have white spotting on the upper wing coverts, as is typical of other young rails.

SANDHILL CRANE
WHOOPING CRANE
KING RAIL
CLAPPER RAIL
SORA RAIL
VIRGINIA RAIL

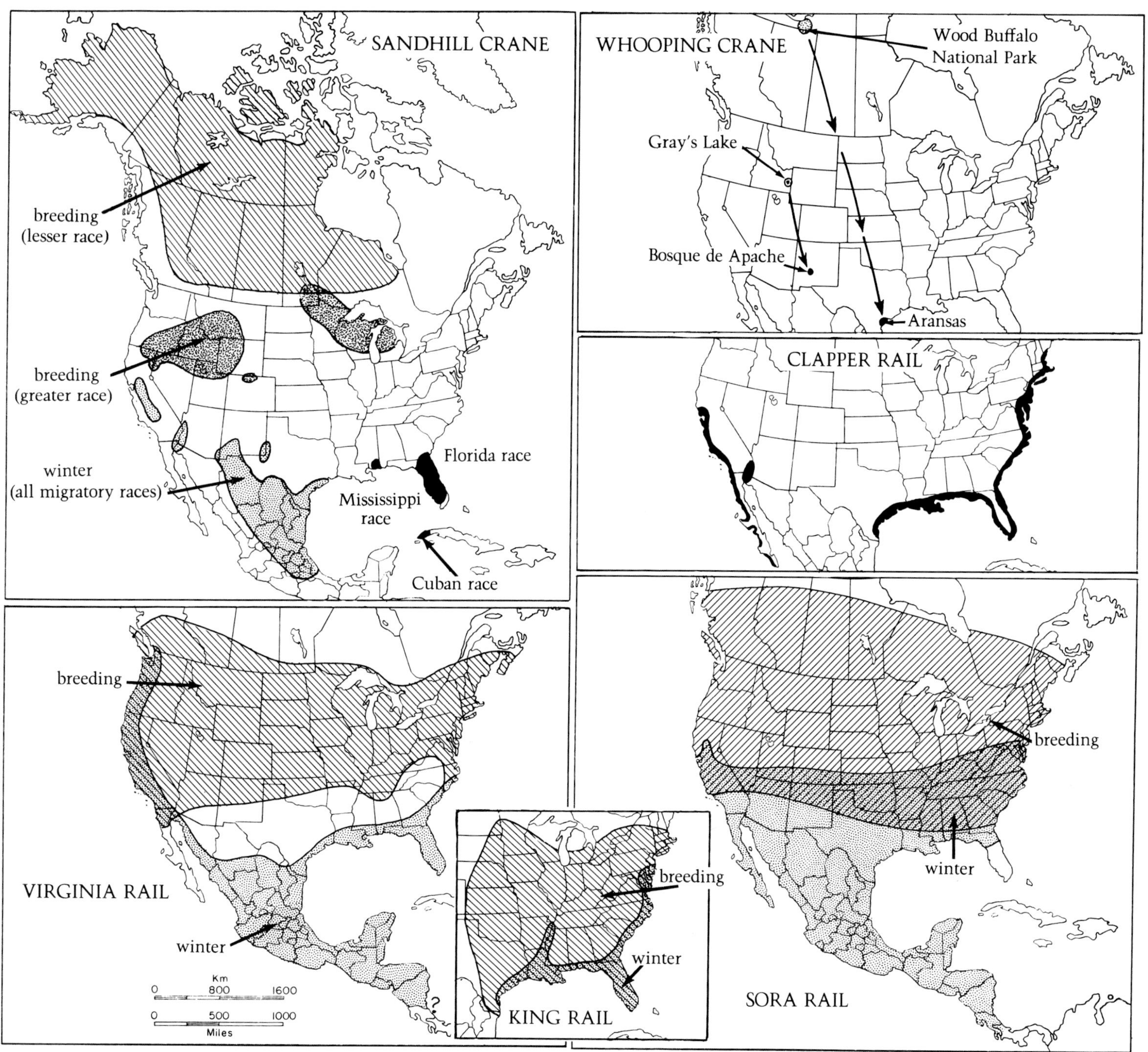

SANDHILL CRANE
breeding
(lesser race)
breeding
(greater race)
winter
(all migratory races)
Florida race
Mississippi
race
Cuban race
WHOOPING CRANE
Wood Buffalo
National Park
Gray's Lake
Bosque de Apache
Aransas
CLAPPER RAIL
breeding
VIRGINIA RAIL
winter
Km
0 800 1600
0 500 1000
Miles
?
breeding
winter
KING RAIL
breeding
winter
SORA RAIL

An adult clapper rail weighs approximately 300 grams. But the breast is small, and there is relatively little edible meat. The poor development of the breast muscles is correlated with the weak powers of flight.

The clapper rail has become rare on the California coast as a result of habitat destruction through landfill of tidal flats and estuarine marshes. The Pacific population is currently listed as endangered. Some hunting still occurs on the Atlantic coast, where the species remains reasonably abundant. Hunting is done from a boat, poled through the marsh at high tide when the birds can be put to flight.

KING RAIL *(Rallus elegans)*

See also pages 16–17.

RANGE: Breeds throughout the eastern half of the United States from North Dakota and New York south to Texas and Florida. Migrates in winter to the Gulf and Atlantic coasts.

HABITAT: Freshwater marshes

REMARKS: This large rail is widely distributed in interior marshlands and well-vegetated swamps. It is often associated with muskrats, utilizing as foraging grounds the waterways and openings created by these mammals. Nests are situated on platforms of vegetation, constructed by the birds themselves. A clutch of 8 to 12 eggs is typical. Incubation period is 21 to 23 days. The black chicks are precocial, able to follow their parents within hours after hatching. Foods of both young and adults are largely crustaceans and aquatic insects. King rails are hunted very little because of the difficulty of forcing them into flight. They are weak flyers, but nonetheless they make long seasonal migrations, flying exclusively at night as is true of other rails.

VIRGINIA RAIL *(Rallus limicola)*

See also pages 16–17.

RANGE: Throughout the United States and southern Canada to southern South America

HABITAT: Freshwater marshes

REMARKS: The Virginia rail is widely distributed and generally common in North America, but—because of its small size and secretiveness—it is hunted very little. The bird is rarely observed in flight; usually, it skulks in the dense vegetation from which it can be routed only by vigorous efforts of a good bird dog. The diet consists largely of insects. The clutch of 8 to 10 eggs is deposited in a well-concealed nest under tules or sedges. Incubation time is 18 to 19 days.

The major challenge in conservation of this species, and all other rails as well, is preserving marshland habitat from drainage and filling.

SORA RAIL *(Porzana carolina)*

See also pages 16–17.

RANGE: Breeds from northern and central Canada south to the midwestern and southwestern United States. Winters in southern United States to South America.

HABITAT: Freshwater marshes and wet meadows; in winter also in salt marshes

REMARKS: The sora rail is the most common rail of North America. It is similar to the Virginia rail in habits, and like it, is more often heard than seen. The common call note is described as a "whinny," descending in scale. In the eastern states, the sora rail is hunted to some extent. But as indicated earlier, none of the small rails are important as game birds.

Sora rails feed primarily on small mollusks and insects, with some seeds added to the diet, especially in autumn. Incubation lasts 14 days. Frequently, the male will tend the first chicks hatched and the female will shepherd the others.

Because of its abundance and wide range, the sora may become more important as a game bird than it has been. For this reason, Odom (1977) recommends an accelerated program of research on this species.

AMERICAN COOT *(Fulica americana)*

See also pages 20–21.

RANGE: Central Canada to northern South America; related species in South America and Europe

HABITAT: Resident on bodies of fresh water bordered by emergent vegetation. Winters also on brackish and salt water.

REMARKS: Coots are equally at home in the marsh and on large bodies of open water. In winter, they frequently form great flocks or "rafts," sometimes intermingling with ducks. Coots fly fairly well and are shot in considerable numbers by hunters in the midwestern United States and in Mexico. Although coots eat more or less the same plant food as grazing ducks (like wigeon), they are often strong in flavor; the flesh should be soaked in salt water before cooking. The derogatory name "mudhen" presumably refers to the muddy flavor.

Coots build floating nests in emergent vegetation on fresh water. Clutch size is 6 to 12, and two broods may be raised in one season by a breeding pair. The chicks are precocial and shortly after hatching can swim and dive almost as skillfully as adult birds. Lobed feet permit effective locomotion in water. Coots are highly territorial during the breeding season, vigorously defending their nest area from other coots and at times from ducks, small birds, and even from such innocent objects as floating tennis balls. When the second brood hatches, the parents drive their first brood off the territory just as though they were trespassing adults.

Most young birds are found in the big winter rafts seen on open water. Young coots have greenish legs, which turn to yellow and then to orange as the birds get older. Some year-old birds nest, but many have difficulty defending territories, the best of which generally are claimed by adults. For this reason, some yearlings do not breed.

The turnover in a coot population is high, judging by the proportion of young in fall populations and by the high productivity of breeding pairs. Some individuals, however, live to a ripe age. A female coot banded at Lake Merritt in Oakland, California, was recaptured 11 years later.

In recent years, large aggregations of wintering coots have caused severe damage to pastures and winter grainfields in California. Hunters are urged to shoot more coots during waterfowl season, and several special coot seasons have been declared in late winter and spring. Comparable damage is not reported in other parts of the range.

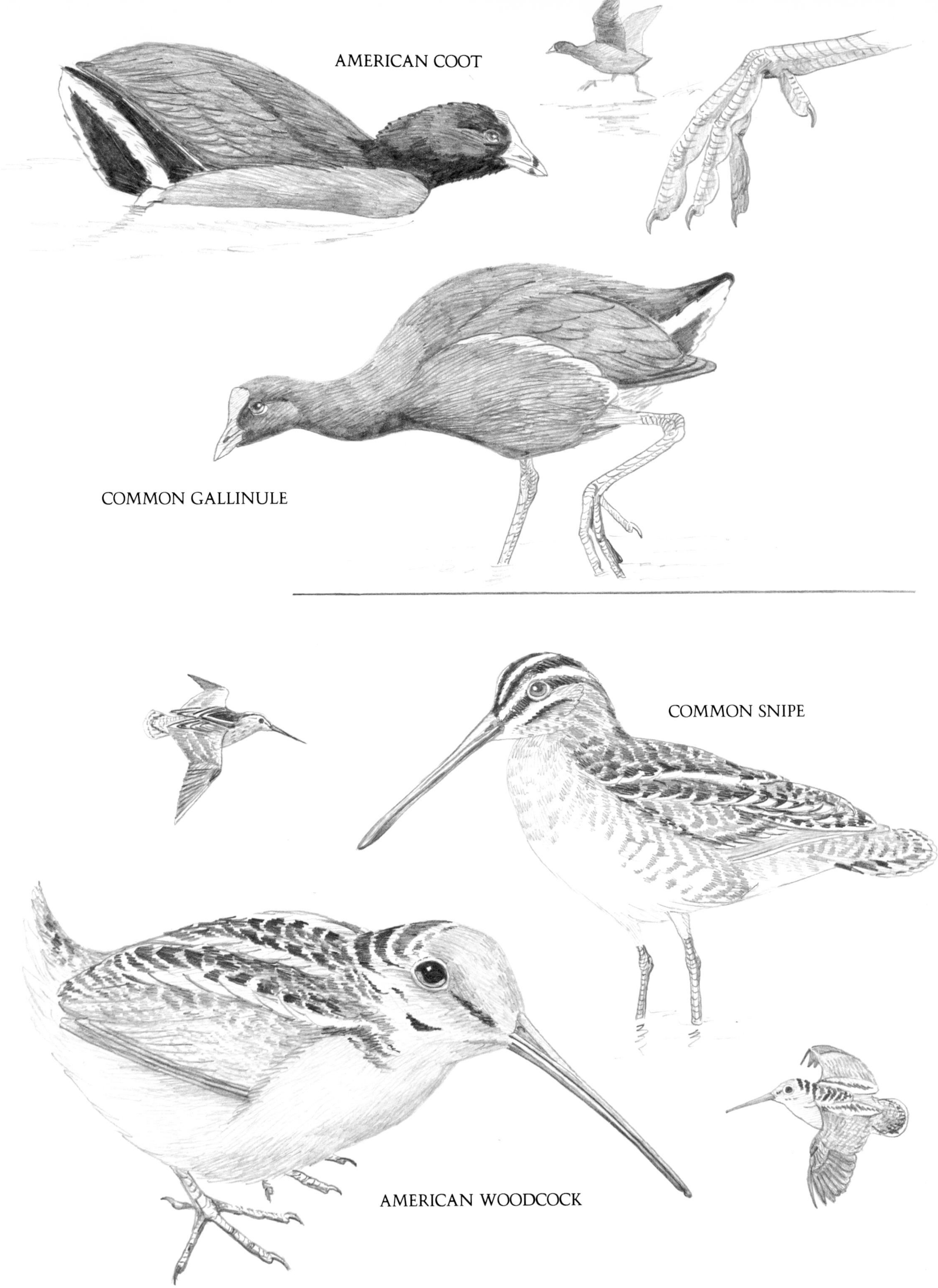

AMERICAN COOT

COMMON GALLINULE

COMMON SNIPE

AMERICAN WOODCOCK

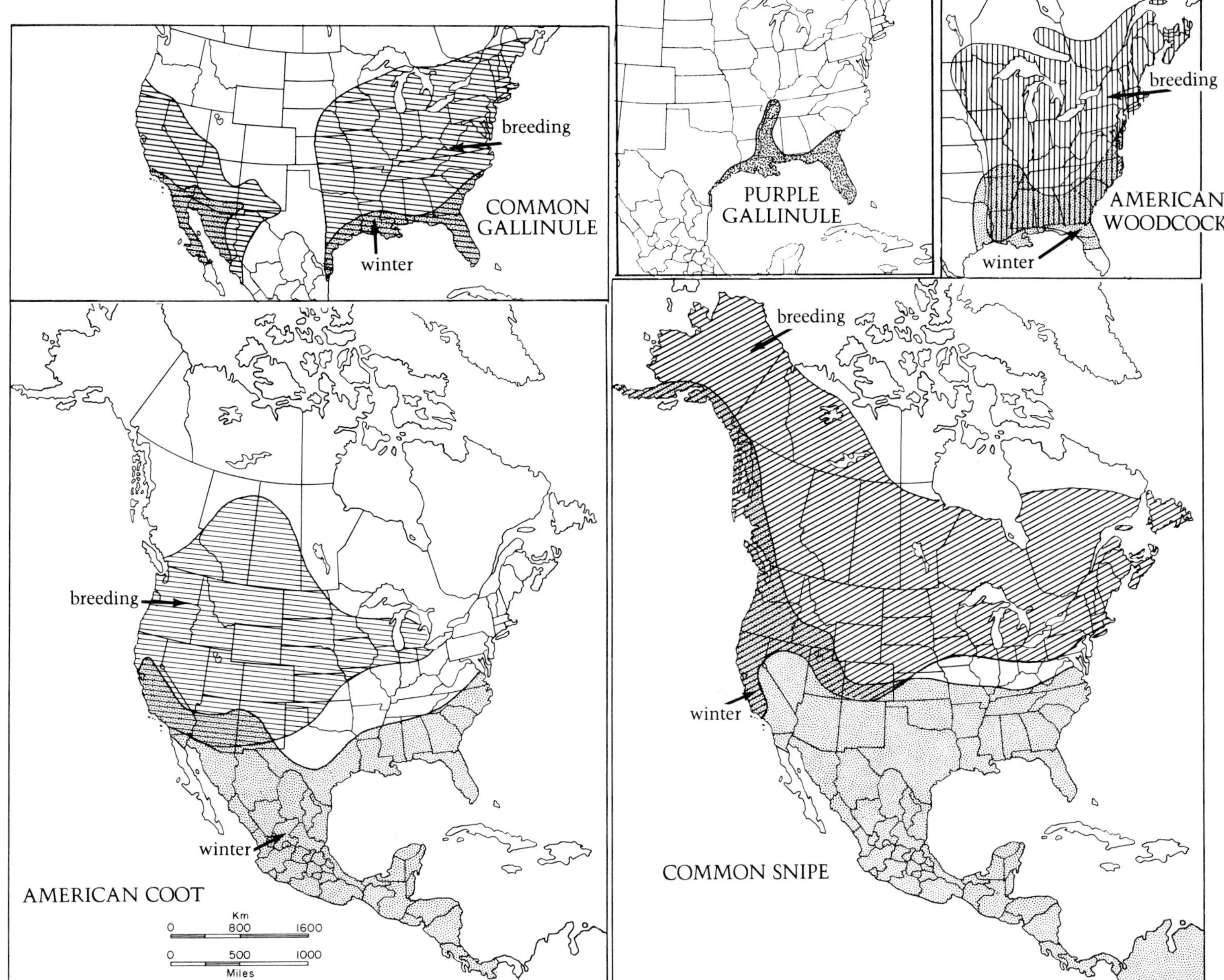

breeding
COMMON GALLINULE
winter
PURPLE GALLINULE
breeding
AMERICAN WOODCOCK
winter
breeding
winter
AMERICAN COOT
Km
0 800 1600
0 500 1000
Miles
breeding
winter
COMMON SNIPE

COMMON AND PURPLE GALLINULES *(Gallinula chloropus* and *Porphyrula martinica)*

See also pages 20–21.

RANGE: *Gallinula* is widely distributed in temperate and tropical America, Eurasia, and Africa; *Porphyrula*, humid and tropical areas of southeastern United States south to northern Argentina.

HABITAT: Swamps and bodies of fresh water where emergent vegetation is abundant

REMARKS: Although gallinules very much resemble the coot, they behave more like typical rails, being secretive and timid and rarely venturing far from heavy cover. The lack of lobed feet, which characterize the coot, is suggestive of the inferior swimming powers of the gallinule. The common gallinule has a bright-red bill and frontal shield; the purple gallinule has a red bill and a bluish-white shield. In contrast, the coot has a white bill and dark red shield.

Gallinule breeding is monogamous. Both sexes build the nest, care for the young, and defend a common territory. Clutch size is 8 to 10, and several broods are raised each year. Incubation is about 19 to 22 days. These birds prefer to nest in dense emergent vegetation.

Sexes are monomorphic, but immature birds may be recognized by their dull, brownish plumage and lack of bright bills.

The purple gallinule is omnivorous, eating seeds of grasses (including cultivated rice) and invertebrates. The common gallinule is primarily a grass and weed-seed eater, taking invertebrates only occasionally.

Gallinules are difficult to flush. Few are killed in the United States and Canada, even though bag limits are normally generous. According to fragmentary records obtained by the U.S. Fish and Wildlife Service, the average annual kill during 1964–75 was 26,400 gallinules, taken largely in Louisiana.

Order Charadriiformes

SHOREBIRDS

Shorebirds once were shot in great numbers, both for the market and for sport. All the larger species were included, the most important being curlews, godwits, yellowlegs, avocets, various plovers, snipe, and — in the eastern United States — woodcock. The Migratory Bird Treaty with Canada (1916) led to complete protection of most shorebirds. Only the snipe and woodcock have continued as objects of sport hunting. These two species are among the sportiest American game birds, supplying the finest of hunting for those aficionados who pursue them. Both species are exceptionally good eating.

The many other species of shorebirds are of special interest to bird watchers and wildlife photographers. They add a touch of grace and beauty to the mudflats and marshlands.

Family Scolopacidae (Snipe, woodcock)

COMMON SNIPE *(Capella gallinago)*

See also pages 20-21.

RANGE: Circumpolar; in North America breeds in Alaska, Canada, and northern United States. Winters in southern United States, Mexico, Central America, and into South America.

HABITAT: Freshwater marshes and wet meadows

REMARKS: The common snipe is probably the most numerous of American shorebirds. It breeds over a tremendous range and migrates in winter to an equally large area in southern North America and into the tropics. Its habit of frequenting vegetated marshland makes it less conspicuous than some of the waders that gather on open mud-flats. A precipitous decline in snipe numbers during the late 1930s led the U.S. Fish and Wildlife Service to close the hunting seasons from 1941 through 1953. But the population has fully recovered, and normal hunting seasons have resumed. The cause of the decline was never ascertained.

Male snipe establish breeding territories, which they advertise by spectacular "winnowing" displays, involving steep downward flight that causes the outer tail feathers to vibrate with a tremolo sound. The female constructs her well-concealed nest and incubates the 4 eggs for about 19 days. The male takes charge of two chicks, the female the other two, feeding and brooding them for some days until they learn to forage for themselves. The diet of both young and adult consists almost wholly of aquatic insects and other invertebrates pulled from the mud by the long flexible bill. The young make sustained flights when they are three weeks old, at which time they become independent. Southward migration begins in late August, the birds flying alone or in small "wisps," but not in large organized flocks like some other shorebirds. The natural history of snipes is well described in the monograph by Tuck (1972).

The jacksnipe has a well-deserved reputation as a fast and sporty flyer, testing the skill of the most experienced hunter. Especially on cloudy or windy days, it flies an unpredictable zigzag course that contributes to many a missed shot. Snipe are normally hunted by wading through the marsh, attempting to shoot the birds that fly out ahead. The sportsman who brings in a limit of snipe can be proud of his shooting and happy with the thought of a fine meal to come.

AMERICAN WOODCOCK *(Philohela minor)*

See also pages 20–21.

RANGE: Breeds from southeast Manitoba and east Texas, eastward to the Atlantic coast. Winters in southern United States.

HABITAT: Moist deciduous forest and alder swamps

REMARKS: The woodcock and ruffed grouse are the two most important upland game birds in the northern, midwestern, and northeastern United States. The woodcock likewise is widely hunted on its wintering grounds in the southeastern United States. Woodcock prefer thick, brushy woods that make for difficult hunting. The species has withstood heavy hunting pressure without apparent population decline. The cutting of virgin forests has resulted in actual improvement of the original environment for this species. Old logging roads bordered by alders are favored haunts.

Woodcocks nest in moist woods or brushy pastures and have 4 eggs. Females are larger than males and outnumber them. Breeding is polygamous (possibly promiscuous) with males establishing "singing" territories, where elaborate aerial displays are performed at dawn and dusk. A displaying male will emit a short buzzing note ("peent") while on the ground and then fly high over his territory producing a twittering sound of wind blowing through his feathers before plunging back to earth, giving a clear, liquid vocal call. This elegant performance presumably attracts females to the mating ground. A patient observer can closely approach a displaying male woodcock by moving toward the point on the ground where the peent call was given while the bird is twittering in flight. Males do not assist the females with incubation or brood care (Sheldon 1967).

Woodcocks move from daytime feeding coverts to roost at night in forest openings and glades. The diet is primarily earthworms, which the birds extract from the moist earth with their flexible bill. The tip of the upper mandible may be bent open to seize food items. It is soft and sensitive—qualities that presumably permit the bird to "feel" underground for its invisible food.

The outer wing primaries are attenuated, perhaps serving as wing slots to facilitate the bird's dodging, twisting flight through a thicket. A brush-dwelling dove in Mexico *(Leptotila verreauxi)* that flies much like a woodcock has identical flight feathers.

Order Columbiformes

PIGEONS AND DOVES

The mourning dove is an important game species throughout the southern half of the United States. It withstands heavy shooting, yet it continues to be abundant and widespread. White-winged doves and band-tailed pigeons are hunted locally in the western United States, but both are limited in distribution and in numbers. The passenger pigeon *(Ectopistes migratorius)* was once the most abundant game bird in North America, but it was exterminated by a combination of habitat destruction and market hunting. Several other species of pigeons and doves occur within the United States, but none of these are currently important game birds. The exotic Chinese spotted dove *(Streptopelia chinensis)* and ringed turtle dove *(Streptopelia risoria)* are classified as game species, but both occur only in urban localities of Southern California and are rarely hunted. The common pigeon or rock dove *(Columba livia)* has adapted to life in the barnyard and in many city streets. It is killed more as a pest than as a game bird.

All members of the family Columbidae (pigeons and doves) to be discussed feed their young with crop "milk," cellular material that is sloughed from areas of specialized epithelial tissue in each lobe of the crop. Pigeons and doves build flimsy platform nests in trees. Both sexes share in incubation, brooding, and feeding of the young. Breeding is monogamous. The pair bond is probably maintained throughout the entire nesting season, which may involve multiple nestings. Young may be distinguished from adults by the presence of buff-tipped wing coverts, which remain until the postjuvenal molt is complete. Pigeons and doves are peculiar in that they drink by sucking a continuous stream of liquid into the mouth without lifting their heads.

The best accounts of the Columbiformes are to be found in the book edited by Sanderson (1977).

Family Columbidae (Pigeons and doves)

BAND-TAILED PIGEON *(Columba fasciata)*

See also pages 28–29.

RANGE: Pacific coast from British Columbia south to Baja California and southern Rocky Mountains; pine oak highlands of Mexico and Central America

HABITAT: Montane conifer and broad sclerophyll forests

REMARKS: The distribution of the band-tailed pigeon is closely related to that of the oaks *(Quercus)*. Bandtails depend to a large extent on acorns for fall and winter food. Other important foods include madrone berries *(Arbutus)*, conifer seeds (*Pinus* sp.), a large variety of summer berries and fruits, buds, tree flowers, and catkins in spring. Bandtails prefer to feed in the trees or bushes, clinging to the branches; they are sometimes guilty of raiding orchards (cherry orchards, for example). Most of their favored foods are unpredictable in their yearly availability, so the species has evolved a nomadic behavior. In winter, large mobile flocks of pigeons follow available food supplies. In spring, pigeons nest in or near areas of plentiful food. Opportunistic breeding (i.e., breeding in response to favorable environmental conditions outside of the "normal" breeding season) in response to a large acorn crop has also been noted (Gutiérrez *et al.* 1975).

Two relatively discrete populations of bandtails are found in the United States, a coastal population and an interior population. The coastal population is much larger than that of the interior and thus sustains a substantially higher annual harvest—500,000 as compared to 4000 to 5000 in the interior (Jeffrey 1977). Although the female usually lays only one egg, up to three broods may be raised during a breeding season. Productivity is sufficient to allow a moderate harvest.

Male pigeons can reliably be distinguished from females by the bluish breast feathers. Females are comparatively drab. Young of the year have gray heads and lack the white collar on the back of the neck.

Since bandtails are fast, high flyers, pass-shooting where the flocks cross low gaps in the mountains can be a difficult and exacting sport. Coastal winter flocks, often numbering in the thousands, are truly impressive as they follow ridge lines searching for food.

MOURNING DOVE *(Zenaida macroura)*

See also pages 28–29.

RANGE: Breeds in southern Canada, throughout the United States (except in high mountains or dense forests), and on the temperate uplands of Mexico. Winters through the southern United States and Mexico, sparingly to Central America.

HABITAT: Prairie, desert, open woodland, agricultural, and urban areas

REMARKS: The mourning dove is probably the most important game bird in North America. It is avidly hunted by millions of sportsmen, and the estimated total annual kill is approximately 50 million birds. Yet the species is so widespread and so prolific as to sustain this kill without impairment of the breeding stock.

BAND-TAILED PIGEON
MOURNING DOVE
WHITE-WINGED DOVE
PASSENGER PIGEON

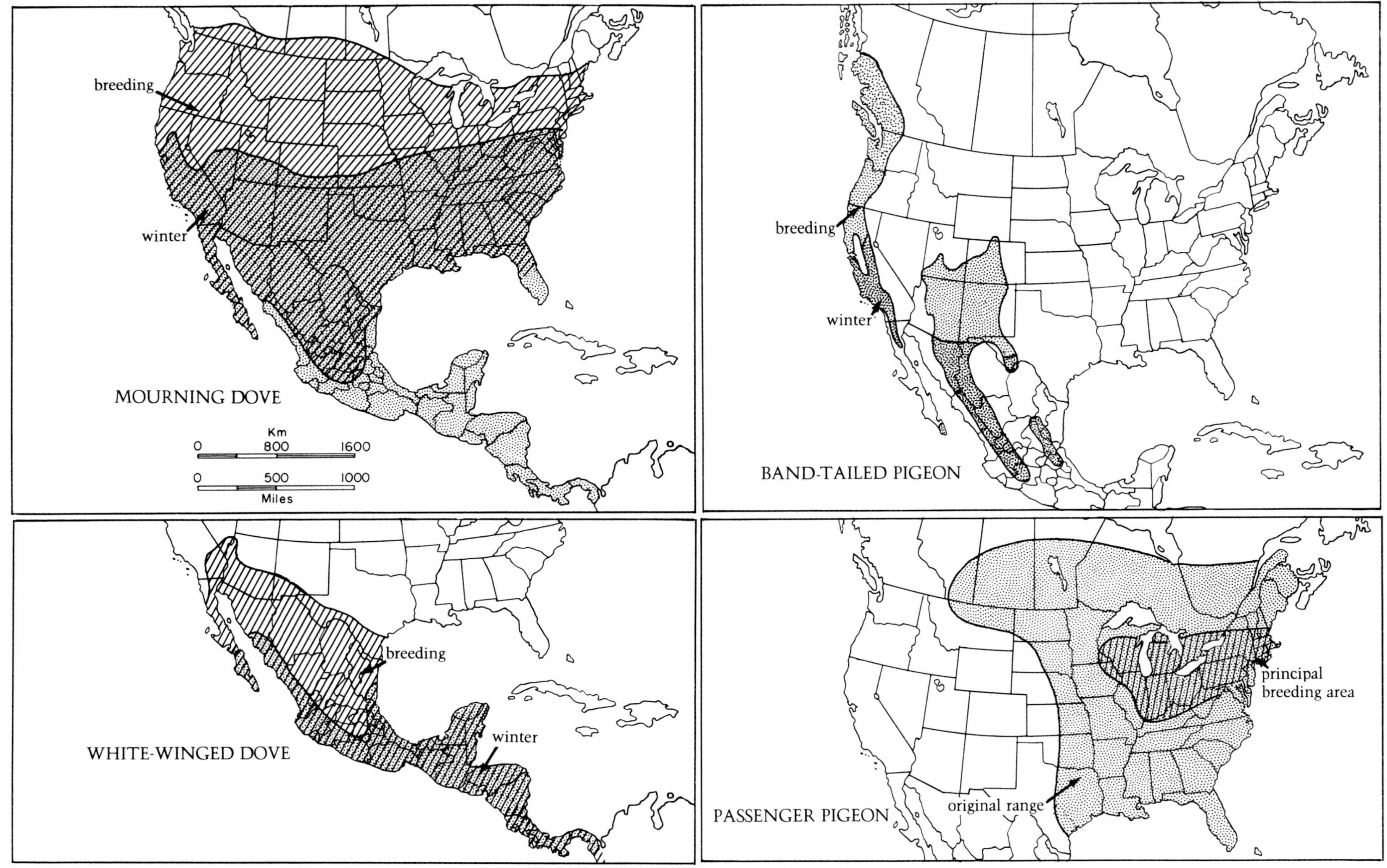
MOURNING DOVE
breeding
winter
Km
0
800
1600
0
500
1000
Miles
BAND-TAILED PIGEON
breeding
winter
WHITE-WINGED DOVE
breeding
winter
PASSENGER PIGEON
original range
principal
breeding area

The mourning dove generally nests several times during a season, laying two eggs in a clutch. A full nesting cycle takes about 30 days (2 to 4 days nest building and laying, 14 days incubation, 12 to 14 days till the squabs are fledged). Pairs occasionally have been known to raise 6 broods (12 young) in a season, but the average is more nearly 6 young. Both parents incubate and care for the squabs. Male doves are distinguished by the blue crown and rose-tinted breast. Females are uniformly brown. The iridescent feathers on the neck occur on both sexes, more noticeably on males.

Mourning doves live principally on weed seeds and waste agricultural grain that has fallen to the ground. Because of their weak feet and legs they cannot scratch, nor do they cling readily to upright stems or twigs in foraging. So they get practically all of their food from the surface of the ground, and the birds are not implicated in grain depredations. Mourning doves must drink daily. In arid regions, a lack of water may limit populations. A single water source, however, may provide drink for birds within several miles.

General farming and the introduction of exotic weeds and agricultural crops has greatly improved the habitat for mourning doves, and there doubtless are many more of these birds in North America now than there were before settlement. Unlike the passenger pigeon, the mourning dove is fully compatible with man and his modern environments. High populations of doves are characteristic of urban and suburban areas as well as farmlands. Many doves have learned to use bird feeders. Also, their strong power of flight enables them to exploit food resources some distance away from the nest. Heavy hunting has not caused any general decrease in the species. All in all, the mourning dove is one of the most successful and persistent game birds.

WHITE-WINGED DOVE *(Zenaida asiatica)*

See also pages 28–29.

RANGE: Breeds in desert areas and river bottoms of southwestern United States (southeastern California to southern Texas) and in Mexico, Central America, and western South America. Winters from Mexico to western South America.

HABITAT: Tropical and subtropical woodlands, thorn forest, and desert scrub

REMARKS: The white-winged dove is primarily a bird of the arid tropics. Its occurrence in the southwestern United States is a marginal extension of the breeding range into the temperate zones. However, several million pairs nest in the southwest, and legal hunting is declared in all the states bordering Mexico. A much larger population exists south of the border. The bird is widely hunted in Mexico, both for sport and for subsistence food.

Whitewings can be either colonial (i.e., more than 10 breeding pairs per acre) or dispersed nesters. Habitat quality is presumably the factor determining which method of nesting is adopted. Dense thickets of thorn scrub make ideal colony nesting sites, and up to 200 nests per acre have been recorded in river bottoms of southern Arizona. The normal clutch is 2 eggs, and 2 to 3 clutches are hatched per year. Since most of the birds have migrated south by the September hunting season, the impact of shooting has a minor overall effect on the population. The primary threat to the future of the white-winged dove is its deteriorating habitat. Federally funded reclamation and agricultural projects claim thousands of acres of prime nesting habitat by eradicating the dense stands of scrub forest in the southwestern bottom lands. The doves suffer accordingly.

Whitewings feed on weed seeds and grain. The birds will perch on the top of stalks such as grain sorghum and remove the still-standing grain. They can cause locally severe agricultural losses. It has been estimated that a flock of 50,000 doves could consume more than a ton of grain in a day (Cottam and Trefethen 1968:171). White-winged doves typically feed in large groups in autumn and winter. Dramatic morning and evening feeding flights are characteristic of this species.

PASSENGER PIGEON *(Ectopistes migratorius)*

See also pages 28–29.

RANGE: Southeastern Canada and the eastern United States; nesting occurred largely in the Lake States south to the Ohio River.

HABITAT: Eastern hardwood forests, especially of beech and oak

REMARKS: The passenger pigeon is extinct. Yet it was enormously abundant through much of the nineteenth century. Schorger (1955:viii) states: "Viewed from all angles, the passenger pigeon was the most impressive species of bird that man has known. Elegant in form and color, graceful and swift of flight, it moved about and nested in such enormous numbers as to confound the senses." Many observers spoke quite literally of flocks of these birds darkening the sky, while their wings roared like constant thunder.

The species was highly specific in its habitat needs. It required as food the mast of the great oak and beech forests of eastern North America. As these forests were cleared for farming, the carrying capacity of the continent for passenger pigeons dropped rapidly. In addition, there was enormous attrition of the nesting colonies by market hunters. Because pigeons tended to nest in concentrated areas, they were peculiarly susceptible to overkill. The birds were shot, netted, poisoned, and trapped, and young were punched out of the flimsy nests. In 1882, during the last great nesting in Wisconsin, for example, it was estimated that over two million birds were sent to market in six weeks. Decimation of the flocks, combined with rapidly shrinking habitat, led to quick extinction. The last passenger pigeon died in the Cincinnati Zoo in 1914. Its death, however, served one important function in dramatizing the need for effective wildlife protection. The conservation movement gained great impetus from the tragedy of the passenger pigeon.

Order Galliformes

GROUSE, QUAILS, PHEASANTS, TURKEYS, AND GUANS

The gallinaceous birds collectively are the most important of the upland game birds. To the array of native species have been added several exotics, the ring-necked pheasant being the most successful. There is scarcely a spot in North America that does not support a population of one or another of the species cited in this section.

Members of the grouse family (Tetraonidae) predominate in the north and in high mountains. As a group, they are decidedly winter-hardy, being able to survive deep snow and extreme low temperatures in boreal, arctic, and alpine habitats. All species of grouse are able to live on buds and green parts of plants, which often are the only available foods in winter. Unusually long intestines and well-developed intestinal caeca are adaptations to survival on such a coarse diet. Certain protozoa and bacteria in the gut help digestion by reducing cellulose to simpler compounds on which the bird can live. The mating system of most grouse is polygamous, with the females accepting sole responsibility for the nest and young. Ptarmigan, on the other hand, are generally monogamous, and in some species the males participate in brood defense. Although renesting may occur if the first nest is destroyed, only one brood per year is raised. All grouse have fully feathered tarsi and pectinate toes.

Quails, pheasants, and partridges (Phasianidae) are distributed in warmer climates, mostly below the tundra and coniferous communities. They are principally seed eaters, although insects, fruits, and tender green leaves often enter the diet seasonally. Four species of quail and the ring-necked pheasant furnish most of the upland game-bird shooting in the United States. The quail and partridges are monogamous breeders, and males generally assist the female in brooding. The pheasant is polygamous, females alone caring for the young.

The turkeys (Meleagrididae) are a very limited family comprising only two species—the common turkey (wild and domestic) and the ocellated turkey of the Yucatan Peninsula. Turkeys are polygamous, like pheasants.

In Mexico and Central America, another family (Cracidae)—which includes the guans, curassows, and chachalacas—is of considerable importance. Only one species of this group, the Texas chachalaca, occurs in the United States.

Two useful volumes giving much additional information about galliformes are those by Johnsgard (1973) and Delacour and Amadon (1973).

Family Tetraonidae (Grouse)

SAGE GROUSE *(Centrocercus urophasianus)*

See also pages 34–35.

RANGE: From southwestern Canada to eastern California and from North Dakota to northern New Mexico

HABITAT: Lives exclusively on sagebrush *(Artemisia)* plains and foothills.

REMARKS: The sage grouse, or "sagehen," is the largest of North American grouse. Males weigh up to 7 pounds (3100 grams) and females up to 5 pounds (2200 grams). The larger size and conspicuous black throat patch and white bristles covering the gular sacs distinguish the male. Immature sage grouse resemble pale females but have pointed and mottled outer primaries and pointed outer wing coverts that are white tipped; young males are larger than females. In common with young of all galliformes, the bursa of Fabricius is enlarged, with a deep lumen. The bursa atrophies in adults (see illustration).

The close ecological association of this bird with sagebrush is an excellent example of extreme specialization to a specific habitat. Sagehens occur only where there are extensive stands of sage. They use the shrubs for nesting, loafing, and escape cover, and they eat the leaves in winter, giving a strong flavor to the flesh. The spring and summer diet includes leaves and seeds of many forbs and grasses.

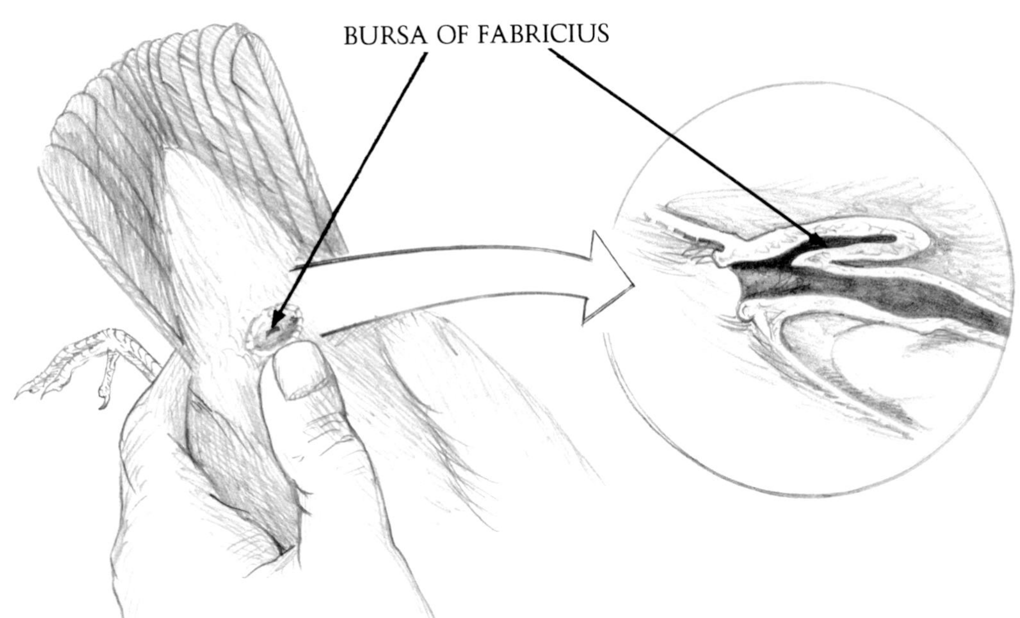

SAGE GROUSE
male
female
BLUE GROUSE
male
female
SPRUCE GROUSE
male
female
male displays

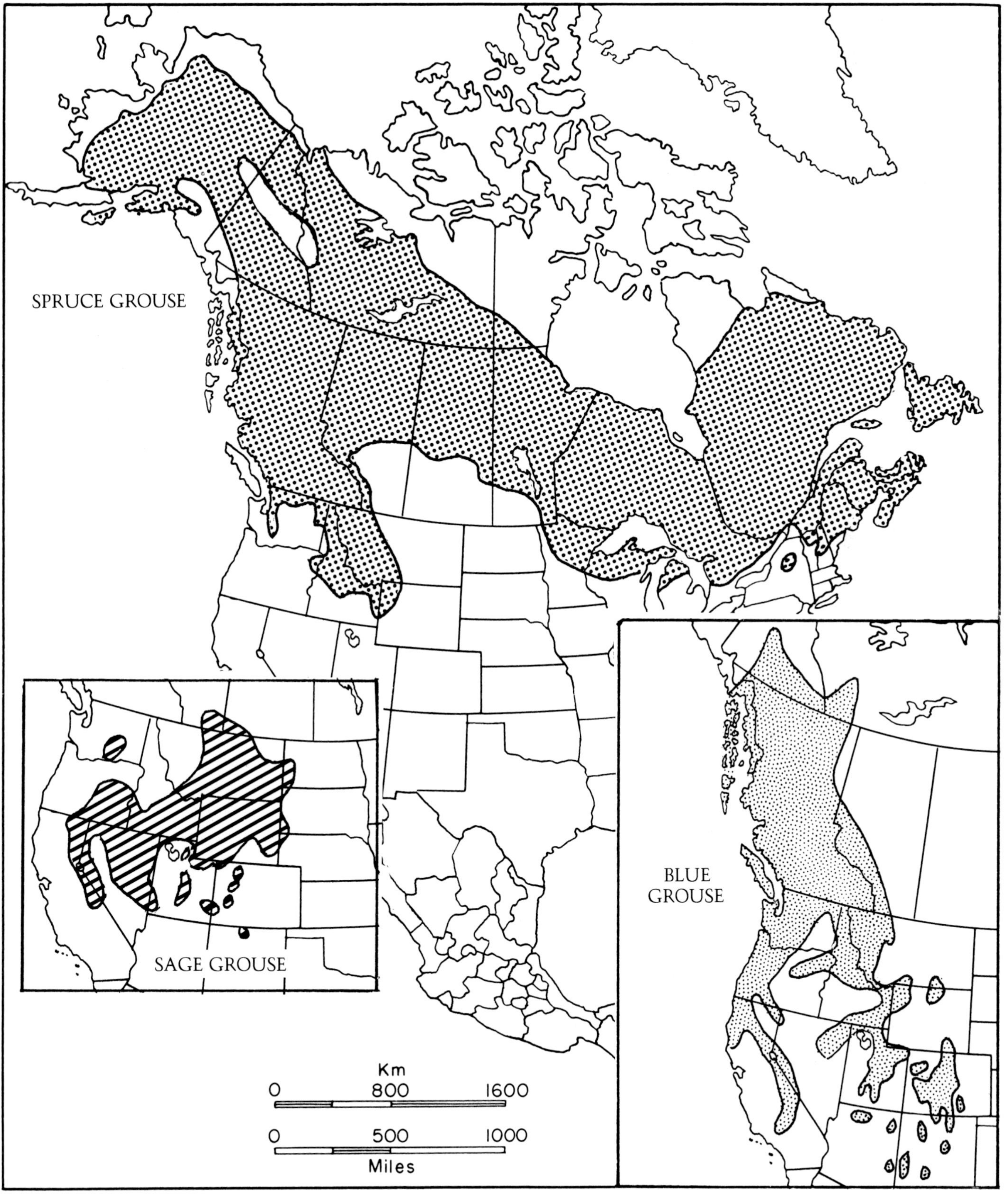
SPRUCE GROUSE
SAGE GROUSE
BLUE GROUSE
Km
0
800
1600
0
500
1000
Miles

Populations decline with livestock grazing, which does little harm to the sage plants but eliminates the forbs and grasses between them. Young sage grouse require green leaves as well as insects for food during the first few months of life. Regulating grazing to stimulate forb and insect production is one of the best management practices. Intensive removal of sage through herbicide spraying and other eradication methods has hastened the decline of the bird (Patterson 1952). It was the major game species in many western states in early American history, but by the late 1960s, the bird was hunted in only five states.

The sage grouse is the classic lek-forming species of North American grouse; its behavior, social system, and life history have been extensively studied (Johnsgard 1973). Males gather on a "lek" (strutting ground) in spring and compete in attracting the females for mating. Males jealously guard their strutting territories, which are 6 to 15 meters in diameter. On each lek, one or two "master cocks" do most of the breeding. The females disperse after breeding and nest and rear young without assistance from the male. Clutch size is 7 to 8; the incubation period is approximately 26 days.

Females and their young flock together in fall and winter, apart from the flocks of adult males.

BLUE GROUSE *(Dendragapus obscurus)*

See also pages 34–35.

RANGE: Mountains of the Pacific slope from southeastern Alaska to the Sierra Nevada of California, eastward to western Alberta and south to Arizona and New Mexico

HABITAT: Coniferous forests containing true firs *(Abies)* or Douglas fir *(Pseudotsuga)* and associated deciduous tree species, shrubs, and forbs

REMARKS: In winter, the blue grouse lives almost exclusively on the needles of *Pseudotsuga, Abies,* or *Tsuga.* An individual bird may remain in one tree for weeks at a time, feeding on the needles and loafing and roosting on the limbs. Windrows of droppings are found beneath these "grouse trees" when the snow melts. The summer and fall diet is more varied, including leaves of herbaceous plants, fruits, berries, and insects (Martin, Zim, and Nelson 1951).

Males are territorial during the spring breeding period. They advertise by a hollow "hooting" call made by puffing air through inflated neck pouches. The sound may be approximated by blowing across the neck of an empty soda-pop bottle. Breeding is polygamous; the male plays no role in nesting or rearing of the young.

Populations of blue grouse are subject to fluctuations in density, but it is not yet documented that the birds are "cyclic" like the ruffed grouse. Clutch size is approximately 6 to 9. The incubation period is 26 days. Although probably less than 50 percent of the nests are successful, there is evidence that unsuccessful females may attempt to renest. The young are precocial, as are all North American gallinaceous birds. Eleven states and two Canadian provinces held hunting seasons in 1970, and 370,000 blue grouse were harvested (Johnsgard 1973:147).

SPRUCE GROUSE *(Canachites canadensis)*

See also pages 34–35.

RANGE: Boreal forests throughout Alaska, Canada, and in the United States the northern Rockies, Lake States, and New England

HABITAT: Spruce, fir, hemlock, and jack pine forests

REMARKS: The spruce grouse has the most extensive range of any of the North American Tetraonidae. It thrives in the extensive boreal coniferous forests; hunting is permitted throughout most of the range. Population density is ordinarily not high—7 to 12 males per square mile (or 3 to 5 per square kilometer) have been reported. Breeding is polygamous, which usually means that females outnumber males. In forest openings, the rather boldly marked males advertise their territories with a variety of displays including strutting, tail-fanning and wing-clapping flights. The females tend their nests with 5 to 12 eggs and rear the chicks without aid from the male.

In winter, spruce grouse eat largely the buds and needles of spruce, fir, or pine. The summer diet is more varied and includes berries and tender leaves, plus available insects and arthropods.

The principal predator is the goshawk *(Accipiter gentilis)*. On the Kenai Peninsula in southern Alaska, Ellison (1974) found that most of the deaths among his study population were attributable to this hawk.

The spruce grouse tends to be very naive and unwary (it is often called the "fool hen") and can be killed with a stick or a thrown rock. Because of its diet of conifer needles, it is not particularly tasty. Of all the forest grouse, this species—because of its northern distribution—has been least affected by man's activity.

WILLOW, ROCK, AND WHITE-TAILED PTARMIGAN (*Lagopus lagopus, L. mutus,* and *L. leucurus* respectively)

See also pages 38–39.

RANGE: In North America: willow ptarmigan ranges from arctic Alaska south to central British Columbia and across Northwest Territories to Newfoundland and associated islands off Alaska and Newfoundland; rock ptarmigan's range is essentially that of willow ptarmigan but with more northern distribution; white-tailed ptarmigan occurs from central Alaska south to Washington state and alpine areas of Rocky Mountains south to northern New Mexico. The willow and rock ptarmigan are circumpolar in distribution.

HABITAT: Tundra, arctic, and alpine

REMARKS: Ptarmigan are unique among grouse in that they undergo an almost complete molt to a white winter plumage and have fully feathered feet. Both characteristics are adaptations to an arctic environment. Since these birds are major game species only in Alaska and the northern Canadian provinces, they are considered collectively in this book. North American ptarmigan have not been so well studied as their European relatives. All species are extremely "tame" in North America, relying on their protective coloration to avoid predators and hunters.

WILLOW PTARMIGAN
ROCK PTARMIGAN
WHITE-TAILED PTARMIGAN

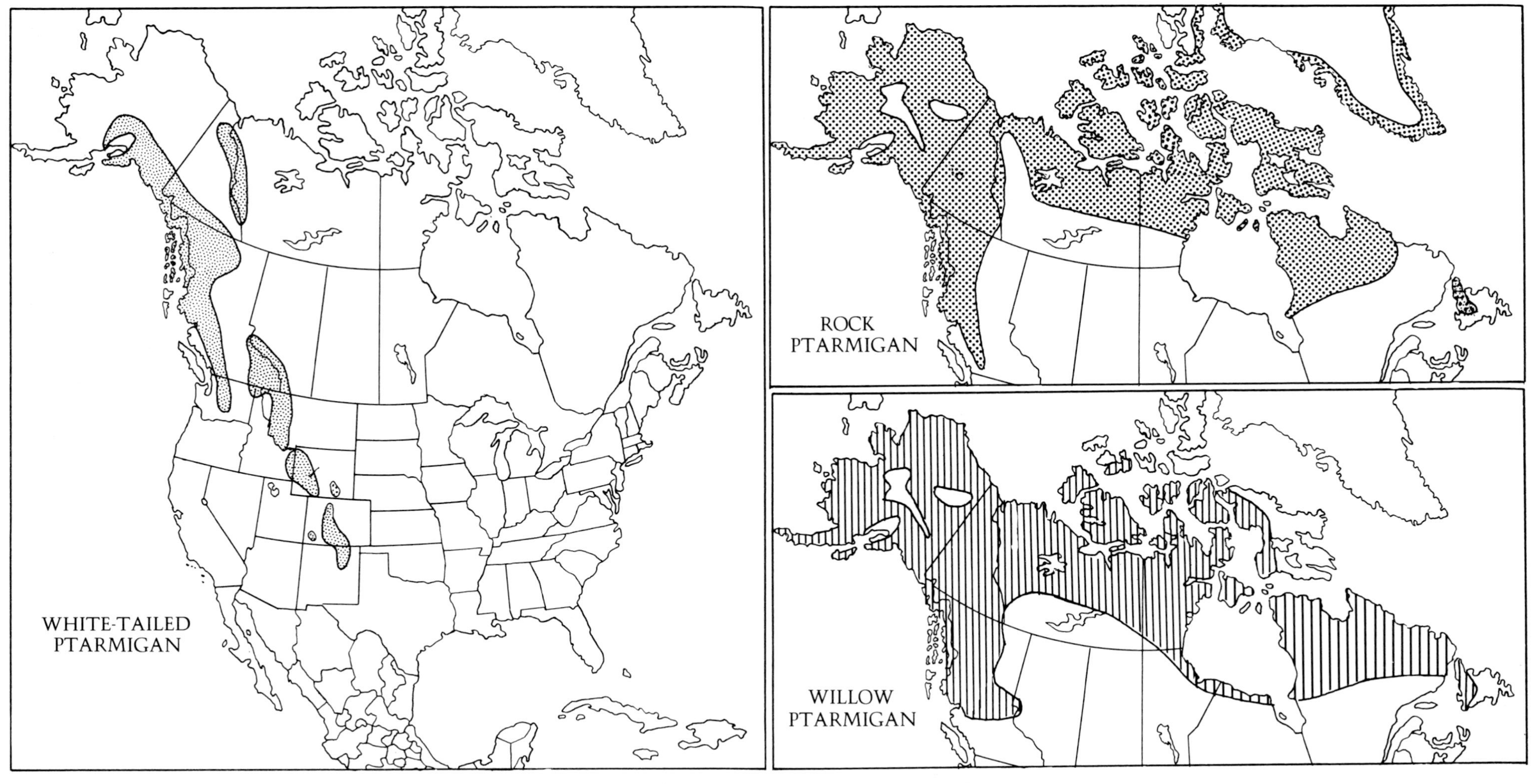

WHITE-TAILED
PTARMIGAN
ROCK
PTARMIGAN
WILLOW
PTARMIGAN

Ptarmigan have in common a winter food dependence upon the buds, twigs, and catkins of willow *(Salix)*, alder *(Alnus)*, and birch *(Betula)*. The proportion of these plant species varies in composition depending on the species and location of ptarmigan studied. Extensive migrations between winter and summer ranges are characteristic of willow and rock ptarmigan. White-tailed ptarmigan exhibit yearly altitudinal migrations in some areas.

The three species differ somewhat in habitat preference. The willow ptarmigan frequents more moist, luxuriant tundra. The rock ptarmigan (considered the most arctic-adapted of the three species) selects harsh, dry highlands. The white-tailed ptarmigan inhabits the alpine zone. Rarely, an observer may find all three species together in some northern areas.

Sex and age determination is difficult. Experience with specimens is necessary to attain competence in segregating these classes. Johnsgard (1973) presents a good summary of these criteria in the three species for all seasons as well as for immature classes. The white-tailed ptarmigan retains a white tail throughout the year that permits distinction from the rock and willow species, which have black inner rectrices. Rock and willow ptarmigan may be distinguished by bill size and color, the rock having a black, weak bill and the willow having a gray, heavier bill.

Males establish and advertise breeding territories in spring. Mating is generally monogamous, although individual male rock ptarmigan may breed with two females. All females nest within the territories of their mates. The highly developed male sexual displays, social hierarchy, and sexual dimorphism common to other species of grouse are not noted among this group.

All males remain with the females until the eggs hatch. European workers (Jenkins *et al.* 1963) have noted that the male willow ptarmigan, unlike other ptarmigan, frequently remains with the female and participates in brood defense. The birds generally segregate into male and female winter flocks. Clutch size varies between 5 and 9 eggs, depending on the species; incubation time is approximately 22 to 24 days.

Unlike many other species of our native gallinaceous birds, the ptarmigans, primarily because of their remote habitat, have been little affected by man's activity. Sheep grazing in the alpine reaches of the Rocky Mountains seems to be detrimental to the white-tailed ptarmigan by thinning or destroying willow patches essential for winter survival.

RUFFED GROUSE *(Bonasa umbellus)*

See also pages 42–43.

RANGE: Alaska, Canada, and northern United States south in mountains or heavily forested areas to northern Georgia, northern California, Nevada (introduced), and Utah

HABITAT: Deciduous or mixed deciduous/coniferous forest communities, of which aspen (*Populus* sp.) is almost invariably a component.

REMARKS: The ruffed grouse is one of the principal game birds in the northeastern United States and eastern Canada; it is less abundant in western North America. Optimum habitat consists of aspen stands of mixed ages. Gullion (1972:4) states: "Ruffed grouse need aspen in three age classes: dense sucker stands less than 10 years old for brood cover; sapling and pole stands 10 to 25 years old for adult wintering and breeding cover; and older aspen for food, and as wintering and nesting cover." The buds and catkins of mature male aspen trees constitute the primary winter food of ruffed grouse. On occasion, catkins of alder, hazel, or birch may be taken. Summer foods include fruits, berries, wild grapes, and succulent green leaves of clover and other forbs. In optimum range, spring breeding stocks may be one pair per 6 to 8 acres (2 to 3 hectares). After a good breeding season, a population can increase by fall to a bird per acre. Normal annual loss of about 55 percent indicates that at least half of the birds present in fall are surplus and may be harvested by hunting. Such high populations decline to very low levels at 10-year intervals (the "10-year grouse cycle"). Reasons for the cycle are not fully understood, but causative factors may include severe predation (Keith 1963) or lack of winter snow cover (Gullion 1972). Deep, loose snow is important for winter survival, as the birds dive into snow for night roosting.

Male ruffed grouse advertise their breeding territories by "drumming" their wings in the air, producing a thumping sound that is audible for long distances. Breeding is promiscuous, the females coming to the drumming log for mating, then nesting and rearing the chicks with no help from the male. An average clutch is 11 to 12 eggs, of which perhaps 3 or 4 chicks may be reared.

Two color phases are common among ruffed grouse—red and gray. Both may occur in the same population and even in the same brood. At higher latitudes and altitudes, the gray phase predominates. Birds of this color may be better adapted physiologically to colder climate.

Several books have been written about the ruffed grouse, of which the volume by Bump *et al.* (1947) is the classic account. A recently organized Ruffed Grouse Society fosters the conservation and management of this fine game bird.

PRAIRIE CHICKEN *(Tympanuchus cupido)*

See also pages 42–43.

RANGE: Originally, Great Plains region west to eastern Alberta, and south to New Mexico, and coastal Texas; an isolated population lived in New England south to Maryland.

HABITAT: Prairies and brushy grasslands

REMARKS: Most of the original prairie habitat of the prairie chicken has been plowed for agriculture. The species now exists only on a remnant of its original range, around prairie marshes, in the sandhills of the Dakotas, brushlands of Wisconsin and Michigan, shinnery oak *(Quercus havardi)* and bluestem *(Andropogon)* grassland sandhills of eastern New Mexico and west Texas. Within these areas, however, it is often abundant during population highs and is regularly hunted in six states. Estimated harvest for 1970 was 85,000 (Johnsgard 1973:147). One subspecies, *T. c. attwateri*, found in isolated populations in Texas, is currently listed as rare and endangered (Lehmann 1941). Of all the grouse, this species has been the most adversely affected by human activity.

Prairie chickens eat 80 to 90 percent plant matter and more seeds and less green plant material than other members of the grouse family. Mast and cultivated crops such as corn, sorghum, and milo are important winter foods. When forced, chickens can subsist on buds like other grouse.

pectinate toe
female tail
male
RUFFED GROUSE
male displays
male
PRAIRIE CHICKEN
SHARP-TAILED GROUSE
male

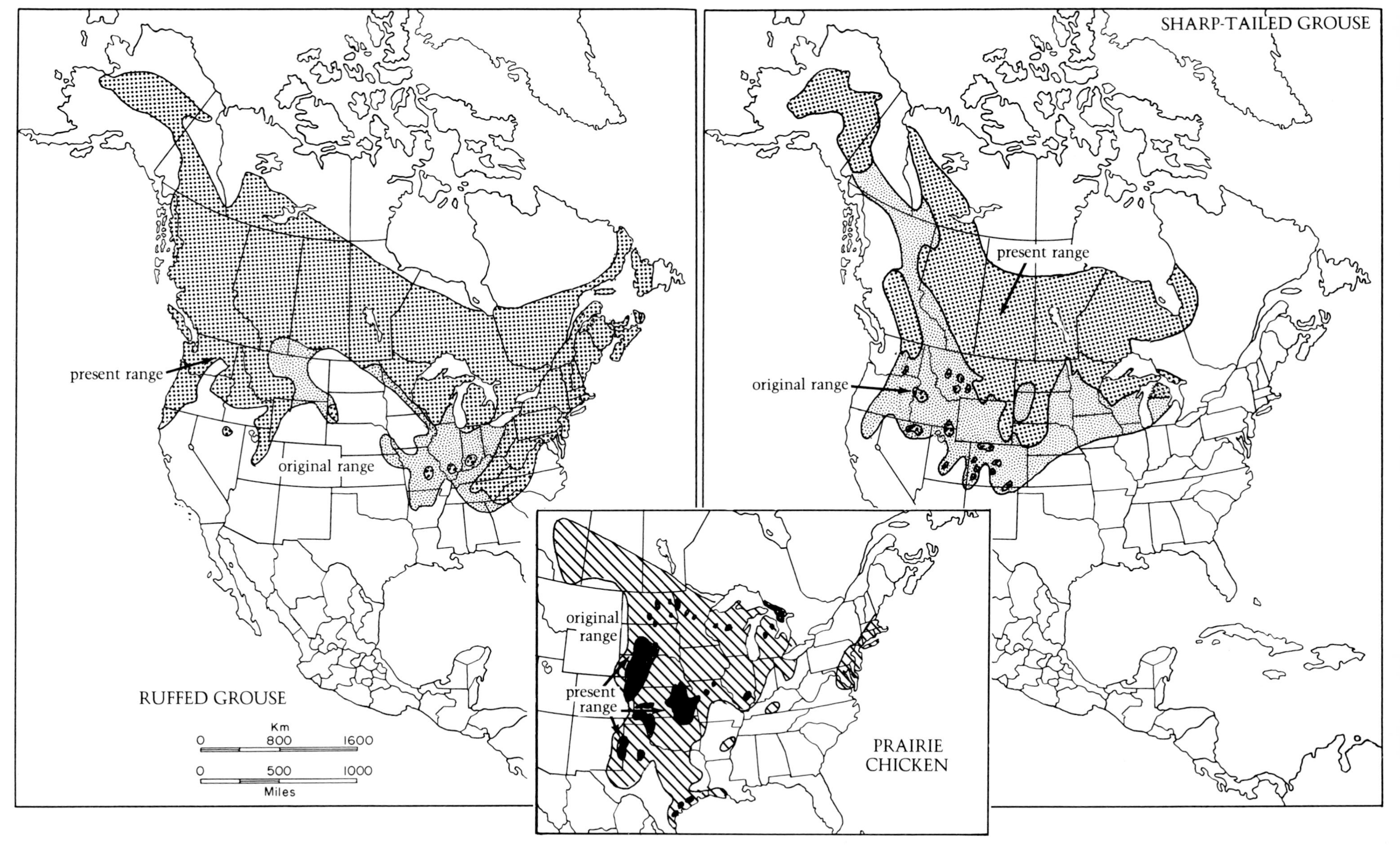
present range
original range
RUFFED GROUSE
Km
0
800
1600
0
500
1000
Miles
SHARP-TAILED GROUSE
present range
original range
original range
present range
PRAIRIE CHICKEN

Prairie chickens and sharp-tailed grouse, like the sage grouse, are polygamous, lek-forming species (i.e., they use traditional display and breeding grounds often referred to as "booming" or dancing grounds). Males defend territories a few meters in diameter while soliciting females, which then select an individual male with which to breed. A few males establish dominance and assume the role of "master cocks" and, thereby, breed with the majority of females. Females, on the other hand, assume an exaggerated behavior of submission presumably to avoid the attacks of males. The cocks use air sacs on the neck to produce the booming sound.

Male prairie chickens can be identified by elongated pinnae, conspicuous yellow comb above the eyes, bare areas (air sacs) of yellow skin on the side of the neck, and solid brown tail feathers. Females have barred outer tail feathers. Average clutch size is 12 to 14 with the female assuming all care for the eggs and young. Renesting may occur if the first clutch is destroyed. The incubation period is 23 to 26 days. Populations undergo 10-year cycles of abundance, concurrent with ruffed grouse and snowshoe hare.

SHARP-TAILED GROUSE *(Pedioecetes phasianellus)*

See also pages 42–43.

RANGE: Northcentral and northwestern United States and southcentral Canada

HABITAT: Mixed prairie and parklands, semidesert scrub, and dry grasslands

REMARKS: The sharp-tailed grouse resembles the prairie chicken in its habitat requirements, and in some places the two occur together. But the sharptail requires more woody vegetation and less grassland than the prairie chicken (Ammann, 1957). The sharptail range extends considerably farther to the north and west. Apparently, this species can endure more severe winter weather than can the prairie chicken, and it has broader habitat tolerances. The sharptail's normal winter diet consists largely of buds and catkins of aspen, birch, and willow. Summer foods are fruits, berries, and tender green leaves.

Habitat alteration in the form of heavy grazing, hay cutting, brush and tree removal, and agriculture has caused extirpation of the species along the former southern border of its range. However, this species remains much more abundant than the prairie chicken.

Males of this species may be reliably identified by the linear markings on the tail feathers; females have transverse barring. Immature birds can be recognized by bursa. Mating system, clutch size, and incubation period, as well as parental duties, are similar to those of the prairie chicken.

Family Phasianidae (Quails, Partridges, Pheasants)

CALIFORNIA QUAIL *(Lophortyx californicus)*

See also pages 46–47.

RANGE: Southern Oregon southward through California to the tip of Baja California; introduced in British Columbia, Washington, Oregon, Idaho, Nevada, and Utah.

HABITAT: Oak woodland, chaparral, brushy foothills, and riparian strips transecting deserts and Great Basin shrublands

REMARKS: The California quail is the west-coast representative of a group of closely related quails that range through the arid and semiarid portions of southwestern North America. When California was in process of settlement, the center of abundance of the California quail was in the rich valley lands partially cleared for agriculture. The bird was widely known as the "valley quail," and its numbers were fabulous. During the late 1800s and early 1900s, market hunters sold millions of quail in the markets of San Francisco and Los Angeles (177,366 in the year 1895–96 alone). But continued clearing of valley lands and intensive grazing of the foothills largely eliminated the cover and food needed by quail. Their population declined to a relatively low level, where it remains today.

This species is highly gregarious, occurring in large coveys, averaging 40 to 60 birds, occasionally reaching hundreds. The birds frequent brushy thickets, which offer cover from hawks and other predators. They feed in adjoining open areas where forbs and weeds scatter abundant seeds on the ground or offer tender green leafage. Some important food plants are clovers *(Trifolium)*, filarees *(Erodium)*, lupines *(Lupinus)*, lotus *(Lotus)*, and fiddleneck *(Amsinckia)*. Acorns are taken avidly when available. Drinking water is essential in hot weather, especially for juveniles. Adults can subsist on moisture derived from green plant foods such as clover leaves. California quail roost at night in trees or tall shrubs with dense foliage that conceals and protects the sleeping birds from owls.

In spring, the birds form pairs. Males attend their mates throughout the nesting period and help to rear the young. In years of exceptionally favorable rainfall and abundant food, a female quail may produce two broods of chicks, the male rearing the first batch while the second clutch is laid and incubated. In such years, all the unmated cocks are drawn into the reproductive effort, either as mates for hens attempting second broods or as guardians of stray chicks. This phenomenon occurs only once or twice in a decade. One clutch of a dozen or so young per pair is the norm.

The most effective management measures to encourage California quail are to supply the necessary kinds of food, cover, and water in close proximity. Good habitat will support populations of up to two birds per acre, and hunting may be permitted to take as much as 25 percent of the autumn population. In California, the statewide quail kill may exceed a million birds some years. In suburban areas, the same management procedures may be followed to produce a backyard quail covey, whose sole purpose is to add a touch of beauty and cheer to the neighborhood.

For a full account of the ecology and management of the California quail, the reader is referred to the book by Leopold (1977).

GAMBEL QUAIL *(Lophortyx gambelii)*

See also pages 46–47.

RANGE: Desert regions of southwestern United States and northwestern Mexico

HABITAT: Sonoran and Mojave desert scrub and desert riparian zones

REMARKS: The Gambel quail is closely related to the California quail and resembles it in its flocking, feeding habits, behavior, preference for roosting in trees, and vocalizations. The Gambel quail differs in being more desert-adapted. It is most abun-

CALIFORNIA QUAIL
male
female
GAMBEL QUAIL
male
female
SCALED QUAIL
MOUNTAIN QUAIL
MONTEZUMA QUAIL
male
female
BOBWHITE QUAIL
male

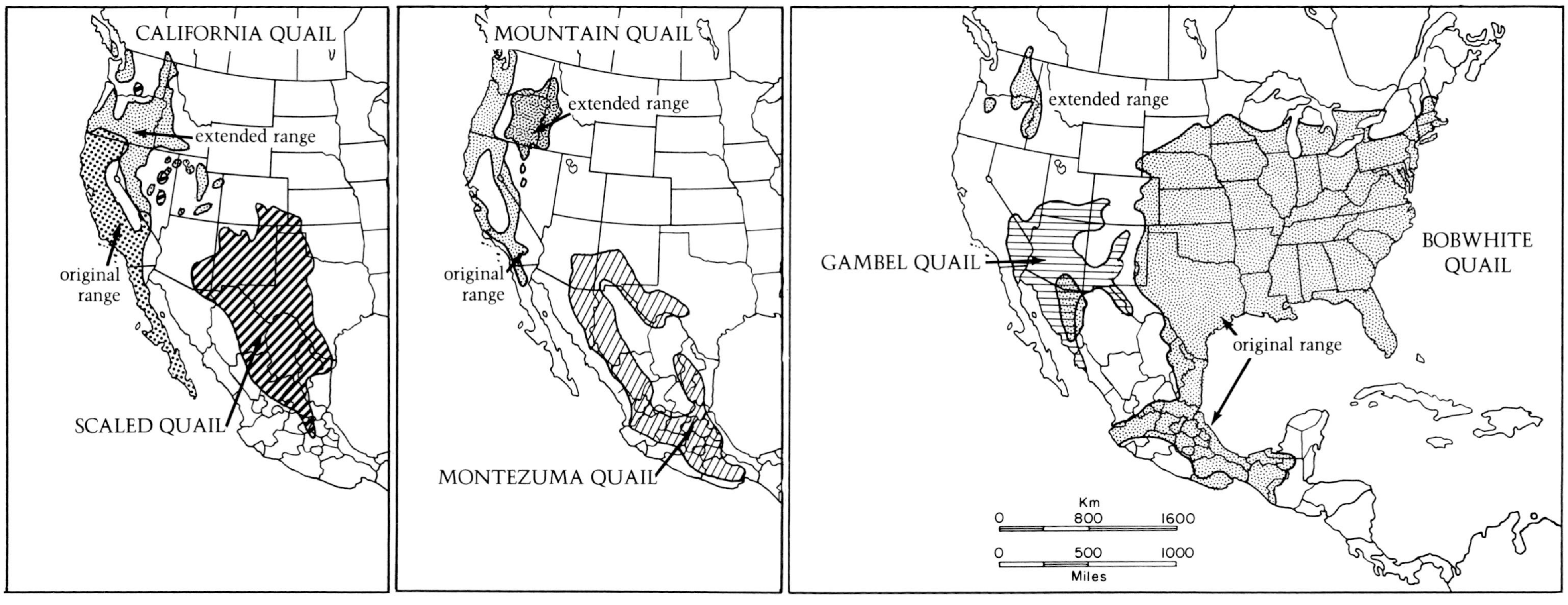
CALIFORNIA QUAIL
extended range
original range
SCALED QUAIL
MOUNTAIN QUAIL
extended range
original range
MONTEZUMA QUAIL
extended range
GAMBEL QUAIL
BOBWHITE QUAIL
original range
Km
0 800 1600
0 500 1000
Miles

dant in Arizona and Sonora, where mesquite *(Prosopis)*, chamisa *(Atriplex)*, catclaw *(Acacia)*, creosote bush *(Larrea)*, tamarisk *(Tamarix)*, prickly pear *(Opuntia)*, and/or other desert shrub vegetation is dominant. The birds feed on the seeds of various desert annuals (e.g., *Erodium, Lotus, Lupinus*) most of the year and on greens and fruits during the rainy season (Gullion 1960). In years when no rain falls, Gambel quail may not pair and nest; the winter coveys simply remain intact through spring and summer. Apparently, some aspect of qualitative nutrition, supplied by green feed, is necessary to complete reproduction. Conversely, in exceptionally favorable, wet years, Gambel quail (like the California quail) may raise more than one brood—a rare occurrence in gallinaceous birds.

Males do not usually incubate, but they do assist the female in brooding the young. Males are distinguished by their black club-shaped crest feathers, black throats, rusty crown, and black "horseshoe" chest patch. Females lack these characters and carry short, brown crests. Coveys consolidate in winter and may contain over 100 birds.

Arizona is the center of distribution for this species in the United States. Grazing and land-reclamation programs are the two primary causes for deterioration of the Gambel quail's habitat.

SCALED QUAIL *(Callipepla squamata)*

See also pages 46–47.

RANGE: Southwestern United States through the temperate uplands of northern and central Mexico; introduced into Washington and Nevada.

HABITAT: Chihuahuan scrub desert and arid grassland

REMARKS: Scaled quail and Gambel quail frequently are sympatric in northern Mexico and in the southwestern United States, but the only quail found on the vast desert areas of central Mexico is the scaled quail. Desert populations exhibit violent fluctuations in numbers, the "lows" apparently following dry years, the "highs" resulting from above-average rainfall. In years of no rainfall (as with Gambel quail), little or no nesting occurs.

Scaled quail eat a wide variety of seeds at all times of year, and—like the California and Gambel quail—they consume quantities of greens during rainy periods.

Much of the range of the scaled quail has been overgrazed by livestock. Desirable cover plants, such as *Atriplex*, often are consumed by the stock; carrying capacity of the range for quail is thereby reduced. Conversely, in well-watered localities moderate grazing may have some beneficial effect on quail range by encouraging the growth of forbs and weeds that provide the basic diet (Campbell *et al.* 1973).

Sexes are very nearly identical. Reproductive biology is similar to the *Lophortyx* species.

MOUNTAIN QUAIL *(Oreortyx pictus)*

See also pages 46–47.

RANGE: Pacific slope from southern British Columbia (Vancouver Island) to Baja California, east to southwestern Idaho (introduced) and Nevada

HABITAT: Evergreen chaparral, evergreen-broadleaf forest, coniferous forest with shrub understory, and pinon-juniper woodland on some desert ranges of California

REMARKS: Mountain quail are unique among United States quail in that some populations undertake annual altitudinal migrations of considerable distance on foot between winter and summer ranges. Sierra Nevada populations breed in coniferous communities and winter in the lower chaparral zone. They may be locally abundant in the Sierra and Coast ranges, but they frequent such dense brush and steep slopes that they are hunted much less than California quail. The birds are very secretive and when pursued tend to run rather than fly, thus further compounding hunting difficulties.

The California quail and mountain quail are sometimes sympatric, but competition between the species is avoided through habitat selection and differences in diet. The mountain quail is a "sequential specialist," hulling acorns in the fall; eating mushrooms, flowers, and greens in winter; and digging for bulbs *(Lithophragma)* in spring and summer (Gutiérrez 1980). Although the mountain quail does consume some seeds and greens of annual plants, it is not dependent on them, as is the California quail. Daily drinking water is necessary during hot weather.

The clutch size of the mountain quail is the smallest of all the species of United States quail, averaging 7 to 9. Fall coveys are also small (6 to 12) and generally represent family groups or aggregations of adults that were unsuccessful the previous breeding season. Pairing is monogamous and males, unlike those of other United States quail, presumably share incubation duties with their mates, as indicated by well-developed brood patches found on most mountain quail males during the breeding season.

The mountain quail and scaled quail are peculiar in that the sexes are very nearly monomorphic. The mountain quail is the largest quail found north of the Mexican tropical forests. Johnsgard (1973) gives an estimated annual harvest figure of 375,000 birds.

BOBWHITE QUAIL *(Colinus virginianus)*

See also pages 46–47.

RANGE: Eastern United States from South Dakota and Maine south to Texas, Florida, and southern Mexico; a distinct subspecies, the masked bobwhite, was native to southern Arizona and Sonora but is now virtually extinct. The bobwhite has been successfully introduced in Washington, Oregon, and Idaho.

HABITAT: Weedy fields bordered by brush or woodlots

REMARKS: Bobwhite is the primary upland game bird of the eastern United States. It is a favorite quarry for hunters who enjoy shooting over pointing dogs. At the same time, its pert demeanor and cheerful call notes bring pleasure to nonhunters as well. Average populations are not dense but are so widely distributed that there are few areas within its range that are out of earshot of the ringing "bobwhite" mating call in spring.

The two components of habitat that are essential to bobwhite are (1) brushy cover, and (2) weedy fields or pastures for feeding. The brush need not be extensive to serve as cover from predators and weather, but it must be dense. Fence rows of *Rosa multiflora* often are planted to separate fields and to serve the cover needs of quail and other birds. Among the favorite foods of bobwhite are the seeds of ragweed *(Ambrosia)*, beggarweed *(Desmodium)*, clovers *(Trifolium)*, and various species of lespedeza *(Lespedeza)*, both native and cultivated. Many kinds of grain crops are utilized (wheat, corn, soybeans, etc.) as well as acorns and other mast. Except in times of severe drought, free drinking water is not generally required. The birds get adequate moisture from dew and green leaves.

Although northern bobwhites are reasonably winter-hardy, they suffer severe losses in years of deep snow or bitter cold. Populations are more secure, and hence more consistent, in southern areas of milder winter climate. Optimum habitat, in Georgia, for example, or in south Texas, may support a bird per acre. Allowable harvest of the fall population is said by Rosene (1969) to be about 40 to 45 percent. With hunting pressure of that intensity, enough breeding stock survives until spring to recoup the losses. Bobwhites are monogamous, each pair raising a brood (or attempting to do so) from a clutch of about a dozen eggs. Nests and eggs are often destroyed by snakes, ground squirrels, opossums, or raccoons. Then the pair will usually renest and try again. Fall age ratios average 300 young to 100 adults, whereas California quail will run about half that many young. The high productivity of bobwhites permits generous hunting regulations. It also buffers normal predation on adults by Cooper hawks, sharp-shinned hawks, and various mammalian predators.

A classic volume on the bobwhite quail, and one of the landmarks of wildlife publication, is that of Herbert Stoddard (1931). A more recent publication is the book by Rosene (1969).

MONTEZUMA QUAIL *(Cyrtonyx montezumae)*

See also pages 46–47.

RANGE: Arizona, New Mexico, and southwestern Texas south to Oaxaca, Mexico

HABITAT: Pine-oak woodlands, and Mexican encinal

REMARKS: Montezuma (Mearn's) quail are dependent upon the bulbs of *Oxalis*, *Cyperus*, and other tuber-producing plants. Their strong, long claws and powerful leg muscles clearly indicate their adaptation to a digging type of foraging behavior. The birds are sedentary and maintain small covey ranges, but in some areas they do undergo altitudinal migration between winter and summer ranges. The species is typically associated with the dense, tall grass understory of the pine-oak woodland or the Mexican encinal (oak woodland) and, therefore, is severely affected by heavy grazing. A decrease in total distribution of the species has been noted since the early 1900s, probably as a result of livestock grazing.

Breeding is monogamous. But although the birds pair in late winter and early spring, they do not nest until the start of summer rains in July and August. The average clutch is 11, and incubation is about 26 days. The male does not participate in incubation but does help brood the young. Fall coveys are small (6 to 10), presumably representing single family units. The natural history of this species is summarized by Leopold and McCabe (1957).

A covey when flushed will usually fly only 100 meters. Then the individual birds hide in dense grass or other ground cover. The scatters hold well for a pointing dog. They are exceptionally fast flyers and offer very sporty and difficult shooting as they dodge through oak or pine forest. Their relatively large size makes them excellent table fare. Arizona and New Mexico are currently the only states that maintain legal hunting of this bird, which, however, is widely hunted in Mexico.

This species represents a different evolutionary lineage than the other quail discussed in this book, being closely related to the tropically distributed quail.

GRAY PARTRIDGE *(Perdix perdix)*

See also pages 52–53.

RANGE: Native to Europe and Asia; successfully introduced in the prairie provinces of Canada, and the northcentral United States as far west as eastern Oregon. In North America, the species is generally called "Hungarian partridge."

HABITAT: Rich prairies, particularly associations of native grasslands, hayfields, and extensive wheatlands

REMARKS: After their introduction, "huns" gradually extended their range over much of the northcentral states and prairie provinces and now form an important part of the game harvest in those areas. Seeds, especially small grains such as wheat, are the principal item of diet. These birds avoid wooded areas and only sparingly use brushy cover. Their nests are generally in hayfields or native grasslands.

The sexes are similar in appearance and cannot always be distinguished by plumage differences. Immatures can be distinguished from adults by their pointed outer primaries. Mating is monogamous; the male does not share incubation duties but helps his mate attend the brood. Clutch size is typically 15 to 17, and the incubation period is 24 to 25 days (Weigand 1980).

Gray partridges are strong, fast flyers. A covey may fly nearly a kilometer before alighting. In good cover, the scattered birds hold well for pointing dogs. The gray partridge is much more satisfactory to hunt than the chukar partridge, which tends to run after completing a flight.

CHUKAR PARTRIDGE *(Alectoris chukar)*

See also pages 52–53.

RANGE: *Alectoris* is native from southern Europe to China. Stock from India—hence, *A. chukar*—has been successfully introduced to all western states and British Columbia. The chukar has spread into northern Baja California.

HABITAT: Rocky desert areas and arid sagebrush lands; rocks constitute primary cover.

REMARKS: Although many introductions of this species have failed throughout the United States, the bird has become firmly established in the west, especially in the Great Basin sagebrush region. The distribution of the chukar closely follows that of cheatgrass *(Bromus tectorum)*, an exotic annual grass, the seeds of which form a staple item of the diet.

Chukars prefer steep slopes, especially if talus or other rocky escape cover is present. They need daily drinking water during hot weather. One effective management technique is spring development or guzzler installation.

Sexes are indistinguishable without resorting to morphological measurements, so the role of the male in incubation and brood care has been difficult to determine. The question is not yet resolved. Mating, however, is monogamous. Clutch size varies between 10 to 20 but 15 is about average. An incubation period of 24 days is typical.

When hunted, chukars fly freely and hit the ground on a dead run, usually uphill. The chukar is fast becoming a popular game bird because of the challenging aspect of the hunt and the bird's relatively large size (600 to 800 grams). A recent harvest estimate of 658,000 birds in the United States attests to this popularity.

GRAY PARTRIDGE
CHUKAR PARTRIDGE
male
RING-NECKED PHEASANT
female
WILD TURKEY
female
male–display

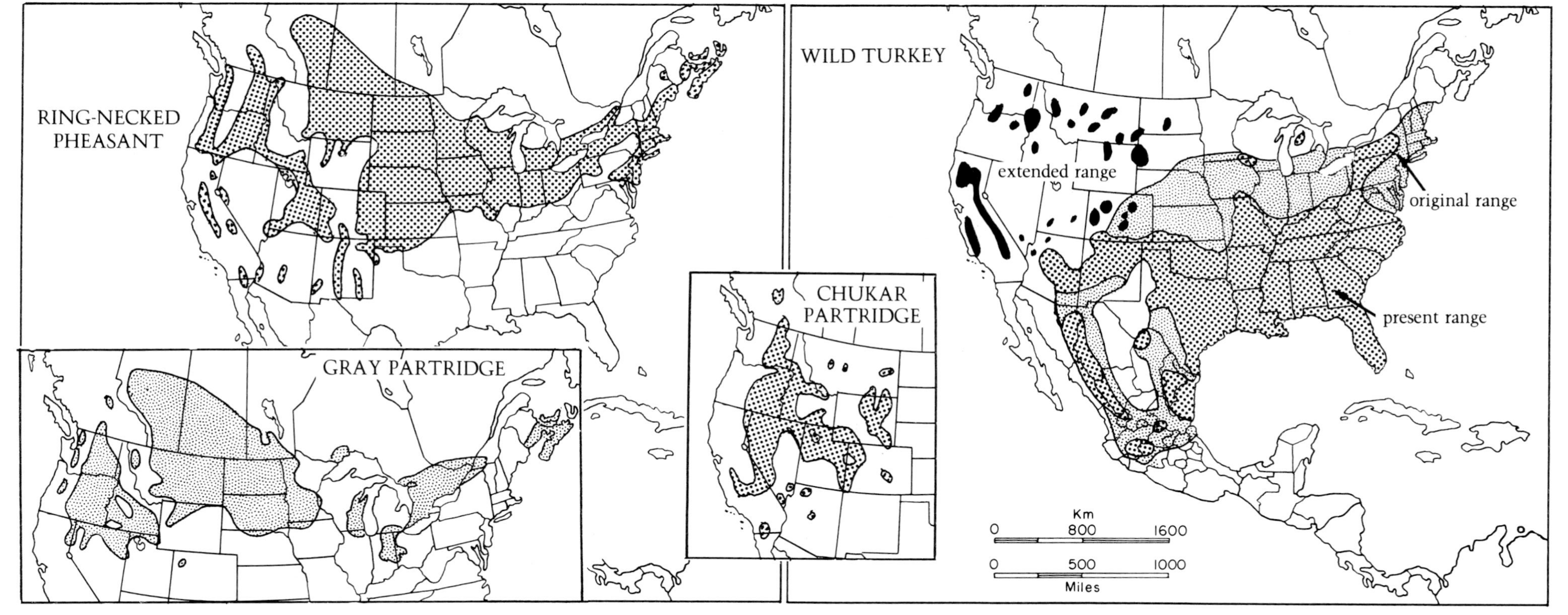
RING-NECKED
PHEASANT
GRAY PARTRIDGE
CHUKAR
PARTRIDGE
WILD TURKEY
extended range
original range
present range
Km
0
800
1600
0
500
1000
Miles

RING-NECKED PHEASANT *(Phasianus colchicus)*

See also pages 52–53.

RANGE: Native of Asia and introduced into Europe by Marco Polo. Further introductions led to establishment in North America, New Zealand, and Hawaii.

HABITAT: Rich farm lands, especially where grains like rice, wheat, or corn are raised. Can exist with a minimum of cover but requires some escape areas such as weedy fencerows or ditch banks, cattail patches, or brushy woods.

REMARKS: Pheasants are much the most successful of the introduced game birds in North America. They have replaced the prairie chicken on farm lands throughout the midwestern United States, where otherwise there would be no abundant gallinaceous bird today. The prairie chicken was driven out by farming before the pheasant was introduced. In irrigated valleys of the western United States, the ringneck is present, often abundant (i.e., the Central Valley of California).

Pheasants feed primarily on the seeds of weeds and cultivated grains and legumes. Greens constitute a minor (although important) part of the diet. In spring, males crow on territories of one to several hectares. Mating is polygamous, and the hens in each harem raise their young without assistance from the cock. Only the most vigorous cocks have harems. The weaker or less aggressive ones go mateless. Because of their mating habit, it is customary to permit legal hunting of cocks only (or mainly cocks), preserving the majority of the hens as breeders. One cock can serve as many as 10 to 20 hens in the wild, and even more in confinement.

For many years, the center of pheasant abundance in North America was in the Dakotas. Birds were there by the thousands, attracting hunters from as far as New York and Los Angeles. But as agriculture intensified, even small strips of cover, such as those along fences or roadsides, were plowed up to put every available square foot of land into crops. In the 1960s and 1970s, the pheasant population declined for lack of cover for rearing chicks. Birds are now relatively scarce in the former "pheasant bowl" of the continent. Similar agricultural trends are threatening pheasant populations elsewhere on rich soils.

Family Meleagrididae (Turkeys)

WILD TURKEY *(Meleagris gallopavo)*

See also pages 52–53.

RANGE: New York, south and west to Arizona through the highlands of western and eastern Mexico to the states of Michoacan and Veracruz, respectively; introduced into 16 states beyond its original distribution.

HABITAT: Pine and oak forests, mixed hardwoods, and oak woodland of upland and lowland

REMARKS: The turkey is our largest upland game bird, with some individuals weighing over 20 pounds (9 kilograms). Its history is woven into the culture of the continent. The Tarascan Indians of the highlands of west-central Mexico probably first domesticated the bird, which has become the most important domestic livestock developed in North America (Schorger 1966). The wild turkey was proposed as our national symbol by Benjamin Franklin but narrowly lost to the bald eagle in a subsequent vote by Congress.

The clearing of land for agriculture, extensive logging, as well as market hunting, and the introduction of a protozoan parasite common to the domestic chicken (called blackhead disease), all served to sharply decrease wild turkey populations and their distribution. The situation became so desperate as to provoke serious concern for the loss of the bird as a game species. However, many of the marginal lands cleared in the early history of the country have been abandoned and have returned to forest. Blackhead is not so prevalent a problem now, because fewer chickens have free range. Concomitant with these changes, wildlife agencies and biologists began an extensive program of research and restoration through trapping and transplanting wild stock. The results rank as one of the great success stories of game management. Within the last 30 to 40 years, the number of states conducting turkey hunting seasons has risen from 19 to at least 35; the annual harvest has increased from 40,000 to 137,000.

Turkeys are polygamous, the males establishing "gobbling" areas, where they attempt to attract hens. The hens lay 10 to 13 eggs and incubate them for 28 days. When you consider the turkey's large size, the nests are surprisingly hard to find. The hens raise the poults without help from males. Often hens and their broods will join to form large winter flocks; males usually gather separately in small flocks after the gobbling season.

Turkeys eat a variety of nuts, berries, seeds, greens, and bulbs as well as insects. Turkey welfare often depends upon the production of mast crops, especially acorns. When foraging, turkeys scratch vigorously in the forest duff, uncovering food items for themselves and leaving clearly visible evidence of their efforts. The bird has demonstrated its adaptability to habitats by occupying a number of vegetation communities throughout its range. The turkey is considered the most wary of all upland game species and ranks as the choicest table fare.

Order Anseriformes

SWANS, GEESE, AND DUCKS

Waterfowl are among the most important game birds in North America. Yet their future seems precarious. Ducks and geese are limited to specific types of water and marshland habitat that are being constantly reduced by drainage, reclamation, and pollution; they are peculiarly vulnerable to hunting, because of their concentration on the remaining marshes; and they attract more hunting pressure than most upland game species, which could better withstand the kill. Under the terms of the Migratory Bird Treaty Act (1918), confirming the Treaty with Canada (1916), the federal government was given jurisdiction over managing and protecting all migratory birds, including waterfowl. Subsequently, it has been the function of the U.S. Fish and Wildlife Service to guard this resource against destruction. By close regulation of hunting and by restoration of all possible breeding and resting marshes, the United States government—in collaboration with the various state, Canadian, and Mexican governments, and private organizations—has struggled to meet the responsibility. Success has been incomplete at best. Marshland habitat is still being drained faster than conservation agencies can acquire it. Some waterfowl species are still declining while others are no more than holding their own. Restoration of waterfowl to their potential maximum is still to be accomplished, and many obstacles stand in the way.

The problem of waterfowl management is international in scope, because most of the ducks breed in Canada and Alaska and then winter in the United States and Mexico. The accompanying map shows the main continental breeding and wintering grounds as well as the four main "flyways" or migratory routes followed in fall and spring. The Canadian prairie (Manitoba, Saskatchewan, and Alberta) is the most important breeding area from which ducks radiate into all the flyways. Most geese are pro-

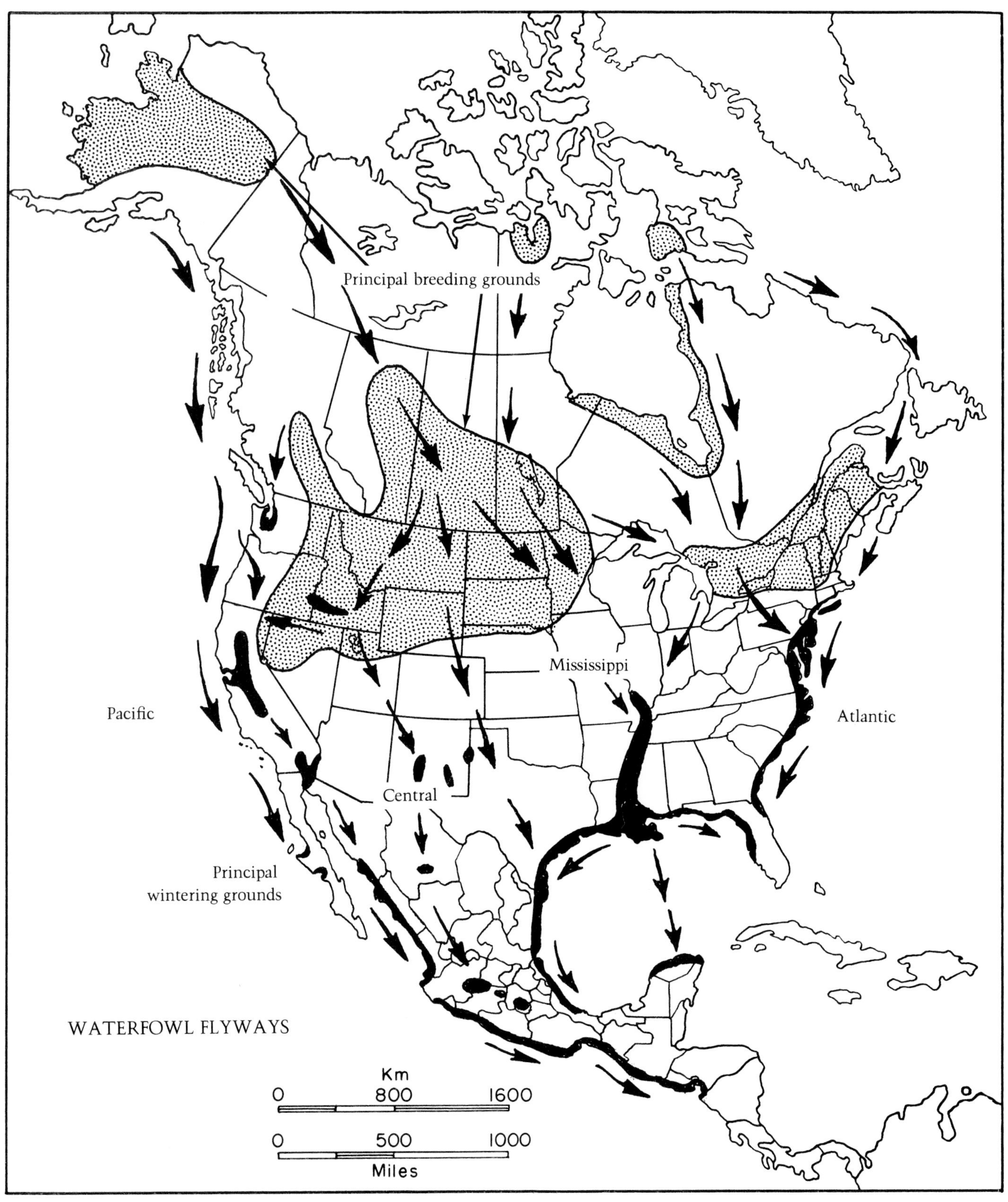
Principal breeding grounds
Mississippi
Pacific
Atlantic
Central
Principal
wintering grounds
WATERFOWL FLYWAYS
Km
0
800
1600
0
500
1000
Miles

duced on tundra to the north of the prairies. Populations in the various flyways differ somewhat in species composition, though many common species are represented in all four. It seems that the populations remain essentially divided into flyway groups by *tradition*, passed from parent ducks or geese to offspring. Each segment of the breeding area has its own clientele that returns annually. A specific group of birds will tend, more or less, to gravitate toward the same winter range each year. Thus if one region—or even one whole flyway—is overshot, it will not draw many ducks or geese from elsewhere because they in turn are "fixed" in using certain traditional areas. Thus an attempt is made to regulate the kill according to *local needs*, insofar as that is possible. The Atlantic and Mississippi Flyways have relatively few birds, and hunting regulations are very restrictive. The Pacific Flyway has more birds, but they do not move east to alleviate shortages there.

Although the Secretary of Interior has primary responsibility for regulating waterfowl hunting, he has arranged for advice from four Flyway Councils made up of representatives from the states and provinces within the flyway and from citizen groups and conservation organizations. Each summer, biologists from the U.S. Fish and Wildlife Service, with assistance from the states, survey the breeding grounds by airplane transects to estimate the success of the year's hatch. In August when the data are assembled, the respective Flyway Councils meet and recommend to the Secretary a set of regulations intended to limit the hunting kill to the estimated surplus, preserving an adequate breeding stock. The system works reasonably well, and hunting is controlled to the point that it no longer is a major factor limiting continental waterfowl populations.

The most serious problem in waterfowl management is to maintain wetland habitat. Both the U.S. Fish and Wildlife Service and the respective states are buying or leasing marshlands for the continued use of waterfowl and other marsh birds. The federal waterfowl refuge system in 1974 consisted of 260 units embracing approximately 4.5 million acres (1.82 million hectares). An additional 1.4 million acres (566,000 hectares) of breeding marsh was under lease, mostly in the Dakotas, Minnesota, and Nebraska. Finance for the federal refuge system derives largely from a tax imposed on all waterfowl hunters in the form of a "duck stamp" purchased for $7.50 (1980) at any post office. Additionally, the states maintain waterfowl refuges that collectively exceed the federal system in number and area. Yet all these habitat units (over 11 million acres or 4.45 million hectares in the United States) are still far from enough to support the continental population of ducks and geese. Especially on the prairie breeding grounds, agricultural drainage is still eliminating marshland faster than conservation agencies can acquire and preserve it. In North Dakota alone, over 45,000 acres of wetland are drained each year!

United States tax funds cannot be spent to buy land outside of national borders, so a private organization called Ducks Unlimited collects donations from hunters to buy and restore duck-breeding marshes in Canada. Since the program started in 1937, these voluntary contributions have totalled $87 million ($16 million in 1978), and have resulted in the acquisition and restoration of 2.5 million acres (over a million hectares) of breeding marsh. Many nongame species of birds and mammals profit by the perpetuation of wetlands.

Extensive marshland is especially needed by breeding waterfowl, since paired birds become fiercely territorial and defend breeding territories from other pairs of their own kind. The result is a spreading of the nesting population over a large area. After breeding is over, the birds become not only tolerant of their neighbors but also highly gregarious. So a much smaller marsh area will serve as living quarters in winter. Small marshlands, however, are quickly stripped of food, forcing birds to forage outside of their designated sanctuaries. The species that have adapted best to the shrinkage of wetlands are those that have learned to forage on crop residues in agricultural lands. Mallard, pintail, wigeon, and some of the geese, for example, live well on wheat, corn, or rice kernels that have dropped to the ground during harvest. Compulsory marsh feeders such as the redhead or wood duck have not done so well.

Although waterfowl generally are tolerated on agricultural lands after the crop has been harvested, the birds can cause great damage to standing crops. One function of waterfowl refuges is to draw birds off agricultural areas when crop damage might occur. In the Sacramento Valley of California, for example, 250,000 pintails generally arrive in late August when the rice is still flooded and the kernels are in milk stage. The state and federal refuges offer attractive flooded fields of millet and other quality foods to keep the birds happy and out of trouble until the rice fields are drained for harvest. During this critical period, farmers hire airplanes to herd the ducks from the rice to the refuges.

An excellent book on waterfowl identification and natural history is that of Bellrose (1976) entitled *Ducks, Geese and Swans of North America.* Two other useful compendia are *Waterfowl of North America* by Johnsgard (1975), and *Handbook of North American Birds: Waterfowl* edited by Palmer (1976). For a full discussion of problems of waterfowl management, we recommend *Waterfowl Tomorrow,* edited by Linduska (1964).

Family Anatidae (Swans, Geese, and Ducks)

Tribe Anserini (SWANS AND GEESE)

TRUMPETER SWAN *(Cygnus buccinator)*

See also pages 60–61.

RANGE: Main breeding areas are the Copper River area of Alaska, west-central Alberta, and the Yellowstone–Red Rocks Lake area of Wyoming and Montana. Winters in Yellowstone–Red Rocks Lake area and Pacific coast from Alaska Peninsula to the mouth of Columbia River.

HABITAT: Breeds on shallow bodies of fresh water with emergent vegetation on shoreline and abundant subsurface aquatic plants. Winters on open freshwater ponds, lakes, slow-moving rivers, brackish and saltwater bays.

REMARKS: The status of the trumpeter swan was once perilous. Market hunting had reduced the continental population to such a low level that only a few birds survived. A small colony was found breeding at Red Rock Lakes, Montana, and a National Wildlife Refuge was subsequently established there for the birds. Subsequently, another breeding population was discovered in southern Alaska and adjoining Canada.

TRUMPETER SWAN
WHISTLING SWAN
WHITE-FRONTED GOOSE
blue phase
SNOW GOOSE
ROSS GOOSE
white phase

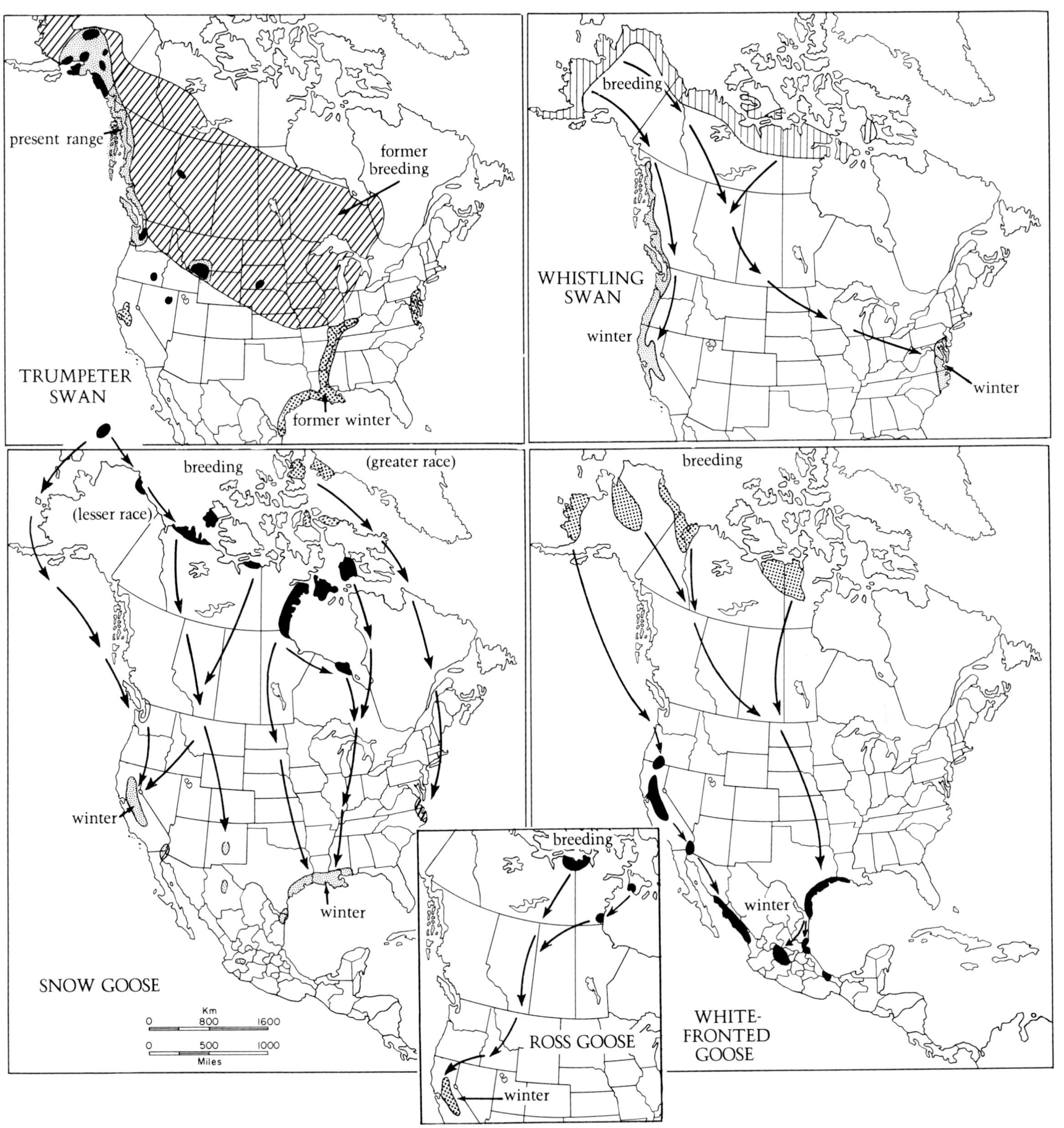

present range
former breeding
TRUMPETER SWAN
former winter
breeding
WHISTLING SWAN
winter
winter
breeding
(greater race)
(lesser race)
winter
winter
SNOW GOOSE
Km
0 800 1600
0 500 1000
Miles
breeding
winter
WHITE-FRONTED GOOSE
breeding
ROSS GOOSE
winter

The strict legal protection and management afforded these birds resulted in an increase of the population to about 4000. The species is no longer considered endangered.

Trumpeter swans are the largest birds in North America, weighing up to 27 pounds (12.3 kilograms). Trumpeters are easily confused with whistling swans in the field. Perhaps the best way to distinguish them is by their voice. The trumpeter's call has been likened to the sound of a French horn (Bellrose 1976); the whistling swan's call is melodious, high-pitched, and quavering. Young swans (called cygnets) are dull gray or brownish in both species. The sexes are alike in both species.

Trumpeters associate in small flocks of 3 to 5 birds, although occasionally up to 50 are found in loose winter aggregations. They mature slowly, probably reaching sexual maturity at 4 to 6 years of age. Pairs mate for life. They are very aggressive, defending a territory for mating, nesting, and cygnet rearing. Territory size seems to be a function of habitat, being smaller in productive, diverse habitats. The male assists the female in construction of the nest, which is built over water in the emergent vegetation. (Whistling swans, by contrast, nest on shore.) The nest may be placed on a muskrat house or constructed on a huge, rounded pile of plant material that the male pulls from a circular area around the nest, thus creating the image of a "moat." Such a nest is quite visible from the air. It is here that the female incubates the clutch of 4 to 5 eggs for 33 to 37 days. The nest site may be used for several years by a pair. Both adults will defend the young. The cygnets grow rapidly from 200 grams at hatching to 8 to 9 kilograms by 9 weeks, yet they do not fledge until 13 to 17 weeks old. Very few nests suffer predation, but some eggs fail to hatch. One or two cygnets usually result from a successful nesting.

Trumpeters eat a variety of aquatic leafy plants, tubers, and seeds. In one study, a captive swan ate 9 kilograms of moist leafy food in a day! When available they prefer tubers of such aquatic plants as pondweed *(Potamogeton)* or duck potato *(Sagittaria)*.

WHISTLING SWAN *(Cygnus columbianus)*

See also pages 60–61.

RANGE: Breeds in Alaska and Canadian Arctic from Aleutian Islands east to Baffin Island. Winters along Pacific coast from Vancouver to central California, and along mid-Atlantic seaboard around Chesapeake Bay.

HABITAT: Breeds on tundra ponds and lakes, slow-moving rivers, and sheltered bays. Winters on freshwater ponds, lakes, flooded lowlands, rivers, and estuaries (rarely on salt water).

REMARKS: The whistling swan, or "tundra swan," like many waterfowl species, was decimated by early unrestricted market hunting. After complete protection was afforded the bird, its numbers rose steadily in the last half century, with as many as 155,000 estimated in the highest year. Recent limited-shooting seasons have been held in Utah, and pressure for seasons elsewhere has arisen because swans are locally abundant on some wintering grounds. Likewise, they purportedly compete with ducks and geese for aquatic foods, and, around Chesapeake Bay, for waste grain.

These white birds weigh up to 20 pounds (9 kilograms) but are still smaller than the trumpeter swan. A yellow spot at the base of the black bill will identify the whistling swan, but frequently this character is not readily visible. Whistling swans are active, noisy birds outside the breeding season and seem to be more gregarious than trumpeters. Flocks of 25 to 100 and sometimes more whistling swans have been reported. During migration, a flock will fly high in a *V* or in an oblique line. But on the wintering grounds, they fly low over the water during local movements, a habit that made them vulnerable to early market hunters.

These swans, like trumpeters, pair for life. When they begin to breed at 3 years of age, they build an elaborate nest on an elevated hummock on the shore or on the tundra nearby. The female incubates the 4 to 5 egg clutch for 31 days while the male stands guard. The pair then defends the young through the 9 to 10 week fledgling period. The family group maintains continuity through the winter. Although nesting success is often high, there are years of low productivity of young because of the short season and frequent poor weather in the far north. The nesting and fledging period is long, so some young die in the fall freeze-up before they can fly or gain enough energy reserves to make the southward migration.

Whistling swans eat mostly tubers and vegetative parts of aquatic plants. They will resort to upland grazing and use of croplands, an aspect of behavior common to most of the successful waterfowl—the ability to use a man-altered environment. The habit of visiting inland cornfields to glean waste grain has developed quite recently among the swans wintering around Chesapeake Bay. When swans are grubbing for aquatic plants in water, some ducks such as wigeons feed among the swans, gathering the loose material left floating on the water surface.

WHITE-FRONTED GOOSE *(Anser albifrons)*

See also pages 60–61.

RANGE: Circumpolar; in North America, breeds from central and northern Alaska eastward in northern Canada to Queen Maud Gulf. Winters in valleys and deltas along the Pacific coast from California to Sinaloa, and along the Gulf coast of Louisiana, Texas, and eastern Mexico.

HABITAT: Breeding areas are largely tundra; winter habitat is agricultural grainland, especially rice stubble.

REMARKS: The continental population of whitefronts is estimated to be about 300,000 in autumn. Of these, the majority are produced on nesting grounds of the Yukon–Kuskokwim Delta, partially contained within the Clarence Rhode National Wildlife Refuge. Most of the delta birds migrate down the Pacific coast in fall to winter in California and western Mexico. A second major production area in Alaska is along rivers east of Kotzebue Sound. In Canada, the primary nesting area is in the Mackenzie Delta–Anderson River area. The birds from the latter two areas migrate south and east to the Gulf coast of Louisiana, Texas, and Mexico. There are, in essence, two quite discrete populations of white-fronted geese in North America, with little mixing (see map).

Unlike many other kinds of geese, whitefronts do not nest in colonies but tend to scatter their nests over an extensive area. An average clutch of 5 eggs is incubated by the female 23 to 25 days. The male assumes the dominant role in rearing and protecting the brood. December families average 2.5 young. Families tend to stay together through the winter and on into spring migration.

Young whitefronts reach breeding age in 3 years. Because of this long period of sexual maturation, only about 100,000 of the population are breeding adults.

On the breeding ground, whitefronts eat greens, fruits, and roots of various tundra plants. In winter, however, they show a decided preference for the seeds of agricultural grain crops. Rice is their universal favorite food in California, Sonora, and Texas. Other seeds taken when rice is not available are milo, corn, barley, watergrass *(Echinochloa)*, and safflower. The birds also graze the tender green leaves of winter grain and legumes.

An exceptionally large race of whitefront, called the tule goose, winters in the Sacramento Valley of California, especially around the Sacramento National Wildlife Refuge. A few are killed by hunters each year. The size of the population is estimated to be 2000 or less. The breeding area was sought for many years and finally in 1979 was located in muskeg wetlands near Anchorage, Alaska.

SNOW GOOSE *(Anser caerulescens)*

See also pages 60–61.

RANGE: Nests in the northern Arctic from Wrangel Island, Siberia, east to Greenland. In recent years, there has been rapid growth of breeding colonies around the fringes of Hudson Bay. Winters along the Pacific Coast, the Gulf Coast, and the mid-Atlantic seaboard.

HABITAT: Breeds in low tundra. Winters in coastal estuaries or on agricultural valley lands.

REMARKS: The snow goose can be divided into three quite distinct populations that mix only peripherally:

(1) Western lesser snow goose—breeds primarily on Wrangel Island, where 300,000 birds and 114,200 nests were found in 1980, or 3000 nests per square kilometer. This population has dwindled since 1960, presumably because of adverse weather that inhibited nesting. Additional nesting colonies occur along the arctic coast of northwestern Canada. In fall, these birds migrate southward and westward to wintering grounds around Puget Sound, in the Central Valley of California, in the delta of the Colorado River, and in a few spots in New Mexico and Chihuahua. The western population, of about half a million birds, is made up entirely of geese in the white plumage.

(2) Central lesser snow goose and "blue goose"—breeds around Hudson Bay and islands to the north. Migrates directly southward across the eastern Great Plains and down the Mississippi River to wintering grounds along the Gulf Coast. This population consists of two color phases—white and blue, in a ratio slightly favoring the blue. The midcontinent population numbers about a million.

(3) Great snow goose—breeds in western Greenland and nearby islands. Migrates down the Atlantic coast to winter grounds along the coast of Virginia and North Carolina. This population is small, averaging about 50,000. The birds resemble the white phase of the lesser snow goose but are considerably larger.

Snow geese are colonial nesters, congregating on breeding grounds in high density. Each pair defends a territory around its nest. Pairs mate for life in their second year and nest in their third. Juveniles can be recognized in their first year by their gray plumage and their dull-gray bill, feet, and legs (which are pink in the adult). Average clutch size is 4.4 eggs, and incubation is about 22 to 23 days. If the nest is destroyed, renesting is unlikely. The short arctic summer provides only enough time for one nesting cycle, about 70 to 80 days from nest building to fledging of the young. When fall arrives, the birds may fly nearly nonstop to their southern wintering grounds.

The bird's strong serrated bill (the "grinning patch") is well adapted for pulling up root stalks of marsh plants and feeding on grasses, which these birds readily do on their summer range. In recent years, snow geese have come to rely heavily on the rice fields of California and Texas, having been able to adjust to the changing land use and having learned to use crop residues.

ROSS GOOSE *(Anser rossii)*

See also pages 60–61.

RANGE: Breeds in northcentral Canada near the Perry River and Queen Maud Gulf. Winters in the Central Valley of California.

HABITAT: Nesting colonies are found on islands in shallow tundra lakes where there is some protection from nest predators such as the arctic fox. Nests are situated close together (4 meters) in sheltered situations among rocks or low shrubs. Winter habitat is agricultural valley lands.

REMARKS: Ross geese are easily confused with snow geese at a distance but are much smaller (less than 2000 grams) and lack a "grinning" patch. Their far northern breeding grounds were not discovered until 1938, and their nesting chronology reflects the constraints of this latitude. The geese begin nesting within one week after their arrival, females laying a clutch of 3 to 4 eggs and incubating for 20 to 22 days. They nest in colonies like snow geese. They enjoy a high nesting success (75 percent), but little opportunity is provided by the short arctic season to attempt another nest if the first is destroyed.

As fall approaches, Ross geese concentrate on staging areas and move in a narrow migration pattern to the Central Valley of California. A few occasionally winter in other flyways. Since they mingle with snow geese on the winter range, a management problem with harvest regulations results. The bag limit presently is less for Ross geese than for snows, but most hunters are unable to determine the species on the wing. To prevent overharvest, the bag is usually set at one Ross goose per day.

Ross geese forage on grasses and sedges during the summer and, like snow geese, favor waste grain for their winter sustenance.

EMPEROR GOOSE *(Anser canagicus)*

See also pages 66–67.

RANGE: Breeds along Bering Sea coast in Alaska (Yukon Delta) and Siberia. Winters in Aleutian Islands, Alaskan Peninsula, Kommandorsky Islands, and perhaps on Kamchatka Peninsula.

HABITAT: Breeds in low, wet tundra and marshes near coast. Winters on ocean bays.

REMARKS: The emperor goose has the most restricted breeding range of any North American goose. It is not a large bird (2600 grams; 6 pounds), but it is striking in appearance. It has a reddish beak without "grinning patch," yellowish feet and legs,

EMPEROR GOOSE
CANADA GOOSE
small race
western race
eastern race
BRANT

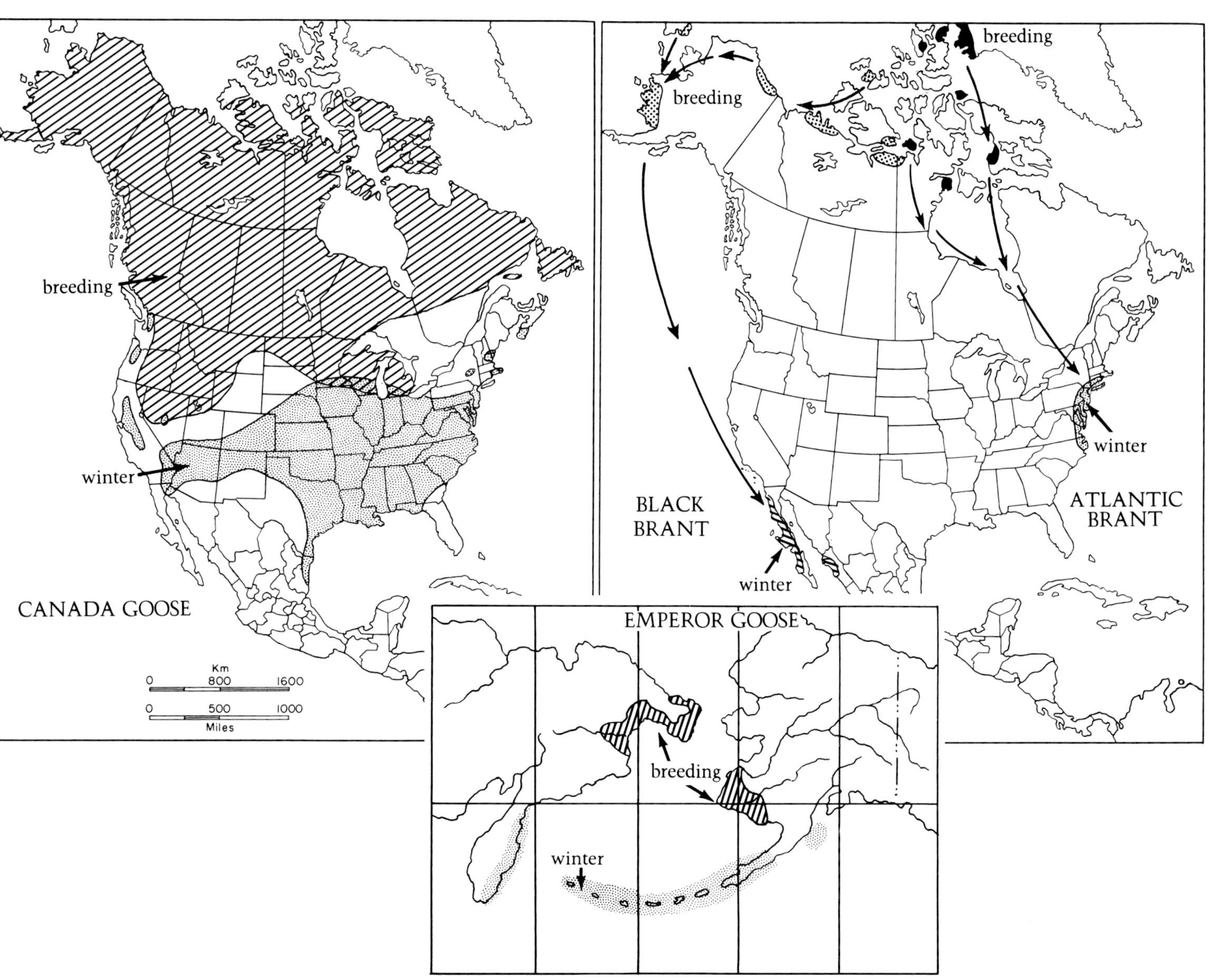

breeding
winter
CANADA GOOSE
Km
0
800
1600
0
500
1000
Miles
breeding
breeding
winter
BLACK
BRANT
winter
ATLANTIC
BRANT
EMPEROR GOOSE
breeding
winter

and a blue-gray, black and white feather pattern. The white head feathers are often stained yellow. The sexes can be distinguished only by cloacal examination. First-year birds, however, can be recognized by the brownish barring on the back and gray on the head and neck, as compared to bluish in the adult.

Eisenhauer and Kirkpatrick (1977) completed an extensive study on the ecology of this previously little-known bird. The chronology of the nesting cycle is such that the birds begin arriving on the breeding grounds before the snow and ice are gone. They probably have a strong permanent pair bond and breed by age three. The female selects the nest site and some sites are reused each year, even by the same pair. Egg clutches average 5 to 6. The male does not help the female incubate the eggs during the 24-day period but will defend the nest vigorously. The brood, once hatched, may move several kilometers to a rearing area.

Nesting success is high (88 percent), which can be attributed to the attentiveness of the pair. Gulls and jaegers account for most of the nonhuman mortality of both eggs and goslings. Eskimos harvest eggs as well as molting geese during the spring and summer; sport hunters take fewer than 5000 birds each season. The entire population is estimated to be 175,000–200,000 birds and is probably limited by restricted habitat. Some concern has been raised over the potential negative impact of future oil exploration and shipping on the very limited nesting area of this species.

Emperor geese eat primarily plant matter—over 90 percent, especially sea lettuce (*Ulva* and *Enteromorpha*), algae, eelgrass, grass, and sedges. Mollusks and crustaceans contribute a limited animal component to the diet.

CANADA GOOSE *(Branta canadensis)*

See also pages 66–67.

RANGE: Aleutian Islands east to the Atlantic Ocean and south to central United States. Introduced to New Zealand and Europe. Isolated breeding populations have been artificially started on refuges outside their historic range.

HABITAT: Breeding—tundra, forest muskeg of far north, tall- and shortgrass prairie marshes, ponds, and lakes. Winter—a body of open water or a refuge near grainfields or coastal estuaries.

REMARKS: More than any other sound in nature, the "honking" of migrating Canada geese signals the changing seasons of fall and spring. A glance skyward on a frosty morning might reveal the characteristic *V*-shaped migratory flight formation. Within the flock are subunits consisting of family groups (a pair and the current year's brood). The pair mates for life and the family stays together until the next breeding season. Familial bonds are strong and are constantly reinforced by social ceremonies. A bird will remate, however, if its partner dies; likewise, the family will often reunite after a temporary breakup.

The Canada goose is the most variable of all North American waterfowl. Eleven subspecies or races are recognized, which vary in size from the giant Canada goose (11 to 13 pounds; rarely, to 20 pounds or 9 kilograms) to the diminutive cackling goose (2.8 to 3.4 pounds). Presumably, each race is in some way adapted to its specific habitat. The smaller races migrate farthest north to breed. Then they leapfrog over the larger birds in fall to winter farther to the south.

Like other geese, the male Canada goose assists his mate in brood rearing. The female incubates the 4 to 7 egg clutch and rarely leaves the vicinity of the nest during the 24 to 28 days of incubation. The male stands guard nearby. The sexes are monomorphic: both have the dark head and neck with white cheek patches; brownish upper breast, flanks, and back; and white or gray underparts. A human observer finds difficulty in distinguishing the members of the pair. In the hand, males can be identified by the presence of a penis. Pair bonds are formed at two years of age, but first nesting usually occurs at three years.

The nesting territory of a pair consists of the nest site and environs, defended from other pairs by threat and display, or rarely by combat. Nesting density does not seem to be a function of territoriality but rather a matter of habitat quality. Densities have been recorded as low as 6 pairs and as high as 130 pairs per square mile. Canada geese will nest in remarkably diverse situations—on the ground, on islands, in cliffside caves, in hawk nests in trees, in washtubs fastened high in trees, or on artificial platforms mounted on 15-foot poles in a marsh. Hatching success is higher in elevated nests (out of reach of predators) than in ground nests. Supplying elevated nests is a widely used management technique.

Young geese, and some adults that do not nest, fly far to the north in spring to molt and spend the summer. Various lakes in the Northwest Territories of Canada are the gathering grounds for great flocks of nonbreeding Canada geese. Why these birds fly thousands of miles north to replace their old feathers is a mystery. One theory is that by removing themselves from breeding marshes, they avoid food competition with the breeders and their progeny.

The Canada goose has adapted well to changes in the landscape that have accompanied settlement. Crop residues now supply winter food for most honkers in the continent, and water reservoirs and refuges serve as safe loafing grounds. The birds are adept at gleaning corn, wheat, milo, rice, or other grains left on the ground after harvest. They are equally comfortable grazing on winter wheat, alfalfa, or other greens. Like the mallard, pintail, and wigeon, the Canada goose shows the adaptability necessary to thrive in a changing world.

BRANT *(Branta bernicla)*

See also pages 66–67.

RANGE: Atlantic brant breed in northern Greenland and winter on bays of New England and the east coast of the United States. Black brant breed mainly in the Yukon–Kuskowim Delta, lesser numbers on Alaska's North Slope and eastward into the Canadian Arctic, where they have nested sympatrically with Atlantic brant. Most black brant now winter in esteros (bays) along the west coast of Baja California and on the mainland coast of Sinoloa, Mexico.

HABITAT: Breeds on tundra, mostly within a half mile of salt water. Winters in bays and estuaries that produce eelgrass *(Zostera)*.

REMARKS: There are two races of this small, short-necked maritime goose, the Atlantic brant and the Pacific black brant. Both have black heads, necks, and chest; dark brown backs; and an incomplete white throat ring. The Atlantic race has a white belly, but the Pacific race is dusky. The sexes are monomorphic, yet juveniles can be distinguished from adults by their white-tipped greater and middle wing coverts, which are brown in the adult. These birds are noticeably the fastest geese in flight.

Brant nest farther north than most waterfowl species. And because they do so, little or no opportunity for renesting is available if a clutch should be destroyed. Brant are determinant layers, however, and will often build a second nest to accommodate the remainder of a 4-to-6-egg clutch if the early eggs are destroyed. (Determinant egg laying means there are a fixed number of developing eggs in the female—6, for example. If the nest is destroyed when 2 eggs are laid, she will renest and produce the other 4. By contrast, domestic chickens are indeterminant layers.) Nesting phenology and pair bonds are similar to those of other geese.

Atlantic coast populations have fluctuated widely since censuses have been taken. Drastic declines in the population have been caused during some years by reproductive failures attributable to bad weather or by early freeze-up in the north. Restrictive hunting is one management tool that can effectively be used to restore brant populations that have suffered from poor production. Another historical factor in the thrift of brant populations is their normal dependence on eelgrass *(Zostera marina)* for food. When stocks of this plant decreased along the Atlantic coast because of a fungus disease, the birds switched to sea lettuce and to upland grazing in pastures and meadows. Pacific populations also resort to these alternative foods when disease depletes the eelgrass beds. A recent major shift in winter range from the Baja California coast to the coast of mainland Mexico may be the result of lowered food supply in the bays and estuaries of the peninsula.

Tribe Dendrocygnini (WHISTLING DUCKS)

FULVOUS WHISTLING DUCK *(Dendrocygna bicolor)*

See also pages 72–73.

RANGE: Worldwide from Indian subcontinent westward through Arabia, East Africa to North and South America. In North America, breeds along coastal plains of Mexico, rice belt of Texas and Louisiana, Imperial and San Joaquin valleys of California, and isolated areas of Florida. Winters primarily on coastal marshes of Mexico; recent winter populations have developed in Florida.

HABITAT: Marshland near rice or grain fields or coastal marshes and swamps

REMARKS: The whistling ducks derive their name from their squealing call notes "pee chee," which they sound frequently while flying. They are peculiar in their resemblance to geese, being long-necked and long-legged, and having some behavioral characteristics common to their larger relatives. Fulvous whistling ducks have a history of erratic population fluctuations in the United States. Their numbers declined in the 1950s but have begun to increase again in Louisiana, though not in California. The reason for these population changes is not clear. They are not, however, caused by hunting pressure; the birds have usually migrated to Mexico before the season opens in the United States. Were it not for this early migration, the whistling ducks would surely have long been shot out, as they are slow of flight and not particularly wary.

The sexes are monomorphic, and they pair at one year of age. It is believed, although not documented, that they mate for life. Once paired, they build a nest on the edge of a field or over water in rice or dense vegetation. Their nests may be elaborate structures with roofs and ramps. Laying begins, however, before the nest is completed, and some eggs may be lost when they fall out of the unfinished cup. The birds do not add down to their nests as do most other waterfowl. Unlike other waterfowl, both parents incubate the 10-to-13-egg clutch and assist in the rearing of the brood. Only a few observations have been made on nesting success, and these have shown it to be relatively low (30 to 55 percent). Most nest losses were through destruction by livestock, farming operations, dogs, and skunks.

Fulvous whistling ducks feed at night and are particularly fond of rice and other waste grain. In marsh areas, they swim and dive for aquatic vegetation, whereas black-bellied whistling ducks tend more to grazing emergent vegetation.

BLACK-BELLIED WHISTLING DUCK
(Dendrocygna autumnalis)

See also pages 72–73.

RANGE: Breeds from south Texas Gulf coast and Sinaloa southward along both coasts of Mexico to northern Argentina. The Texas population winters in eastern coastal Mexico.

HABITAT: Agricultural lands, mangrove swamps, and coastal marshes

REMARKS: Black-bellied whistling ducks are more abundant than fulvous whistling ducks in North America. Both, however, are relatively unwary and easily killed. Both undergo only one annual molt. The black-bellied species has been extensively studied by Bolen *et al.* (1964) in south Texas.

They pair in the winter and breed in their first year. Bolen presented strong evidence that they establish lifelong pair bonds and that they have high breeding-area fidelity. Both sexes incubate the 13 to 14 eggs for 25 to 30 days and care for the young. The adults remain with the brood for 6 months (4 months after they fledge). The birds will renest if the first clutch is destroyed.

The birds nest primarily in tree cavities but occasionally on the ground. They will accept artificial nest boxes. As with wood ducks, dump nesting occurs regularly; more than 100 eggs have been observed in one box, contributed by many hens (Bolen, in Bellrose 1976:83). But they do not require nest material in their cavities nor do they add down to the nest. The young whistling ducks remain in the cavity for 12 to 24 hours after hatching before they plunge from the nest hole. When they nest on the ground, the birds build a shallow bowl of woven grass.

The ducks feed on waste grain and rice seeds and graze emergent aquatic plants such as water-stargrass *(Heteranthera)*. They may consume as much as 9 percent animal matter, primarily snails and insects.

Much needs to be learned about the ecology and evolutionary relationships of these interesting ducks. Particularly fruitful research locations might be the mangrove swamps of Sinaloa and Nayarit in western Mexico, where many thousands of black-bellied whistling ducks are found.

FULVOUS
WHISTLING DUCK
BLACK-BELLIED
WHISTLING DUCK
WOOD DUCK
female
male
male
female
AMERICAN WIGEON

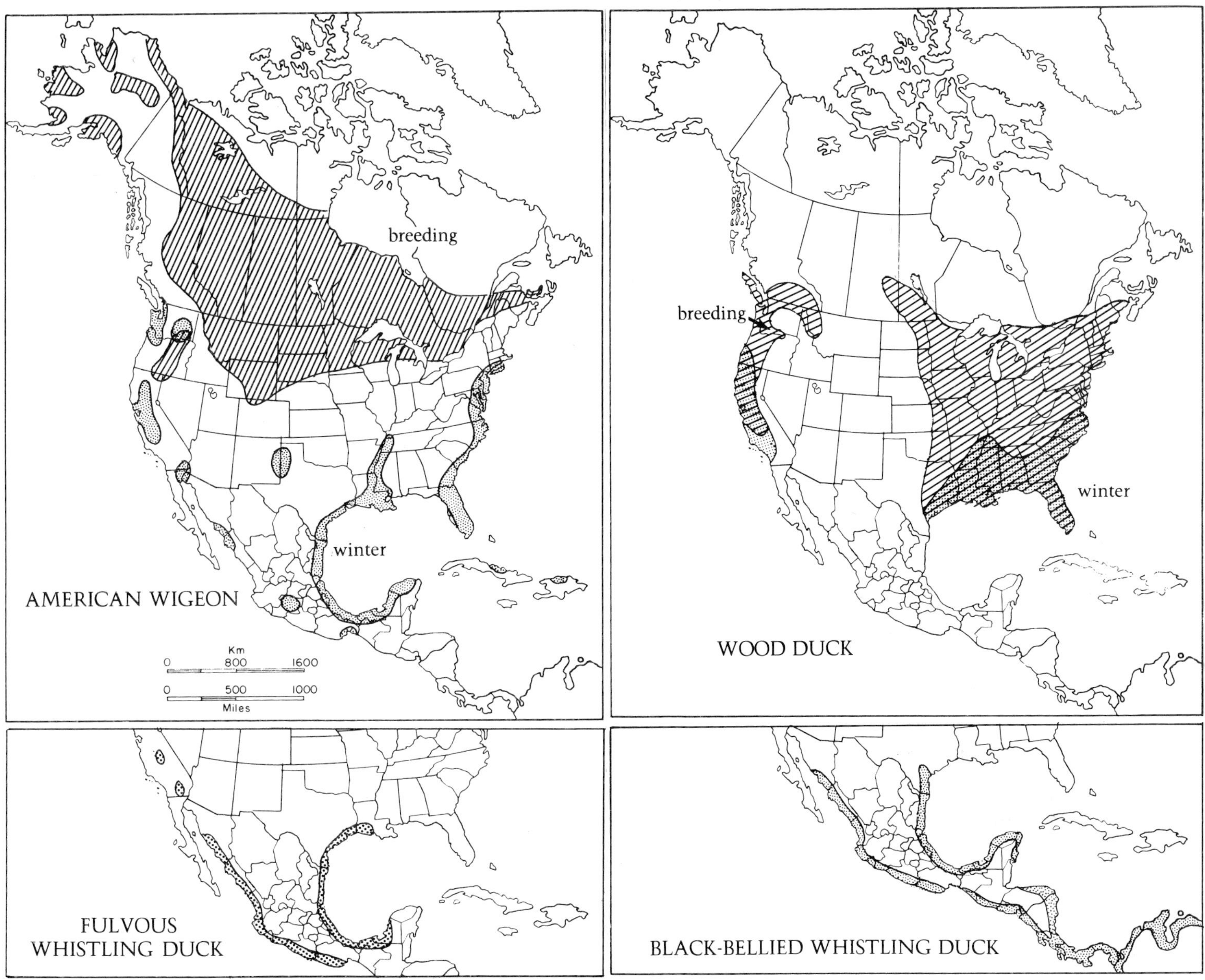
breeding
winter
AMERICAN WIGEON
Km
0
800
1600
0
500
1000
Miles
breeding
winter
WOOD DUCK
FULVOUS
WHISTLING DUCK
BLACK-BELLIED WHISTLING DUCK

Tribe Cairinini (PERCHING DUCKS)

WOOD DUCK *(Aix sponsa)*

See also pages 72–73.

RANGE: Breeds in eastern half of North America in deciduous forest from Nova Scotia to Florida. A small Pacific coast population exists. Winters along waterways in southern hardwoods and in central California.

HABITAT: Rivers, lakes, and swamps that are usually associated with deciduous woods

REMARKS: The recovery of wood duck populations in the recent past has been a most successful waterfowl-management effort. Heavy hunting and habitat destruction through the early 1900s caused the population to decrease dramatically—to the extent that extinction seemed imminent. Rigid hunting restrictions and habitat manipulation (creating artificial nest sites) has led to a rapid recovery in wood duck numbers. The bird is now the most numerous duck bagged in some of the southeastern United States.

Males are the most strikingly colored of our ducks. Even the female has a crest and a noticeable eye ring and eye stripe, which relieves the drabness so common in other female puddle ducks. Their white bellies and long rectangular tails are noticeable in flight. The squealing alarm call of the hen and the drake's goldfinchlike call further serve to identify these unique dabbling ducks. Woodies occur in small groups or pairs outside the nesting season. On occasion, they form large concentrations at favored roosting sites during fall and winter, and local populations can then be censused. The birds are generally secretive and would be extremely difficult to count were it not for communal roosting behavior.

Wood ducks are cavity nesters. Ideal nesting habitat should contain snags or trees with cavities in forest stands open enough to allow the female to see the cavity and select it. Additionally, these sites should be within one half mile of sheltered water, where the adults feed and where young can be taken for rearing. Once a nest site is selected, the female lays 10 to 14 eggs, which she incubates for about 30 days. The males, like most other ducks, do not help in incubation or brood rearing. Dump nests (nests in which more than one female lays) are a common phenomenon in wood duck populations. Combined clutches of 30 to 50 eggs are common in dump nests. Sometimes one hen will incubate such a clutch, but often the eggs are simply abandoned. It has been noted that dump nests can depress the productivity of a population (Jones and Leopold 1967). But if dump nests are successfully incubated, production can be increased (Clawson *et al.* 1979).

The female calls the ducklings from the cavity when they hatch. It is a surprising feat for a little ball of fluff to jump out into the world from heights of up to 65 feet (or 20 meters)! Once on the ground the brood follows the hen to water, which may be a hazardous journey if the nest is far inland.

These birds readily accept artificial nest boxes that simulate cavities. Various designs have been tried, but some general points should be noted by people attempting to encourage wood duck nesting: wooden boxes are initially more acceptable to the birds, but metal structures are safer from predators; predator shields below the nest boxes help reduce predation; nesting material (sawdust) must be present in the box since the ducks do not carry nest material; and nest boxes should be placed in open woods or on a pole in standing water where the prospecting pair can see the nest opening.

Wood ducks are primarily vegetarian except for the young who eat mostly invertebrates. Adults eat more acorns and fruits than do other ducks, but they will feed on waste grain when mast is in short supply.

Tribe Anatini (SURFACE-FEEDING DUCKS)

AMERICAN WIGEON *(Anas americana)*

See also pages 72–73.

RANGE: Breeds largely on the Canadian prairie and northern Great Plains of the United States. Lesser numbers occupy tundra lakes in Alaska and Canada. Winters from Puget Sound and Connecticut south along both coasts to southern Mexico. Principal winter concentrations occur in the Central Valley of California and the coastal marshes of Louisiana.

HABITAT: Nests are situated in rank vegetation near shallow ponds. Winter habitat includes sloughs, ponds, saltwater marshes, and agricultural valleys.

REMARKS: On the wing, wigeons are best identified by the white shoulder patch on the drakes; the patch is indistinct on hens. Likewise, the very short bill is diagnostic. At close range, the white crown of the drake is unique to this species, giving rise to the alternate name "baldpate." The piping whistle of three syllables is distinctive.

In food habits, wigeons are much more prone to graze leafy green foliage than are other dabbling ducks. Wigeons eat copious quantities of aquatic plants such as pondweeds, coontail, wild celery, and even filamentous algae. They are often observed to pilfer vegetation brought to the surface by swans, coots, and diving ducks. In the Pacific Flyway, wigeons gather in great flocks on clover and grass pastures, alfalfa stubbles, and sprouting grainfields where they cause substantial damage by their trampling. In the Imperial Valley of California, wigeons created so much havoc in commercial lettuce fields that the local waterfowl refuge had to be opened to public hunting to disperse the concentration. In recent years, wigeons have begun to fly with mallards and pintails to grain stubbles, thus further demonstrating their adaptability to man-made habitats. The result is a general increase in wigeon populations while many other species are still decreasing.

The European wigeon *(Anas penelope)* is occasionally observed as a vagrant in North America, usually in company with American wigeons. The drake is readily recognized by its bright russet head, topped with a cream-colored pate.

GADWALL *(Anas strepera)*

See also pages 78–79.

RANGE: Breeds in western North America from Alaska south to Oregon and Colorado, with maximum density in the Canadian Prairie Provinces and the Dakotas. Since 1939, breeding has been observed in scattered localities in the Lake States and Mid-Atlantic States. Gadwalls winter largely around the Gulf of Mexico, concentrated especially in Louisiana. Lesser numbers occur along both coasts south to Guatemala.

HABITAT: Shallow marshes and ponds with abundant aquatic vegetation and rank upland vegetation for nesting

REMARKS: The gadwall, like the wigeon, seems to be holding its own in North America, or even increasing. Since the late 1950s, the number of gadwalls recorded during winter waterfowl surveys has risen substantially. Part of this apparent increase might have been caused by improved winter habitat in Louisiana, resulting from hurricanes that opened ponds in the coastal salt marshes. Birds attracted to these areas would be more easily detected and counted than if they were scattered over Mexico. Most of the wintering gadwalls are found in the Central and Mississippi Flyways; only 4 percent winter in the Pacific Flyway. The status of this species is highly satisfactory.

Gadwalls, like wigeons, are grazers, utilizing green leaves and stems of aquatic plants such as pondweeds, naiads, coontail, wigeongrass, and filamentous algae. They eat the seeds of aquatic plants such as alkali bulrush, smartweeds, and buttonbush. But gadwalls have shown no propensity to graze on dry-land plants or to utilize waste grain. The diet of aquatic plants and algae often imparts a strong taste to gadwalls, and they are not a preferred eating duck.

GREEN-WINGED TEAL *(Anas crecca)*

See also pages 78–79.

RANGE: Breeds throughout Alaska, most of Canada, and the northwestern United States, with greatest concentration in the Canadian parklands and Northwest Territories. Winters in the central United States, south to Central America.

HABITAT: Ponds, potholes, sloughs, and shallow marshes

REMARKS: The green-winged teal is the smallest North American dabbling duck, averaging less than a pound (400 grams). The male has a chestnut head with a green eyestripe; the female is drab brown. Both sexes have a bright green speculum. The birds mate and breed as yearlings. Nests are well concealed in heavy vegetative cover and are difficult to find. Clutches average 8.6 eggs. The incubation period is 21 to 23 days. Of 104 nests studied, 31 percent hatched successfully. Females rear their broods without aid from the males, who have deserted their mates and gathered for molting early in summer. The proportion of immature to adult green-winged teal found in hunters' bags over a 12-year period was 1.69 young per adult.

Greenwings are fast and shifty flyers and are not easy to hit. But because they tend to fly low and are not especially wary, they absorb a substantial amount of hunting mortality. Yet the continental population is not declining, perhaps because of the northerly breeding grounds, which have not been substantially reduced by drainage or agricultural development.

Greenwings prefer to feed on mud flats, where they pick up seeds of marsh plants such as millets, smartweeds, bulrushes, and spike rushes. Under favorable circumstances, greenwings will utilize grain residues in flooded fields, but they do not regularly glean in dry stubbles.

MALLARD *(Anas platyrhynchos)*

See also pages 78–79.

RANGE: Arctic and temperate regions of Europe, Asia, and North America; on this continent, breeds throughout Alaska, Canada, and the northern United States; winters in the southern and western United States, south to the Mexican border.

HABITAT: Principally, freshwater marshes, lakes, ponds, sloughs, rivers, and irrigation canals; occasional in brackish estuaries and bays; tule and cattail marshes are preferred to open water.

REMARKS: The mallard is the most abundant and most successful duck in North America. It has adapted well to changes in land use and makes full use of waste agricultural grain dropped to the ground during harvest. By frequenting refuges or natural sanctuaries such as sand bars or large lakes, the mallard successfully eludes hunters during the day and flies to agricultural fields to feed at night. The average breeding population in the central part of the continent is 8.7 million birds, outnumbering any other species of duck.

Mallards breed in their first year and are seasonally monogamous. Each pair establishes a breeding territory along the edge of some body of water, but the nest is situated on land, frequently far from the defended territory, which is principally a feeding, loafing, and courting area. The female incubates the clutch of 8 to 10 eggs for 28 days. During this period the male loses interest and deserts his mate, gathering with other males. The female rears the young alone. If the nest is destroyed before hatching, the hen may mate and nest again, sometimes with another drake if the first mate has deserted. Second clutches are normally smaller. Many nests are lost to flooding, drought, agricultural practices (mowing and such), or predation. Some hens are killed by farm machines or ground predators. Average nest success is about 50 percent, typical of ground-nesting birds.

Male ducks molt their plumage twice a year, except the wing feathers, which are replaced only once. Drake mallards begin to molt immediately after leaving their mates and assume a summer plumage (called "eclipse" plumage) almost indistinguishable from the hens. They are flightless while the wings are being molted. Then, in the fall, a new typical drake plumage is acquired by another molt. The historic and physiologic reasons for this seemingly illogical procedure are unknown. Females molt after the broods are reared and again (partially) during winter and spring.

In addition to feeding on crop residues, mallards eat the seeds and tender shoots of many aquatic plants such as pondweeds, rushes, tules, and smartweeds. They consume some animal foods (insects, sowbugs, snails), and, rarely, shell fish or fish eggs, which impart a distinct flavor. Normally, however, mallards are among the most tasty of waterfowl, and they are much sought by hunters. But the birds are adept at avoiding hunting pressure. We recall many instances when mallards have poured out of protected areas five minutes after the close of legal shooting, seeming to know precisely when it is safe to venture forth.

Mallards have colonized many areas of the world in temperate and subtropical climates where they can live year-round. These nonmigrating local populations have evolved into separate species or subspecies that have one character in common: the males have lost their gaudy plumage and closely resemble hens. North America has three such endemic populations:

Florida Duck *(Anas fulvigula fulvigula)* — Florida Peninsula
Mottled Duck *(Anas fulvigula maculosa)* — Gulf Coast, Louisiana to Nuevo Leon
Mexican Duck *(Anas diazi)* — Mexican highlands north to central New Mexico

Similar endemics have evolved in Hawaii, Laysan Island, New Zealand, and Australia.

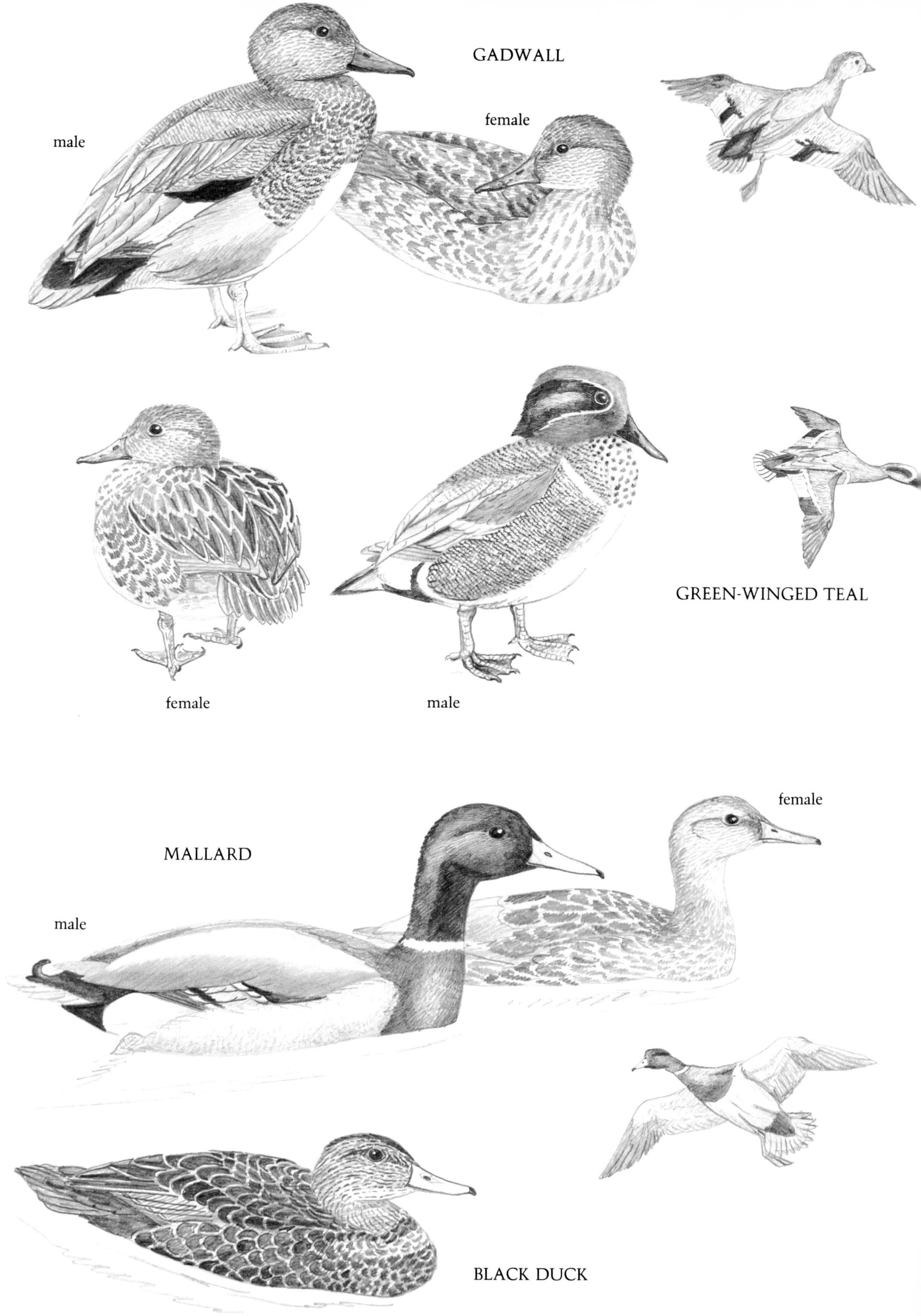
GADWALL
female
male
GREEN-WINGED TEAL
female
male
female
MALLARD
male
BLACK DUCK

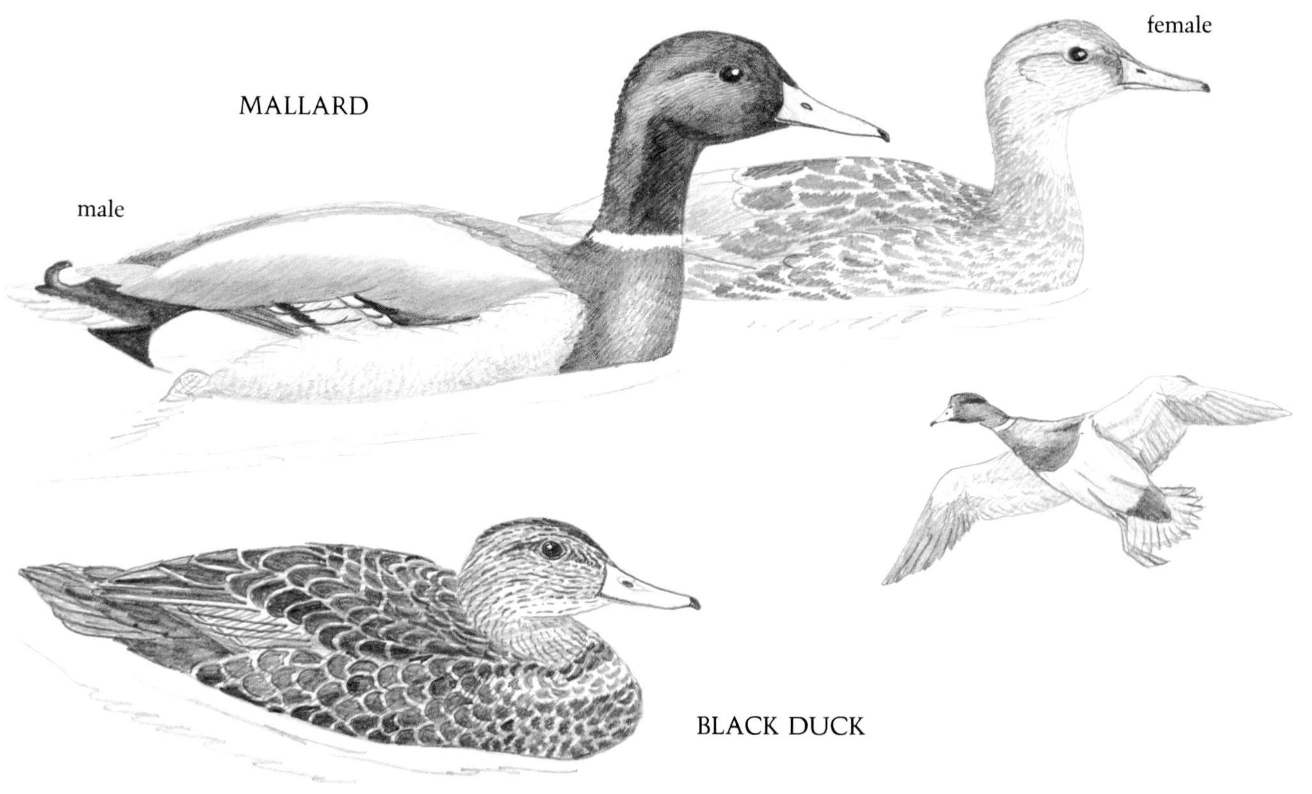

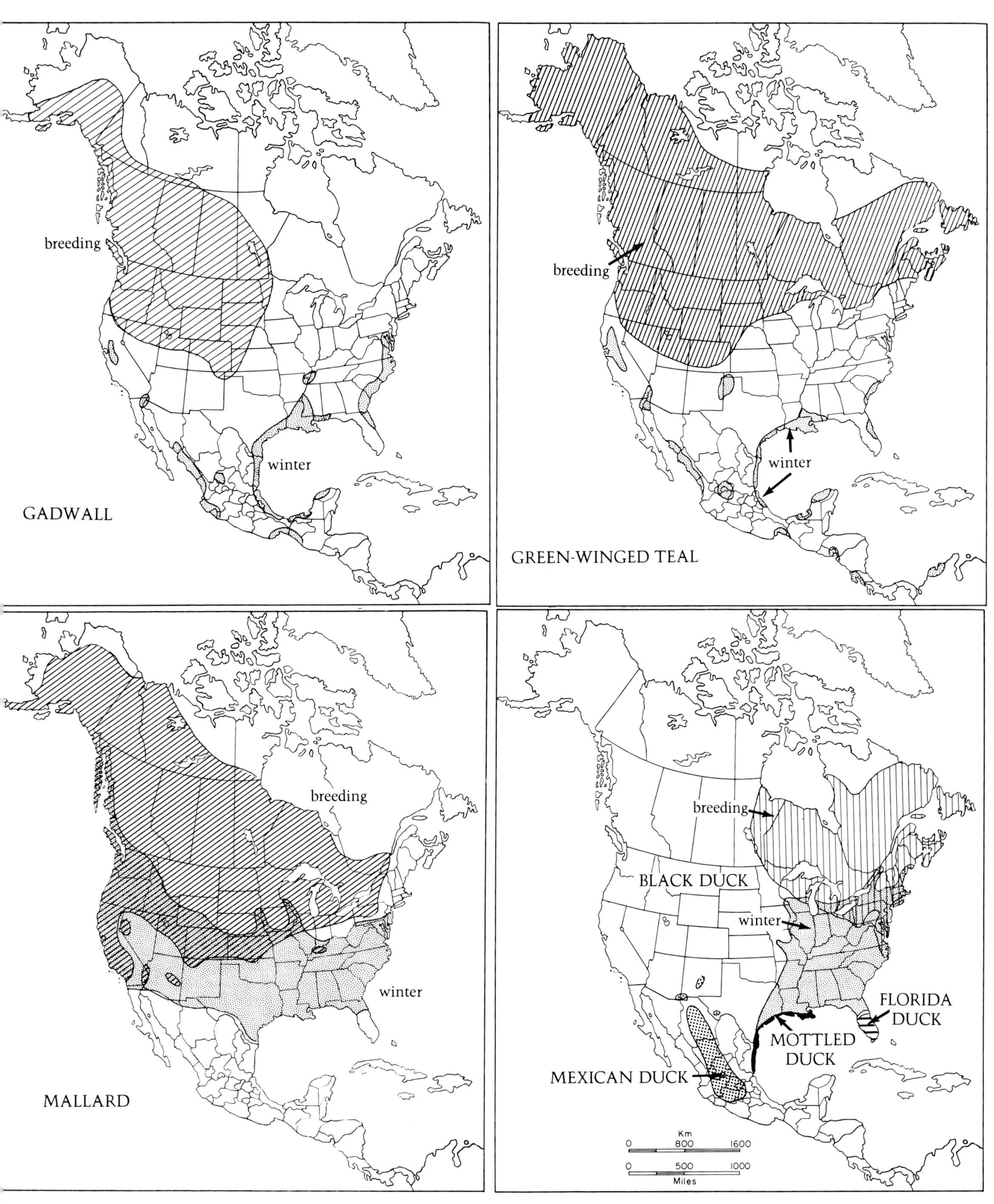
breeding
winter
GADWALL
breeding
winter
GREEN-WINGED TEAL
breeding
winter
MALLARD
breeding
BLACK DUCK
winter
FLORIDA DUCK
MOTTLED DUCK
MEXICAN DUCK
Km
0
800
1600
0
500
1000
Miles

BLACK DUCK *(Anas rubripes)*

See also pages 78–79.

RANGE: Breeds in northeastern North America east of the Great Plains and south of Hudson Bay and Labrador to the Lake States and New England. Winters in the southeast from Illinois and Massachusetts south to the Gulf of Mexico.

HABITAT: Ponds, streams, wooded lowlands, and coastal marshes; more than any other duck, the black duck frequents small wetlands in the eastern forested portion of the continent.

REMARKS: The black duck has the conformation of a mallard, but the plumage is dusky brown, appearing almost black in flight. The purple wing speculum lacks the white borders of the mallard. The sexes are virtually indistinguishable except for some details of bill and leg color.

The black duck historically was the principal game species in New England and the northeastern forest region. But populations have been decreasing steadily since the mid-1950s for causes unknown. Concurrently, the mallard has been extending its range in the northeast. Perhaps habitat changes have induced these shifts in species abundance. Mallards and black ducks hybridize commonly, and up to 4 to 9 percent of black ducks show some mallard characteristics. The black duck apparently is suffering both from competition of mallards and from genetic miscegenation. Eventual assimilation by the mallard is a distinct possibility. Hunting regulations have been set to favor the black duck by closely limiting the kill (bag limit of one per day) in an effort to stem the decline.

Black ducks eat a wide variety of fruits, nuts, berries, seeds, eelgrass, and other aquatic plants, and invertebrate animals. They utilize grain residues but to a lesser extent than mallards. Perhaps this is one of their failings.

PINTAIL *(Anas acuta)*

See also pages 82–83.

RANGE: Circumpolar; in North America, breeds from Alaska through the prairie pothole country to the Great Lakes, eastern Canada, and south to Colorado. Winters primarily in California, Texas, Louisiana, and along both coasts of Mexico, and as far south as Panama and Colombia.

HABITAT: Breeds on arctic tundra, marshland, and in pothole country. Winters on bodies of water near agricultural land.

REMARKS: The handsome pintail or "sprig" is the most widespread of the waterfowl and vies with the lesser scaup for the status of second most abundant duck in North America. It is the most common dabbling duck breeding in the Arctic. Likewise, it is the most abundant duck in the Pacific Flyway (over 2 million winter in California) and is second to the mallard in the Central Flyway.

The chronology of nesting of the pintail is similar to that of other dabbling ducks. Nests are often situated far from water, but close enough for the hen to lead her hatchlings there afoot. During drought years in the prairie nesting area, some pintails will continue their northward flight far into the Arctic (even to Siberia), seeking favorable nesting sites. Males desert their hens during incubation and gather in bachelor groups for molting. When their flight feathers have regrown, many of these birds migrate southward. In California, it is common for 250,000 male pintails to arrive in late August, where they may cause considerable damage to growing rice.

The pintail, like the mallard, has learned to make good use of grain residues fallen to the ground during harvest. The birds will rest in security in a refuge or on a large body of water, flying out to the stubble fields at dusk to forage under cover of darkness.

BLUE-WINGED TEAL *(Anas discors)*

See also pages 82–83.

RANGE: Breeds from central Alaska and Quebec south to northern New Mexico, with principal production area in the northern Great Plains. Winters in the southern United States south to South America.

HABITAT: Small, shallow ponds, sloughs, and lakes surrounded by herbaceous vegetation

REMARKS: The blue-winged teal is one of the most common breeding ducks in the prairie pothole country of the midwest and Canada, with as many as 60 pairs per 100 acres (40 hectares) recorded during the breeding season. As with all North American teal, the males migrate first. Both sexes winter farther south (Chile and Argentina) than any other North American duck. This trait is presumed to be a cold-sensitive response.

Blue-winged teal are small, brownish dabbling ducks weighing less than a pound (450 grams), distinguished by blue upper-wing coverts and a green speculum. Males in breeding plumage have a white crescent on their faces and white rump patches. Females are brownish with dark bills and can easily be confused with cinnamon teal in the field or even in the hand. Notched tail feathers indicate immature birds of either sex.

These ducks are paired during spring migration and disperse over available breeding habitat as migration ends. Males will defend the female but not a territory; hence, the high breeding densities, noted above, are achieved. Once the female has laid a clutch of 10 to 11 eggs, and before she has incubated the eggs for the necessary 21 to 27 days, the male deserts her. Nesting success varies from 21 to 60 percent; if the nest is destroyed up to 40 percent of the hens may renest.

Bluewings characteristically "tip up" when foraging for aquatic plant parts and seeds that make up 75 percent of the diet. Their small size in concert with their feeding behavior dictates that they must feed in shallow water.

Because of their abundance, and their tendency to migrate before regular duck-hunting season begins, an early teal season has been declared in recent years in the eastern and midwestern United States.

PINTAIL
male
female
BLUE-WINGED TEAL
male
female
male
CINNAMON TEAL
"tipping"
NORTHERN SHOVELER
female
male

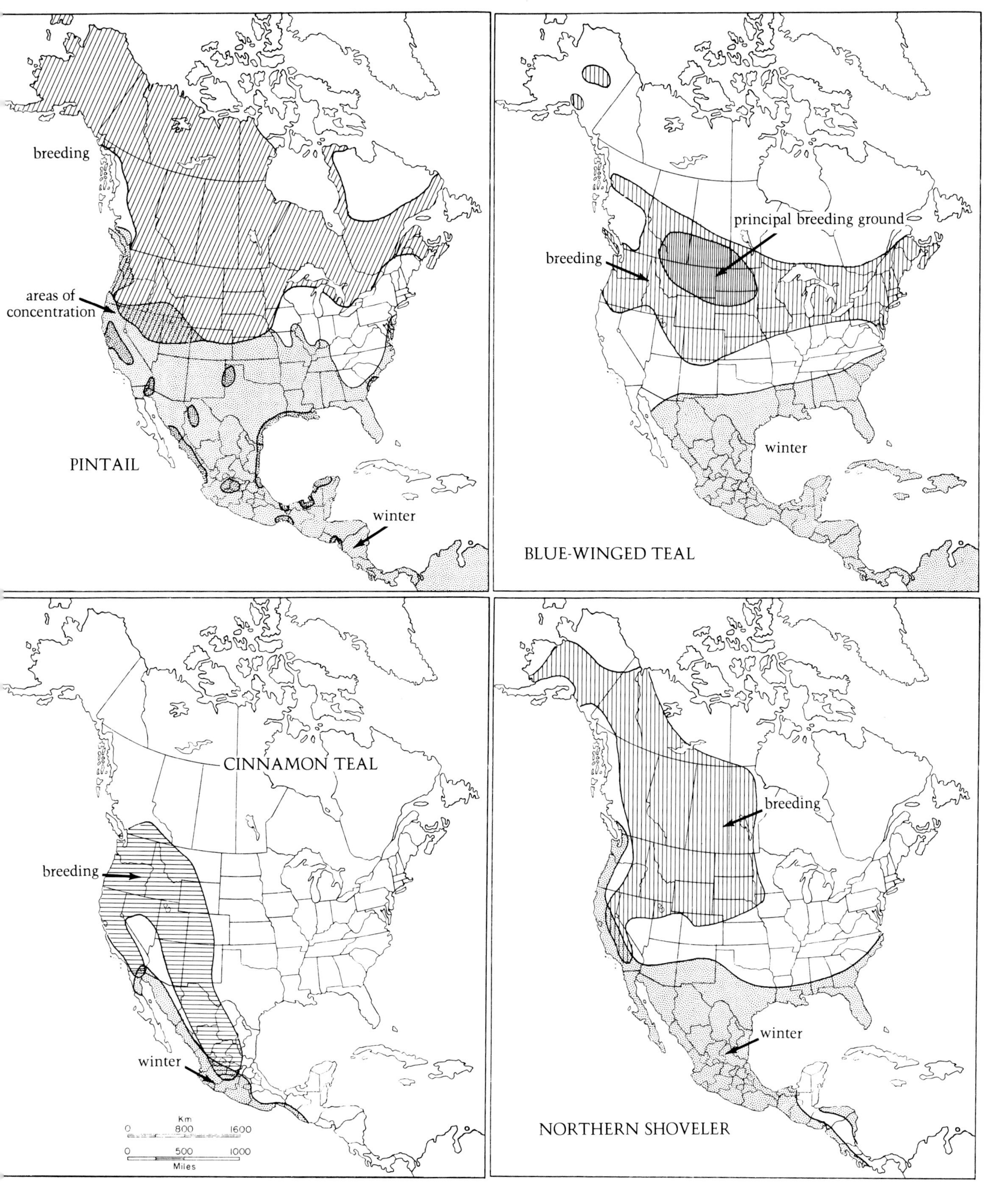

breeding
areas of concentration
PINTAIL
winter
principal breeding ground
breeding
winter
BLUE-WINGED TEAL
CINNAMON TEAL
breeding
winter
Km
0 800 1600
0 500 1000
Miles
breeding
winter
NORTHERN SHOVELER

CINNAMON TEAL *(Anas cyanoptera)*

See also pages 82–83.

RANGE: Western North America from British Columbia south to Guatemala

HABITAT: Breeds in small, shallow marshes (preferably alkaline) with emergent vegetation. Winter habitat along west coast of Mexico; largely, brackish coastal marshes.

REMARKS: These small ducks (less than one pound, or 450 grams) have blue upper-wing coverts, and the males are a bright cinnamon color with a reddish eye. The females are drab and are virtually indistinguishable from female blue-winged teal. The bills of cinnamon teal are slightly longer and wider, but these are not good field characters. Breeding characteristics are similar to the blue-winged teal. On the better breeding areas in Utah, more than 100 pairs per square mile have been found nesting in a given area. Presumably, the limited marsh habitat accounts for this high nesting density.

Migration is early and rapid. The departure of adult males is underway in August. Thus cinnamon teal do not figure prominently in the hunting kill in the United States. They eat primarily seeds and plant parts of aquatic vegetation such as pondweeds but take little animal matter.

NORTHERN SHOVELER *(Anas clypeata)*

See also pages 82–83.

RANGE: Resident throughout the northern hemisphere. In North America, breeds in the western and central United States north to interior Alaska and the northern Great Plains. Winters along the Pacific coast and through southern United States and Mexico south to Panama.

HABITAT: Breeds in shallow water marshes with an abundance of pondweeds and water weeds; winter habitat, freshwater ponds and shallow lakes.

REMARKS: Shovelers are medium-sized ducks (about 600 grams, 1.3 to 1.4 pounds) that sport conspicuous spatulate bills. In flight, the underwing surface is white and the upper primary coverts are bluish. Breeding males have iridescent-green heads, pure white breast feathers, and rusty-brown flank feathers. Immature birds have notched tail feathers. Shovelers arrive on the breeding grounds later than other puddle ducks. Migratory flocks break up, and pairs disperse, searching for suitable nest sites. Experienced breeders often return to the same nest site each year. Males remain in the nesting area while the female lays her clutch of 9 to 10 eggs. She incubates them and takes care of the young without help from the drake. Breeding pairs have large ranges (approximately 50 acres or 20 hectares) and 2 to 10 pairs are found per square mile of nesting habitat (Stoudt 1969).

These ducks eat more animal matter than other surface feeding ducks, and they rarely "tip up" or dive. The bill is adapted for straining aquatic vegetation and insects from the water surface, and thus little food competition with other dabbling ducks occurs. In brackish water, shovelers often take on a strong flavor from invertebrate animals consumed. They are not rated a prime eating duck by most hunters.

Tribe Aythyini (POCHARDS)

CANVASBACK *(Aythya valisineria)*

See also pages 86–87.

RANGE: Breeds from central Alaska (Yukon Flats) south and east to western Ontario, the Prairie Provinces, and northern Great Plains (Dakotas, Montana). Winters mostly along coasts, with major concentrations in Chesapeake Bay and San Francisco Bay.

HABITAT: Breeds on freshwater marshes, ponds, and potholes. Winters largely on saltwater bays and brackish estuaries, with lesser numbers on interior large lakes and impoundments.

REMARKS: Like most other members of this tribe of ducks, the canvasback is a bird of open, deep water, often feeding on bottom plants at depths of 20 to 30 feet (6 to 9 meters). In fresh water, the principal foods are pondweeds, wild celery, duck potato, and sedges. On such a diet, the canvasback is one of the best table ducks. However, it is not averse to living on mollusks, aquatic insects, or, rarely, even small fish, in which event the flesh becomes strongly flavored. Declines in aquatic plant foods on important wintering grounds (e.g., decline of wild celery in Chesapeake Bay) have dictated consumption of more animal foods. In San Francisco Bay, the newly arrived canvasbacks are fine eating, but by late in the hunting season they are quite unpalatable because of a diet dominated by small mollusks dug from the tidal mudflats. When canvasbacks are diving for wild celery, they frequently are accompanied by wigeons and coots that literally steal the tender shoots from their bills, the intruders being incapable of diving as deep as the canvasback to gather their own celery.

Pochards as a group differ from the surface-feeding ducks in some details of breeding. Nests of canvasbacks and other divers usually are situated over water in emergent vegetation. Furthermore, the nest is often within the large home range of the male. Territoriality is weak in this species. (By contrast, typical surface-feeding ducks such as mallards usually nest far from the male's territory.) A normal clutch is 7 to 12 eggs. Incubation (24 to 28 days) is performed entirely by the female, the male abandoning his mate long before hatching and joining other males on larger bodies of water to begin the eclipse molt. Adult males generally are through molting and on the way south before the females have finished their family duties and molted. Consequently, hunting on the breeding marshes results in a disproportionately high kill of females. A spring sex ratio of two males to one female is not uncommon in this species and in the redhead—a factor that seriously inhibits productivity in the breeding populations.

Canvasback populations have declined during the past 20 years, a trend that has led to closed or restricted seasons and low bag limits. Factors besides hunting that may be acting in concert to cause this decline are: (1) Habitat deterioration—"cans" require a diverse habitat for breeding, which may include several types of water areas; habitat alteration for croplands or grazing may not provide these diverse requirements. (2) Poor weather conditions—too much rain or wind may cause nest flooding; drought makes nests accessible to predation by skunks, raccoons, magpies, and crows. (3) Raccoons have been extending their range northward, sometimes causing heavy nesting losses among the birds. (4) The loss of favored foods (e.g., wild celery and wigeongrass) through

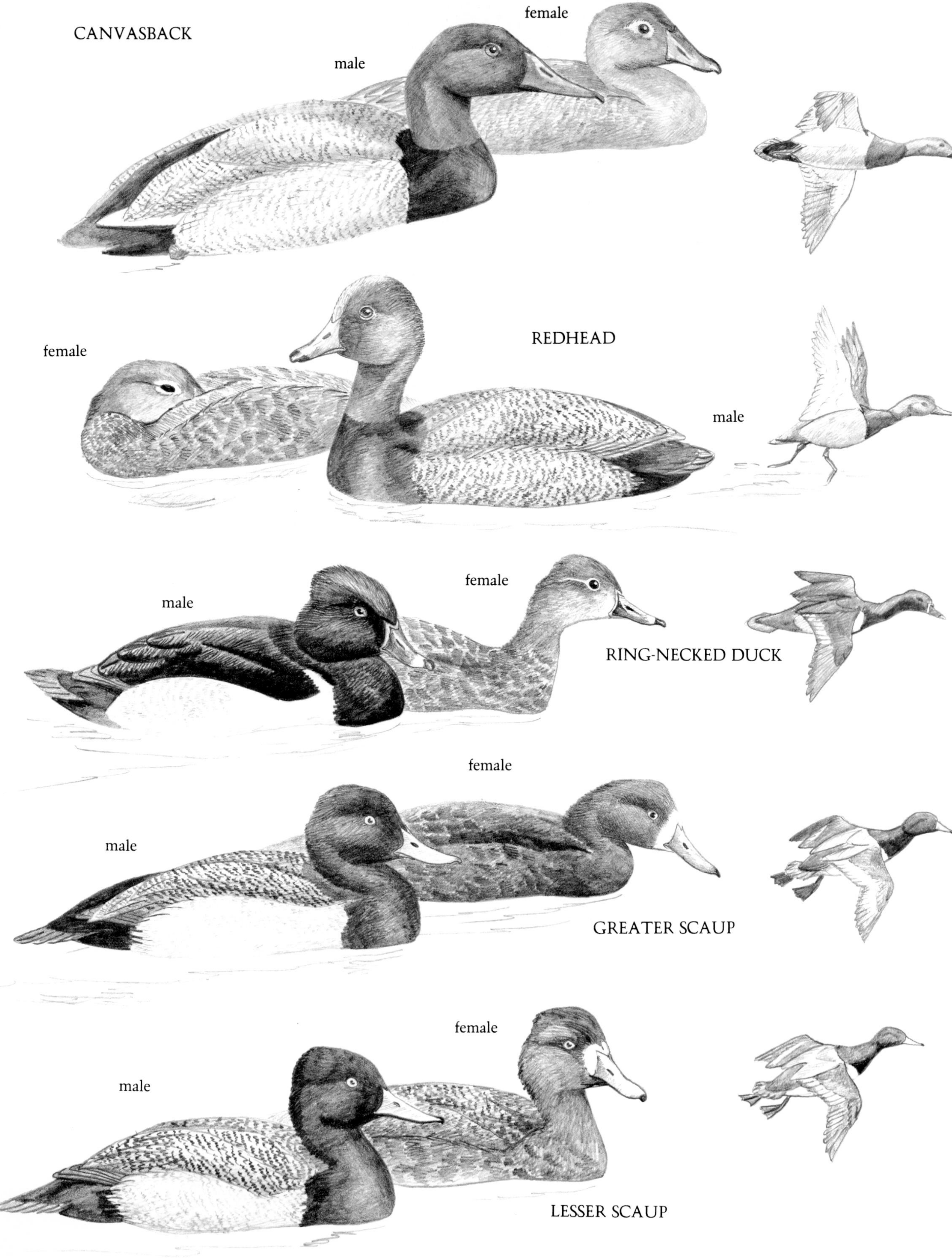
CANVASBACK
female
male
REDHEAD
female
male
RING-NECKED DUCK
male
female
GREATER SCAUP
female
male
LESSER SCAUP
female
male

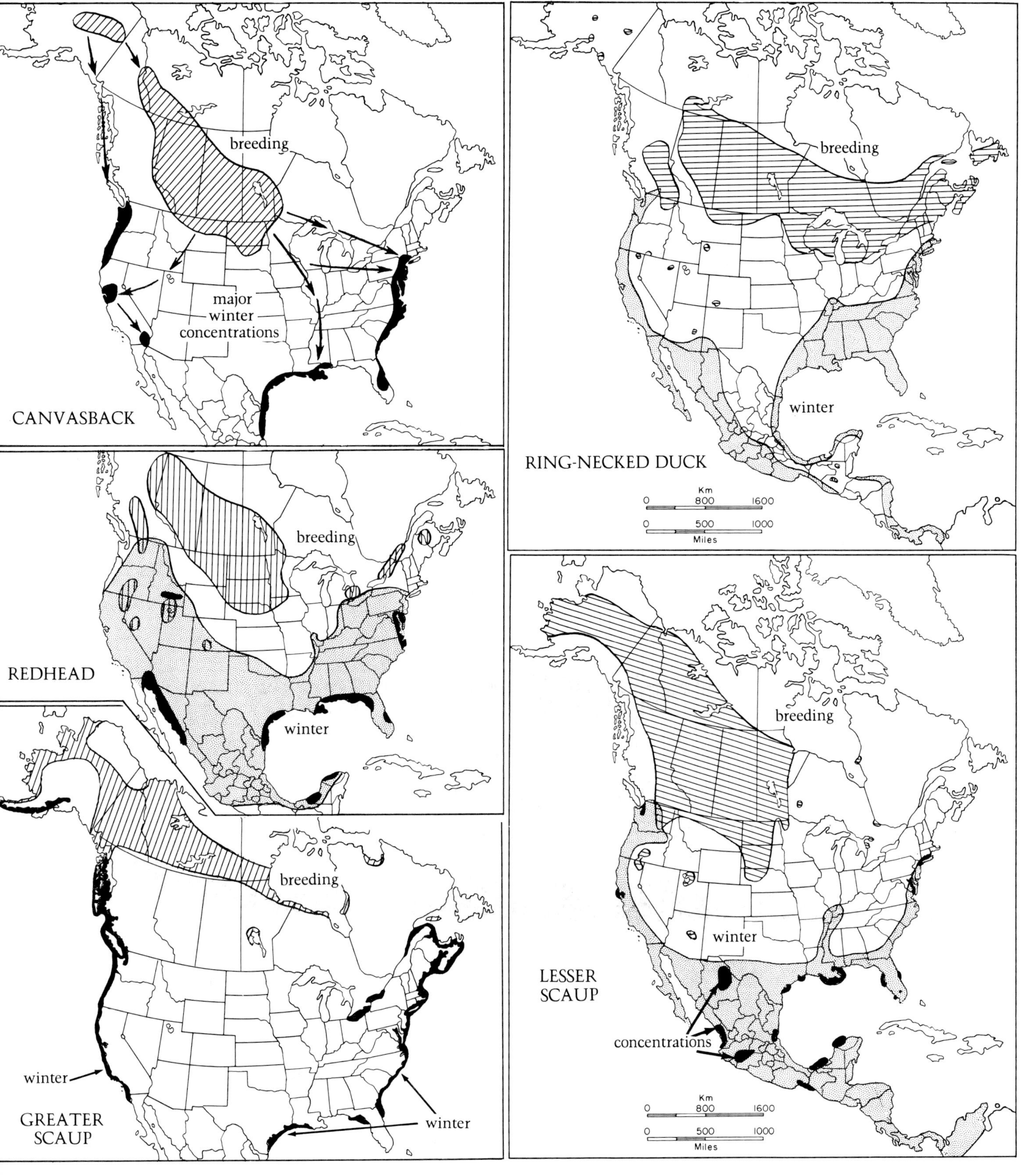

breeding
major
winter
concentrations
CANVASBACK
breeding
winter
RING-NECKED DUCK
Km
0
800
1600
0
500
1000
Miles
breeding
REDHEAD
winter
breeding
winter
GREATER
SCAUP
winter
breeding
winter
LESSER
SCAUP
concentrations
Km
0
800
1600
0
500
1000
Miles

environmental deterioration in major wintering areas such as Chesapeake Bay may have a deleterious effect on their survival. (5) Nest desertion caused by redhead nest parasitism. Some of these mortality factors have probably operated on canvasback populations for thousands of years, yet perhaps as a complex they are now more serious.

Hochbaum (1944) has written a classic account of the canvasback.

REDHEAD *(Aythya americana)*

See also pages 86–87.

RANGE: Breeds primarily in the Prairie Provinces and intermountain valleys as far south as Nevada, Arizona, and Colorado, and as far east as New York. Winters primarily along the Gulf coast of Texas and northeastern Mexico, with lesser concentrations off Florida and the Yucatan Peninsula. Secondarily, winters on coastal bays of the Pacific coast, especially in Sonora and Sinaloa.

HABITAT: Breeds on freshwater marshes and potholes. Winters on coastal bays and larger lakes.

REMARKS: The life cycle of the redhead is similar to that of the canvasback, although redheads breed and winter farther south. Many of the factors contributing to low productivity in "cans" also affect the redhead, including a high desertion rate caused by interspecific nest parasitism. Breeding characteristics also are similar to those of canvasbacks except that redheads prefer deeper potholes and larger marshes in which to nest. The redhead resembles the canvasback in appearance but is distinguished by its small bill and "dished" profile (the canvasback's bill and forehead are long, and they join in a straight line). On the wing, the redhead is smaller and darker than the canvasback.

Like ring-necked ducks, redheads tend to feed in shallower waters of marshes, ponds, and sloughs than do most other divers, often feeding by tipping up in very shallow water. They eat more aquatic plants (90 percent) than do their close relatives. Pondweeds constitute a major food in many localities, shoalgrass being the prime resource on their most important wintering ground at Laguna Madre, Texas.

The annual mortality of redheads is at least 80 percent in immatures and 40 percent in adults. This high mortality plus low productivity—and consequent decline in numbers—has led to closed seasons and restricted bags as well as to serious concern for the future of this fine duck.

RING-NECKED DUCK *(Aythya collaris)*

See also pages 86–87.

RANGE: Breeds mostly in the boreal forest zone of central Canada, New England, and the northern Lake States. Winters primarily in the southeastern United States, with major concentrations in Florida and Louisiana. Small numbers are scattered along the Pacific coast from British Columbia to Guatemala.

HABITAT: Freshwater lakes, ponds, and rivers, with preference for forested areas rather than open grasslands. Even in winter this inclination is evident, although brackish coastal estuaries are used to some extent.

REMARKS: Ringnecks are partial to small clear-water ponds such as storage reservoirs, stock tanks, wooded lakes, or open areas within emergent vegetation of marshes and swamps. These birds occur in scattered small flocks on many little ponds too small to attract other diving ducks. The name "ringneck" is unfortunate since the brownish ring is discernible only on full-plumaged males. The distinctive ring on the bill is more diagnostic.

Mendall (1958) has written the most extensive account of this species's biology. The ringneck has successfully pioneered the northeast United States since the 1930s, until today it is a common breeder in that area. In his study, Mendall noted that the birds prefer to nest in marshes bordered by woods. The females will select a nest site on floating islets of aquatic vegetation (particularly sedge) or even dry land, floating logs, or in wet meadows. Egg laying and nest building commence simultaneously, with an average of about 9 eggs being incubated for 25 days. If the nest is started early, the male may remain with the hen until hatching, and he may even stay with her into the molt if she is unsuccessful in hatching a clutch.

Ringneck populations fluctuate widely on the winter grounds, but no consistent trend has shown over recent years. Although they are affected by occasional inclement weather on the breeding grounds (especially flooding), they do not seem to suffer such drastic loss in productivity as the redhead or canvasback from drought or predation. Perhaps ringneck nest sites are on waters of more permanent nature. Bellrose (1976) estimated that the fall population contains the highest ratio of immatures to adults of any of the ducks (1.7 : 1).

The ringneck feeds in shallower water than does any other diving duck. The diet varies by area and season, but seeds and vegetative parts of pondweeds, wild rice, sedges, and other aquatic plants make up most of the diet. Snails, insects, and clams are favored animal foods and constitute over 30 percent of the food in some areas and seasons.

GREATER SCAUP *(Aythya marila)*

See also pages 86–87.

RANGE: Breeding is circumpolar, except Greenland and Canada north and east of Hudson Bay. In North America, primarily Alaska and northern Canada, east as far as James Bay (very minor colonies). Winters along Atlantic, Pacific, and Gulf coasts, as far south as Florida and Baja California.

HABITAT: Breeds on tundra and in boreal forest zones. Winters on larger saltwater bays, brackish lagoons, and, to a much lesser extent, on large freshwater lakes.

REMARKS: The greater scaup prefers a marine environment for its wintering ground. Nevertheless, during migration, it is found associated with the much-more-abundant lesser scaup in the freshwater areas of the northeastern United States. At a distance, the two are indistinguishable. Yet when they are together, the greater scaup is noticeably larger. Its greenish iridescent head is also in contrast with the purplish head of the lesser scaup. In flight, the white wingbar of the greater scaup extends to the middle of the primaries; on the lesser scaup, the white bar covers only the secondaries.

The greater scaup is not a well-studied bird, yet a few points of interest have been observed. Little aggression or territoriality have been noted among nesting birds. Nests are often close to one another. Yearling hens probably do not breed. Adult hens lay a clutch of 8 to 9 eggs, which they incubate 23 to 28 days. They prefer to nest on an elevated site in rank tundra vegetation close to water.

Greater scaups are strong divers, able to feed in deeper water than close relatives. Animal matter constitutes more than 70 percent of the diet of these divers, with mollusks being the most important food items. In fresh water, greater scaups are more likely to partake of plant foods, which may at times approach 50 percent of the diet.

LESSER SCAUP *(Aythya affinis)*

See also pages 86–87.

RANGE: Breeds in the Alaskan Arctic and western Canada south to Minnesota and west to northeastern California. Winters principally in Mississippi Flyway, particularly the Gulf Coast, with lesser numbers on the Pacific and Atlantic coasts, and southward through interior areas to South America. In Mexico, they are common. (The greater scaup is rare in Mexico.)

HABITAT: Freshwater ponds and marshes in summer. Winters on large bodies of fresh or salt water.

REMARKS: The lesser scaup or "blue-bill" is the most common of diving ducks in North America, with an average of seven million breeding birds. In fact, the lesser and greater scaup together are more abundant than all other ducks except the mallard. Lesser scaups are more commonly found breeding on the river deltas and boreal forests of Alaska and Canada than on marshlands to the south. They also prefer to nest along the deeper ponds found in their habitats. This trait, in combination with their more-northern distribution, lessens the effects of drought. Thus their populations seem relatively stable. They have been shown to have the highest proportion of surplus drakes in any common duck population. Sometimes as high as 80 percent of the lesser scaups in a given area and time will be males.

The scaup ducks, like other divers, have relatively small wings, and ordinarily patter along the water to reach flying speed. Once underway, however, they fly faster than any of the pond ducks except teal and furnish very sporty shooting. They decoy readily to blocks and ignore even the crudest and most obvious blinds. Thus, immature scaup suffer heavy hunting losses, and a high 50 to 70 percent first-year mortality.

The lesser scaup, like other divers, ordinarily builds nests over water. But not uncommonly, it nests in uplands some distance from water in the manner of pond ducks. Although a few first-year hens may nest, most females and probably all males do not nest until their second or even third season. These birds also are less likely to attempt nesting during a drought.

They are strong divers, capable of feeding in relatively deep water. Their main foods are animals such as clams, crabs, crayfish, insects, and snails. Yet in some areas and at certain times, lesser scaups will use plant foods heavily.

Tribe Mergini (SEA DUCKS)

EIDER DUCKS:
- COMMON EIDER *(Somateria mollissima)*
- KING EIDER *(Somateria spectabilis)*
- SPECTACLED EIDER *(Somateria fischeri)*
- STELLER EIDER *(Polysticta stelleri)*

See also pages 92–93.

RANGE: All eiders are primarily Arctic in distribution. They breed along the coasts of the continents and the arctic islands, and winter as far north as open water persists. The common eider migrates in winter as far south as New England; the king eider as far south as the mouth of the Columbia River in Washington. They spend the winter months at sea, often out of sight of land.

HABITAT: Nests on coastal tundra. Winters along ocean shores and bays.

REMARKS: Eiders are large sea ducks of arctic affinities. The common and king eiders are the most abundant of the four species and they are the largest (some males weigh up to 6 pounds; 2.7 kilograms). The spectacled eider is somewhat smaller, and the Steller eider is smaller still (2 pounds; .9 kilograms). The larger species are awkward flyers, alternately flapping and gliding low over the water like cormorants. The males of all species are strikingly colored, but females and juveniles are dull brown in color and difficult to tell apart.

Most eiders breed as two-year-olds, but some males do not mature until the age of three. Their large size no doubt contributes to slow maturation. Pairs mate for one season only, the males abandoning the hens during the period of incubation. Nests are situated on the tundra near water; the larger species have clutches of 2 to 6 eggs; the Steller eider, 7 to 8. Incubation is 26 to 28 days. Broods often join together into aggregations that may include several hens and a gaggle of youngsters of varying ages. Eider nests are lined with a luxurious layer of down, which keeps the eggs warm during the absence of the hen. The down has superb thermal properties and has long been used by natives of Iceland and arctic North America for the manufacture of clothing and bedding. In both Iceland and Greenland, the people have learned to construct artificial rock shelters in which the eiders will nest, thus facilitating the gathering of eider down.

Eiders are strong divers, feeding in deep waters on mollusks, crustaceans, echinoderms, and other bottom animals. Blue mussels seem to be a preferred food. Very little plant material is eaten except during the brief nesting period. The preference for animal food gives the flesh a strong flavor, which, however, does not discourage consumption by Eskimo peoples. Hunting of eiders and egg collecting have long contributed to the summer diet of aborigines, especially in Greenland. Very few eiders are taken by sport hunters.

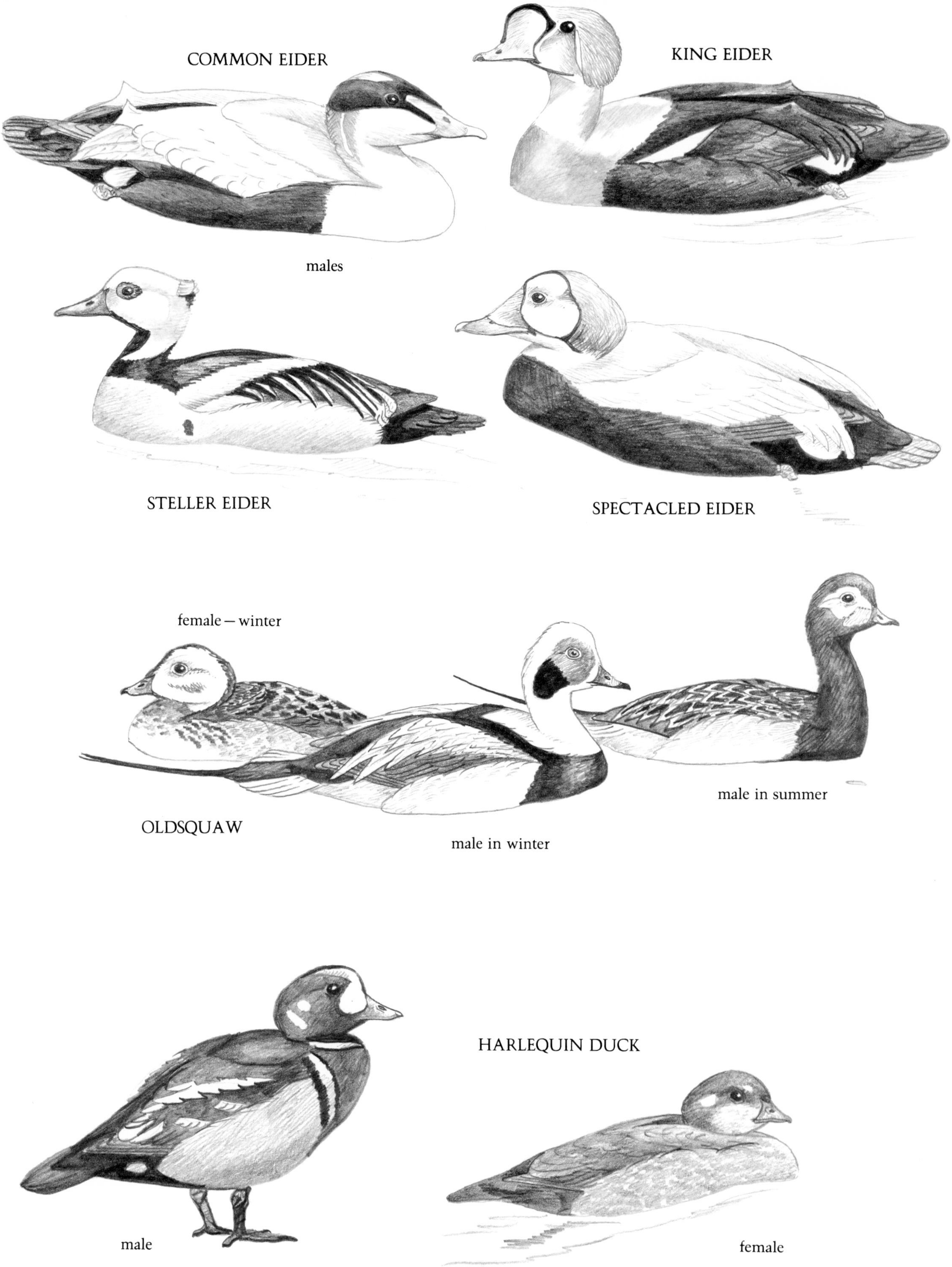
COMMON EIDER
KING EIDER
males
STELLER EIDER
SPECTACLED EIDER
female — winter
OLDSQUAW
male in winter
male in summer
HARLEQUIN DUCK
male
female

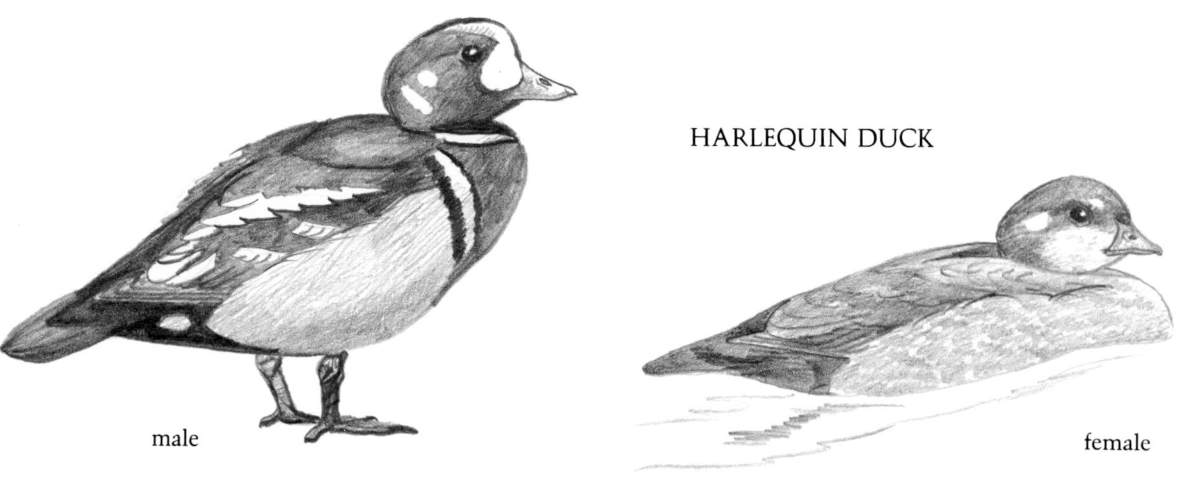

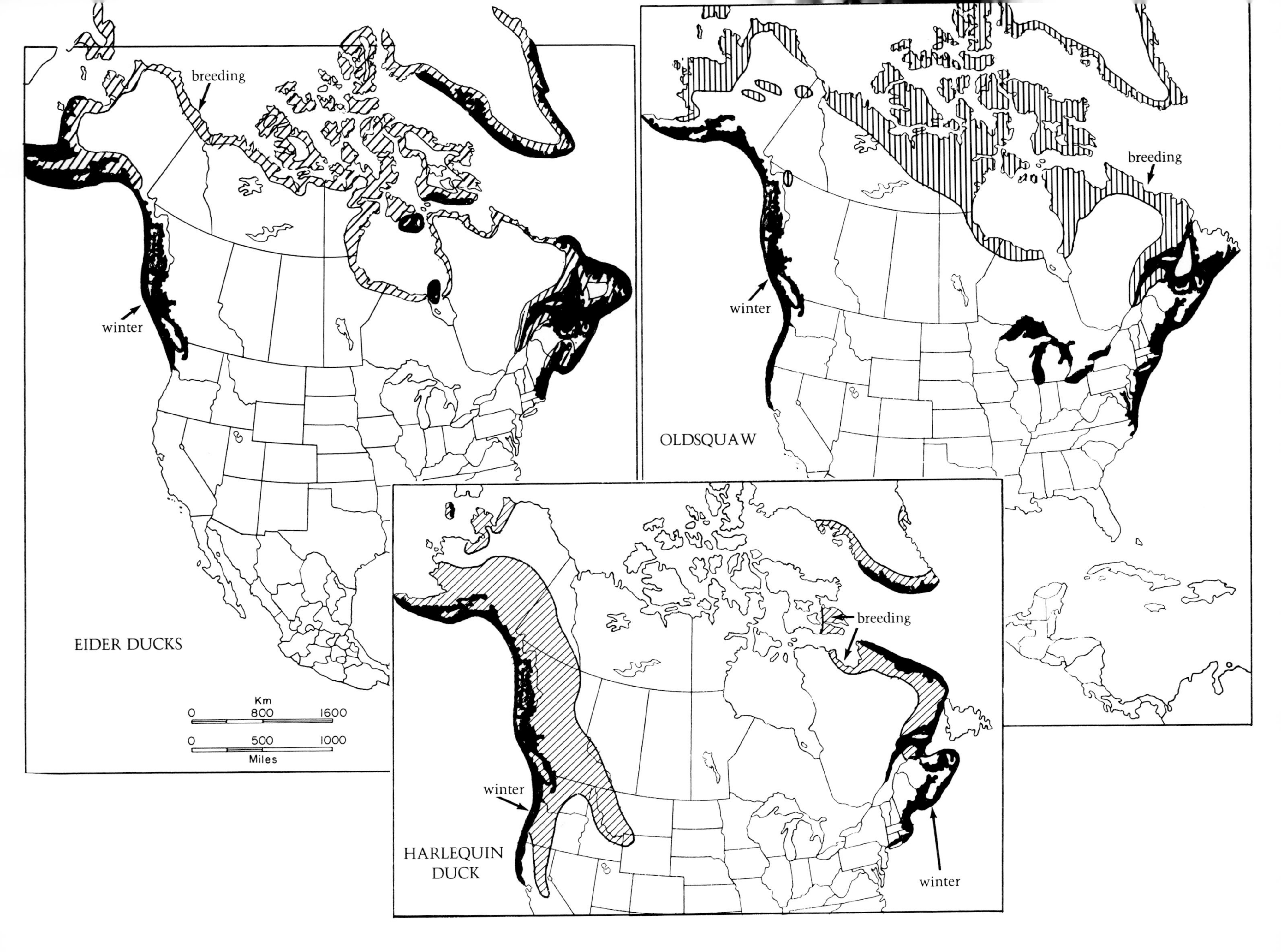
breeding
winter
EIDER DUCKS
Km
0
800
1600
0
500
1000
Miles
breeding
winter
OLDSQUAW
breeding
winter
winter
HARLEQUIN
DUCK

HARLEQUIN DUCK *(Histrionicus histrionicus)*

See also pages 92–93.

RANGE: Breeds in coastal and mountainous areas of northeastern and northwestern North America as far south as Labrador and central California, respectively. Winters off upper Atlantic and Pacific coasts.

HABITAT: Nests near rapidly flowing mountain or coastal streams. Winters on salt water.

REMARKS: The male harlequin is appropriately named. Its bluish body—dashed with white and russet patches and stripes—presents a gaudy spectacle indeed. The female, on the other hand, is drab and lays claim to only a few white head patches, a feature that distinguishes her from the female bufflehead. The eastern harlequin population is not nearly as abundant as the western one, yet the major study done on this species was conducted by Bengston (1966) in Iceland. The harlequin is quite common in certain areas, such as its principal breeding and summering range on the Aleutian Islands National Wildlife Refuge, but it is not often seen in the contiguous United States or inland Canada.

These birds nest along the turbulent rapids of mountain or coastal streams. The female selects a nest site in a rocky crevice or under a bush. The male, like most other divers, defends only a small area around the female during the nesting season and deserts her after she begins to incubate, tenaciously, her clutch of 5 to 6 eggs. Observers have nearly been able to touch the broody hen before she flushed from the nest. Once the eggs hatch, the hen leads her brood to a secluded part of the river. Often the broods aggregate, and unsuccessful hens may join the broods.

Once the clutch has fledged, the females and young depart their streams for the sea, where they spend the winter. Presumably, the males have already undergone their molt on their saltwater wintering grounds. Harlequins apparently winter along the coast adjacent to their known summer range.

Harlequin ducks feed in the turbulent water of the streams where they nest. Diving into the swift current, they somehow maintain their position against this water force to surface in the same area from which they dived. This feat no doubt requires a considerable expenditure of energy or else the harlequins have evolved some mechanism, such as walking on the bottom, for circumventing the force of the water. They eat animal matter almost exclusively (e.g., crustaceans, mollusks, insects, echinoderms, and a few fish). About 2 percent of the diet is vegetable. Harlequins favor chitons as a food item, a mollusk not readily eaten by other divers because of its firm attachment to the rocks.

OLDSQUAW *(Clangula hyemalis)*

See also pages 92–93.

RANGE: Circumpolar; in North America, breeds throughout the Arctic. Winters offshore along the Atlantic and Pacific coasts and on the Great Lakes.

HABITAT: Breeds on tundra snowmelt ponds. Winters at sea along the continental coasts and in the middle of the Great Lakes.

REMARKS: Oldsquaws are remarkable as well as beautiful birds. They are the most abundant duck nesting on the high Arctic, and characteristics of their breeding biology demonstrate their adaptations to this harsh environment (Alison 1975). They begin nesting as soon as snow begins to melt on the tundra. Pairs of oldsquaws are dispersed throughout suitable tundra on small ponds and lakes. Intense intraspecific aggression occurs between males. The female selects a nest site on an island in a tundra pond and hatches a clutch of 6 to 8 eggs in 26 days. If she is unsuccessful, no renesting occurs, because of the brief arctic summer. Even if successful, the female may desert her brood as early as the downy stage. These orphaned youngsters then gather in large groups without shepherding parents. Their survival rate under these seemingly adverse conditions is not known. Natural selection, however, has favored an extremely rapid growth rate. Young birds reach flight stage in about 35 days. Even though the pair bond deteriorates, some pairs reunite to nest again another year. The sex ratio is almost even, which is unusual among North American ducks.

Oldsquaws are the deepest-diving ducks, with records of birds being caught in fishing nets more than 150 feet deep (45 meters). These ducks seek animal food on these phenomenal foraging escapades. Crustaceans are the most important food items; fish, mollusks, and insects are secondarily taken. Plant material when taken makes up less than 20 percent of the diet. The ability to dive so deeply accounts, in part, for oldsquaw scarcity near shorelines. The ducks may be present and abundant, yet rafted some distance from land.

SCOTERS

BLACK SCOTER *(Melanitta nigra)*
SURF SCOTER *(Melanitta perspicillata)*
WHITE-WINGED SCOTER *(Melanitta fusca)*

See also pages 96–97.

RANGE: Black scoters are circumpolar in distribution; the surf scoter incompletely so. The white-winged scoter is indigenous to North America. All species breed in Alaska and Canada and winter along both seacoasts.

HABITAT: The black scoter generally breeds on the tundra while the others nest in the boreal forests around freshwater ponds and lakes. All species winter in coastal estuaries and bays and along open seacoasts.

REMARKS: Scoters are medium-large (2 to 4 pounds; 1 to 1.8 kilograms) black sea ducks. Flocks can often be distinguished by their irregular, wavering low-flight pattern. The white-winged scoter is easily identified by its flashing white speculum on a black wing; the other species have no wing markings. The male black scoter has a small, round, black head and bill, the base of which is bulbous and orange. The surf scoter has a massive wedge-shaped head and bill, with a white forehead and back-of-head patches. Scoters are not as closely linked to the sea as eiders, but nevertheless they spend much of their lives at sea, wintering and molting.

The scoters are the least-studied group of ducks in North America, and the surf scoter is least known of all. Scoters arrive late at their breeding grounds. They breed at age two, their nests being well hidden in the forest or in clumps of tundra grass. Clutches are 5 to 10 depending on the species, with an incubation time of 25 to 28 days. Because they nest later than other waterfowl, scoters have little chance for renesting. Little else is well documented in their nesting phenology.

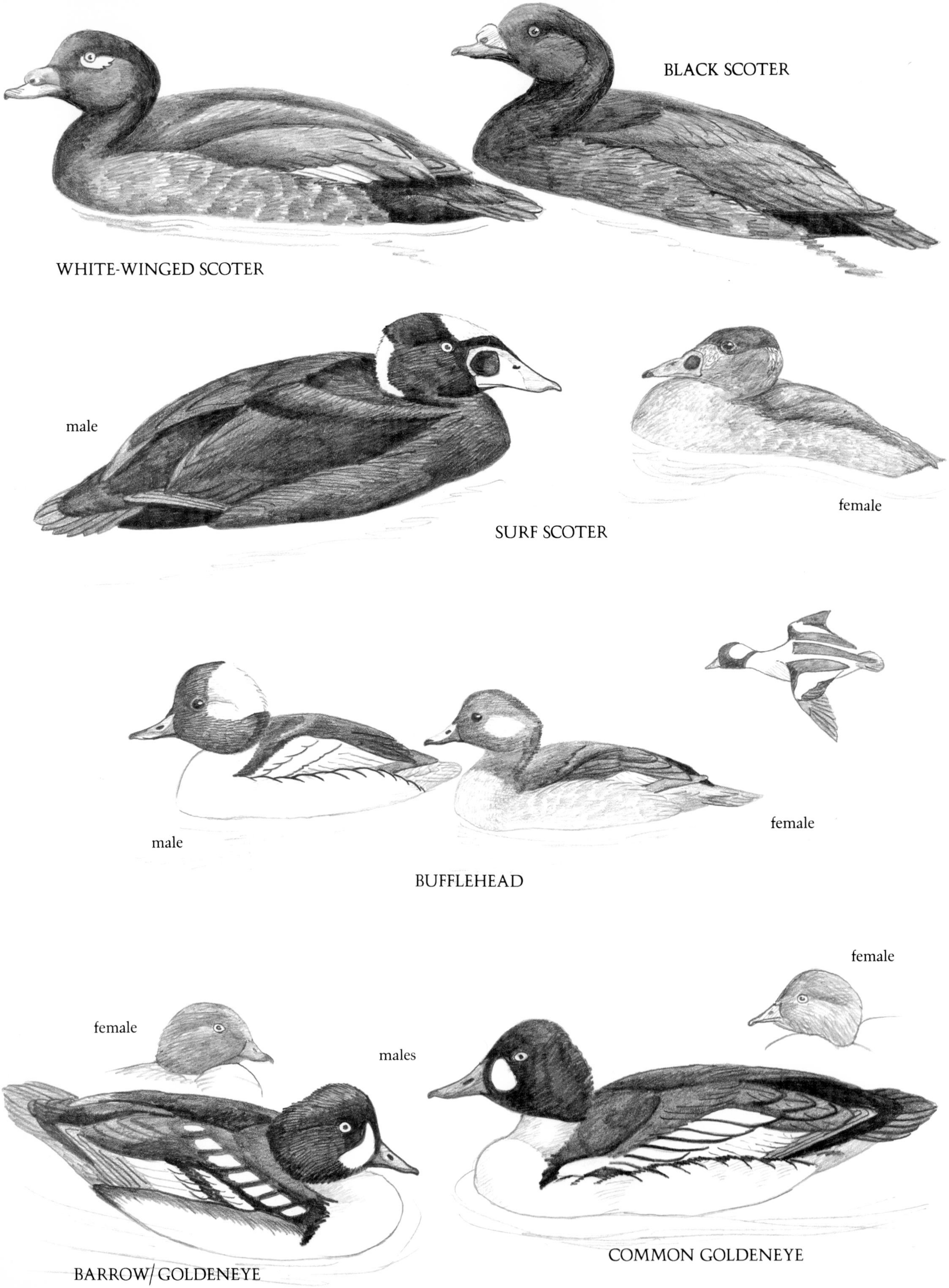

BLACK SCOTER

WHITE-WINGED SCOTER

male

female

SURF SCOTER

BUFFLEHEAD

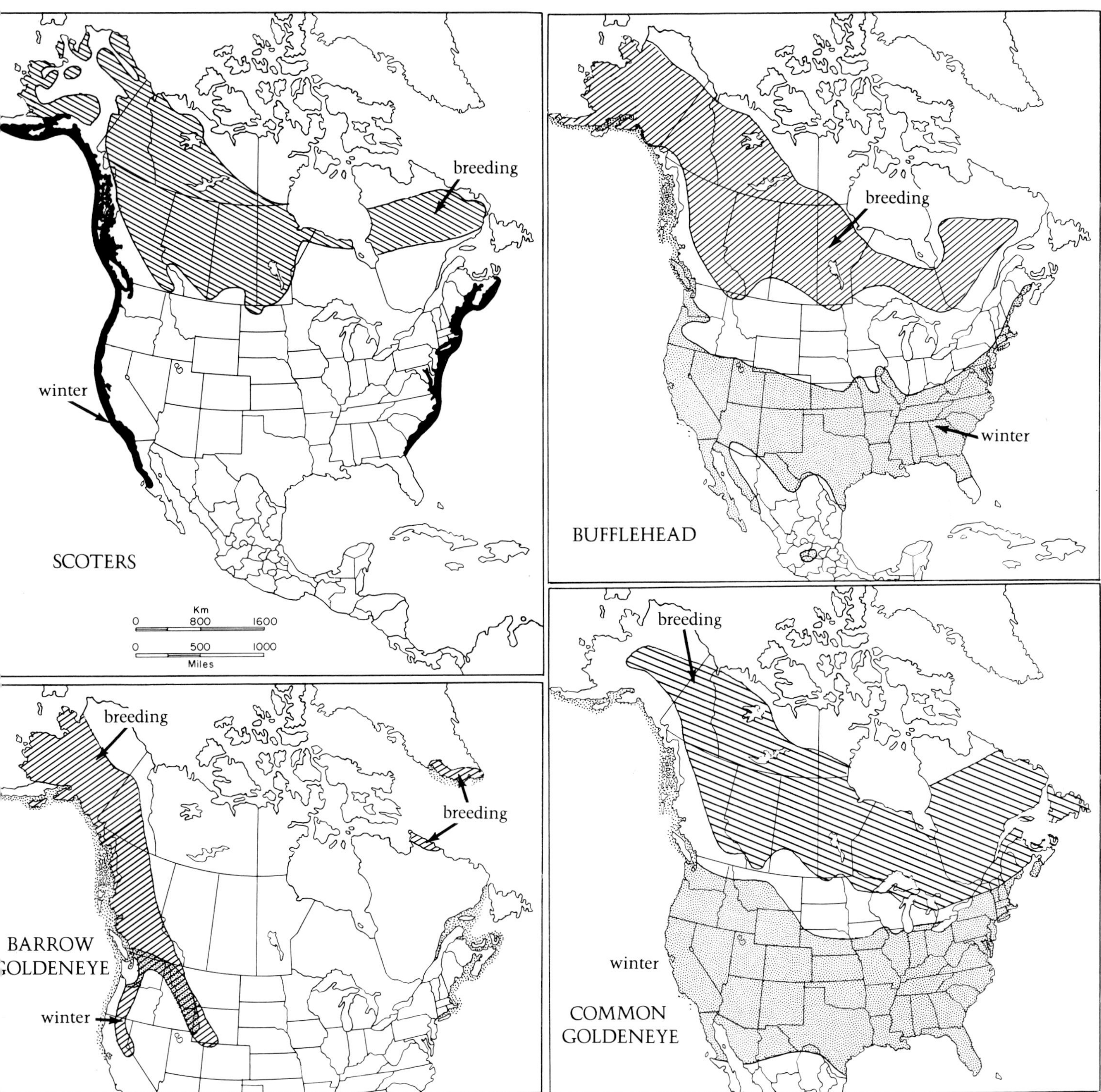

SCOTERS
breeding
winter
Km
0
800
1600
0
500
1000
Miles
BUFFLEHEAD
breeding
winter
BARROW
GOLDENEYE
breeding
breeding
winter
COMMON
GOLDENEYE
breeding
winter

Surf scoters are most common wintering on the Pacific coast, but the white-winged scoter dominates on the Atlantic coast. Major winter concentrations of whitewings and blacks occur in the Aleutian Islands. Little reliability can yet be given to numerical estimates for individual species but perhaps collectively they number between 1.5 million and 2 million birds.

Scoters eat primarily animals, particularly mollusks, blue mussels, clams, oysters, scallops, and lesser numbers of crustaceans and insect larvae. Eelgrass and wigeongrass are among the plant foods recorded from gizzard samples. Some of the clams taken are amazingly large—up to 54 millimeters or over 2 inches in length and 45 millimeters in width. The proclivity for eating shellfish gives scoter flesh a strong flavor. The birds are hunted for sport only in eastern Canada and New England. Few people have any desire to eat scoters more than once, although some cooks in New England persist in publishing recipes alleged to reduce this lively meat to a state of edibility.

BUFFLEHEAD *(Bucephala albeola)*

See also pages 96–97.

RANGE: Breeds from Alaska east across forested areas of Canada to Ontario and Quebec. Winters primarily along both coasts and secondarily on continental waters from the central United States south to northern Mexico.

HABITATS: Ponds and lakes in forested areas in summer. Winters on coastal bays, brackish estuaries, and fresh waters.

REMARKS: The bufflehead is one of the smallest ducks (362 to 630 grams); it is also one of the fastest flying of the waterfowl. Pairs and small groups are often seen flying rapidly over the water's surface. Male buffleheads are easily distinguished from other ducks by a fan-shaped white head patch extending from below the eye to the back of the head. Females are not as sharply marked as the males, being more brown and dull gray with a white dash behind the eye.

Erskine (1971) published a comprehensive study of the bufflehead. As with a number of other game birds, heavy hunting at the turn of the century caused buffleheads to decline noticeably. Because of protective legislation, however, their numbers have since climbed to the point where there are now between one half million and one million breeding birds. Buffleheads nest on ponds and lakes larger than one hectare throughout a great area of forested Alaska and Canada, wherever suitable tree cavities are to be found. These ducks nest in small cavities primarily excavated by woodpeckers; they frequently compete for nest sites with the woodpeckers themselves or with the introduced starling or other passerine birds. As with many northern ducks, nesting is initiated soon after spring arrival, and little, if any, renesting occurs. Once the clutch of about 9 eggs is laid, the male leaves his mate and begins the eclipse molt. Like some other cavity-nesting ducks for which nest sites are sometimes limiting, buffleheads occasionally have dump nests. Females have high nest-site fidelity. The female incubates her clutch for 29 to 31 days and is remarkably successful in her endeavor (over 78 percent of nests are successful). Once the eggs hatch, the young leave the nest after 1 to 1½ days but apparently are not called by the hen as is true of wood ducks and goldeneyes. The hen leads her brood to an open-water rearing area in a lake and remains with them until she molts.

The food of the bufflehead is predominantly insects, crustaceans, and mollusks. Relatively little plant food is taken. The species is only of incidental importance as a game duck, the small size and strong flavor discouraging most hunters from killing it. Also, it flies so fast that not many hunters can hit it.

BARROW GOLDENEYE *(Bucephala islandica)*

See also pages 96–97.

RANGE: Primarily northwestern North America, breeding in arctic and mountain ponds and wintering in coastal Pacific waters. In the northeast, a small population breeds in Greenland and Labrador and winters in eastern Canada and New England.

HABITAT: Breeds on freshwater ponds and lakes with abundant submerged vegetation. Winters largely in coastal bays; a few birds frequent open waters in the northern Rocky Mountain states.

REMARKS: The Barrow goldeneye occupies a restricted range, being common only in British Columbia and a few areas of the northern Rockies and Alaska. The breeding range of the species is mostly in timbered areas, and nests normally are situated in tree cavities. Where there are no trees, the females resort to holes in the ground, holes in cliffs, or other sheltered nooks. Most breeders are two years old or older. Females have a high fidelity to their nesting sites, returning to the same cavity each year as long as it is suitable. Clutches average 9 eggs; incubation is 32 to 34 days. Nest success was found to be high (90 percent) in a study in British Columbia. Nest losses are typically quite low in hole-nesting birds. Ducklings often are deserted by the hen at six weeks of age. They frequently gather into loose bands, sometimes in company of one adult. One unusual trait is the group search for nest cavities by adult and yearling females. This occurs when the adults have nests and are in the process of laying. They seem to lead the yearlings in a quest for unoccupied cavities, an experience that may serve to imprint on the young birds the locations and characteristics of suitable nest sites for future reference when the young reach breeding age (Bellrose 1976:425).

Barrow goldeneyes eat mostly animal foods—aquatic insects, crustaceans, mollusks, and fish. Aquatic plants such as pondweed are used to some extent in summer. Relatively few of these birds are taken by hunters, either for sport or for subsistence.

COMMON GOLDENEYE *(Bucephala clangula)*

See also pages 96–97.

RANGE: In North America, breeds from Alaska to New England, predominantly in the boreal forests of Canada. Winters along both coasts and on ice-free lakes and rivers inland.

HABITAT: Breeds along timber-bordered ponds and lakes. Winters on fresh or salt waters.

REMARKS: Goldeneyes are among the ducks that habitually nest in tree holes. Common goldeneyes breed in small numbers over a vast timbered area. Nowhere are they concentrated in abundance, even on the wintering grounds. Common goldeneyes are more widespread and much more abundant, however, than the Barrow goldeneye. The two goldeneyes share many breeding and behavioral characteristics.

Goldeneyes prefer open-top tree cavities rather than side-entrance cavities. These holes are traditionally occupied each year and may accumulate an incredible record of repeated use. In one deep cavity nest that was opened in the Soviet Union, there was 2 to 3 meters (6.5 to 9.8 feet) of goldeneye nest accumulation. Included in this debris were two abandoned clutches and the bones of two goldeneyes. As if this were not enough, 14 eggs were laid by two females on top of it all (Semenov-Tian-Shanskii 1960, in Palmer 1976). In areas where cavities are scarce, two or more females may lay in the same nest, resulting in some very large clutches. It is not surprising, therefore, that they would readily accept nest boxes. The Lapps and Karelians have provided nesting structures for these ducks for several hundred years.

Because so much of their food consists of animal matter, goldeneyes are prone to have a fishy flavor. An average diet, based on the contents of several hundred stomachs, as reported in the classic account of waterfowl food habits by Cottam (1939) is crustaceans, 32 percent; insects, 28; mollusks, 10; fishes, 3—total animal foods about 75 percent of the diet. Various aquatic plants (pondweeds, wild celery, and so on) constitute the remainder.

Goldeneyes are called "whistlers" because of the distinctive noise their wings make in flight. Goldeneyes are among the last of the migrants to come south in autumn, and they winter in ice-free waters farther north than most ducks.

HOODED MERGANSER *(Mergus cucullatus)*

See also pages 102–3.

RANGE: Breeds from southeastern Alaska south to the Coast ranges of Oregon and across eastern Canada from Manitoba to Nova Scotia. Winters primarily in coastal waters, especially along the Atlantic seaboard.

HABITAT: Nests along wooded sloughs, streams, beaver ponds, and swamp ponds; in winter, saltwater bays and estuaries.

REMARKS: Mergansers are fish-eating ducks that can be recognized by their long, narrow, serrated bills. Hooded mergansers are medium-sized ducks that are not especially gregarious. They frequently travel alone, in pairs, or in small flocks, flying with fast wing beats low over the water. The hooded merganser is the least abundant of the three native mergansers (about 8 percent of American mergansers are hooded). Their numbers seem to have declined as a result of snag removal, logging, and swamp drainage. The adult male is a beautiful black and white bird, which is readily identified by a large, white crest bordered by black. Females and juveniles are dull grayish birds with reddish-brown heads and smaller crests.

Hooded mergansers breed when two years old and prefer the seclusion of a clear, wooded stream or pond, where they nest in tree cavities. They share many of the characteristics of wood ducks, including use of artificial nest boxes, dump nesting (not only in their own species nest, but also in wood duck nests), and incubation period. The females have a strong homing tendency to their breeding area. Once the hen lays her clutch of 10 to 11 eggs, her mate deserts her and seemingly vanishes to the seclusion of a woody abode to molt. The chicks remain in the nest box for 24 hours before they leave to face the world.

Hooded mergansers feed almost exclusively on small fish, crustaceans, and insects. They have been recorded, however, to eat copious quantities of acorns.

RED-BREASTED MERGANSER *(Mergus serrator)*

See also pages 102–3.

RANGE: Circumpolar; in North America, breeds from the Aleutian Islands south and east to the Great Lakes and the Laborador Peninsula. Winters along the Atlantic, Gulf, and Pacific coasts as well as on the Great Lakes.

HABITAT: Nests on the ground near tundra ponds, in boreal forests, marshes, vegetated islands in lakes, and on rocky islets. Winters most commonly on coastal seas and to a lesser extent on the Great Lakes.

REMARKS: Red-breasted mergansers are the most numerous mergansers wintering on ocean waters. The bright-red bill and eyes, green head with its posterior tuft of feathers, white throat and flanks, and dark chest band all serve to distinguish the male. Female and immatures have dull-red bills and eyes, gray sides and backs, and brown heads. The females and immatures are nearly indistinguishable from female and immature common mergansers, but can be identified by the gradual phasing of brown head and white throat feathers. This color change is more abrupt in the common merganser.

Like other mergansers, the red-breasted merganser breeds at 2 years of age. The female lays an average of 7 to 8 eggs in a down-lined hollow on the ground. She incubates her clutch for about 30 days. Once the ducklings hatch, broods aggregate very early, sometimes in large numbers. Apparently, one female may serve as a foster parent for more than her own brood. Red-breasted mergansers nest much later than the common merganser, and since they also tend to nest farther north, there is little time to renest if their first clutch is destroyed. Some records of very late broods, however, indicate that renesting may occur rarely.

Red-breasted and common mergansers are said to have similar food habits when on fresh water. But since the red-breasted merganser primarily winters on salt water, some degree of competition is avoided by their different locations. Both birds eat a variety of fish species as well as shrimp, prawns, crabs, salmon eggs, and crustaceans. Red-breasted mergansers have been known to use a hunting strategy whereby they line up and herd fish into shallow waters, where the fish are more easily caught.

COMMON MERGANSER *(Mergus merganser)*

See also pages 102–3.

RANGE: Circumpolar, nesting in North America from southern Alaska and central Canada south to the Sierra Nevada, Rocky Mountains, and northeastern United States. Winters largely on fresh water in the United States (except Deep South) as far south as northern Mexico.

HABITAT: Nests in trees or along the banks of mountain lakes and streams. In winter, descends to ice-free rivers, lakes, and, occasionally, to the sea.

REMARKS: This largest and most abundant of mergansers (sometimes called "goosander") has a strong predilection for clear water and often is accused of decimating populations of trout. That they do eat trout cannot be denied. But they also consume many minnows and rough fish, and it is doubtful that they really harm the wild-trout population except in rare instances. Fish hatcheries are another matter. The common merganser that pays a visit to a rearing pond ordinarily does not live to repeat the experience. Various scare devices have been tried, however, to alleviate the unnecessary

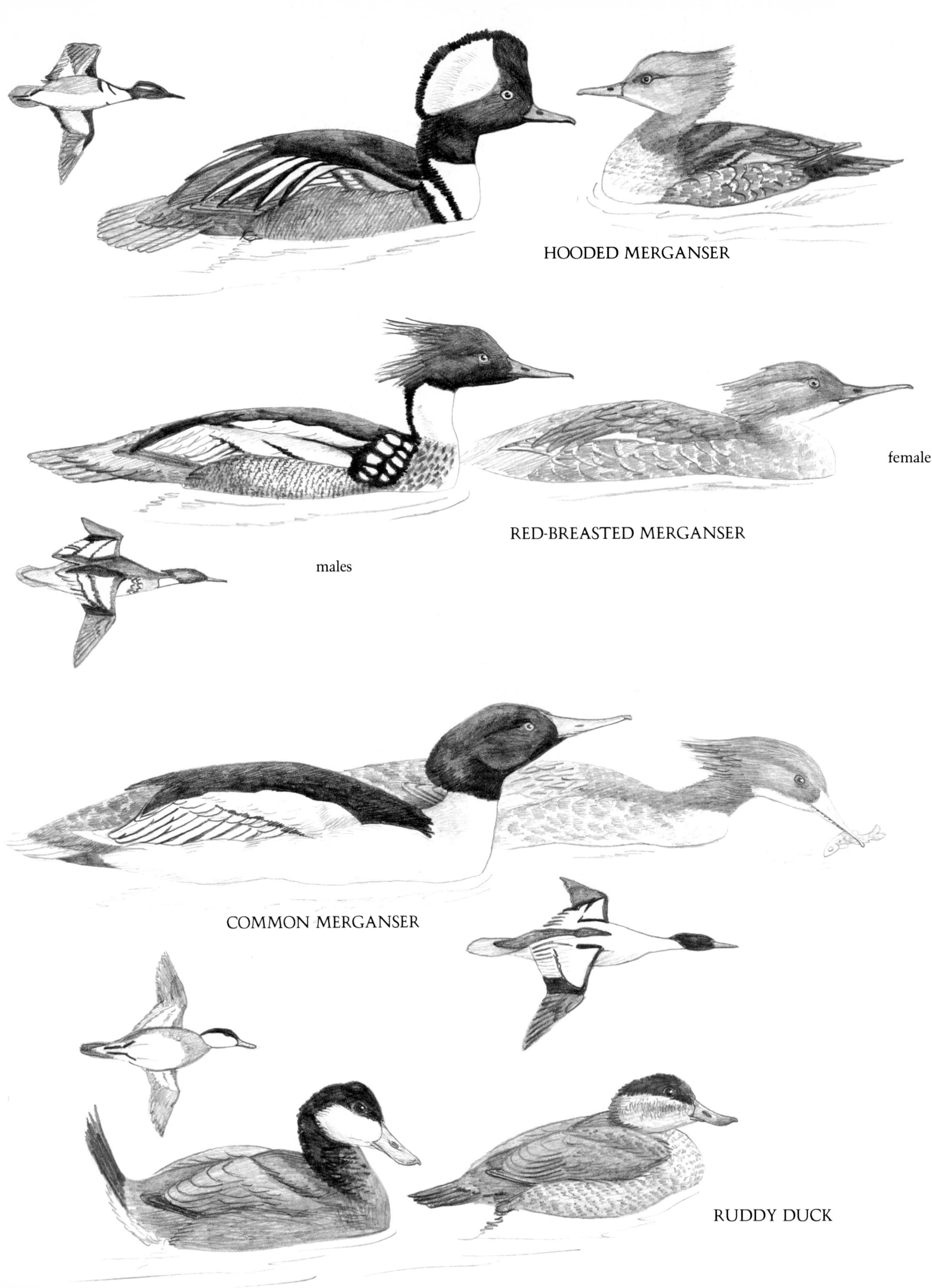
HOODED MERGANSER
female
RED-BREASTED MERGANSER
males
COMMON MERGANSER
RUDDY DUCK

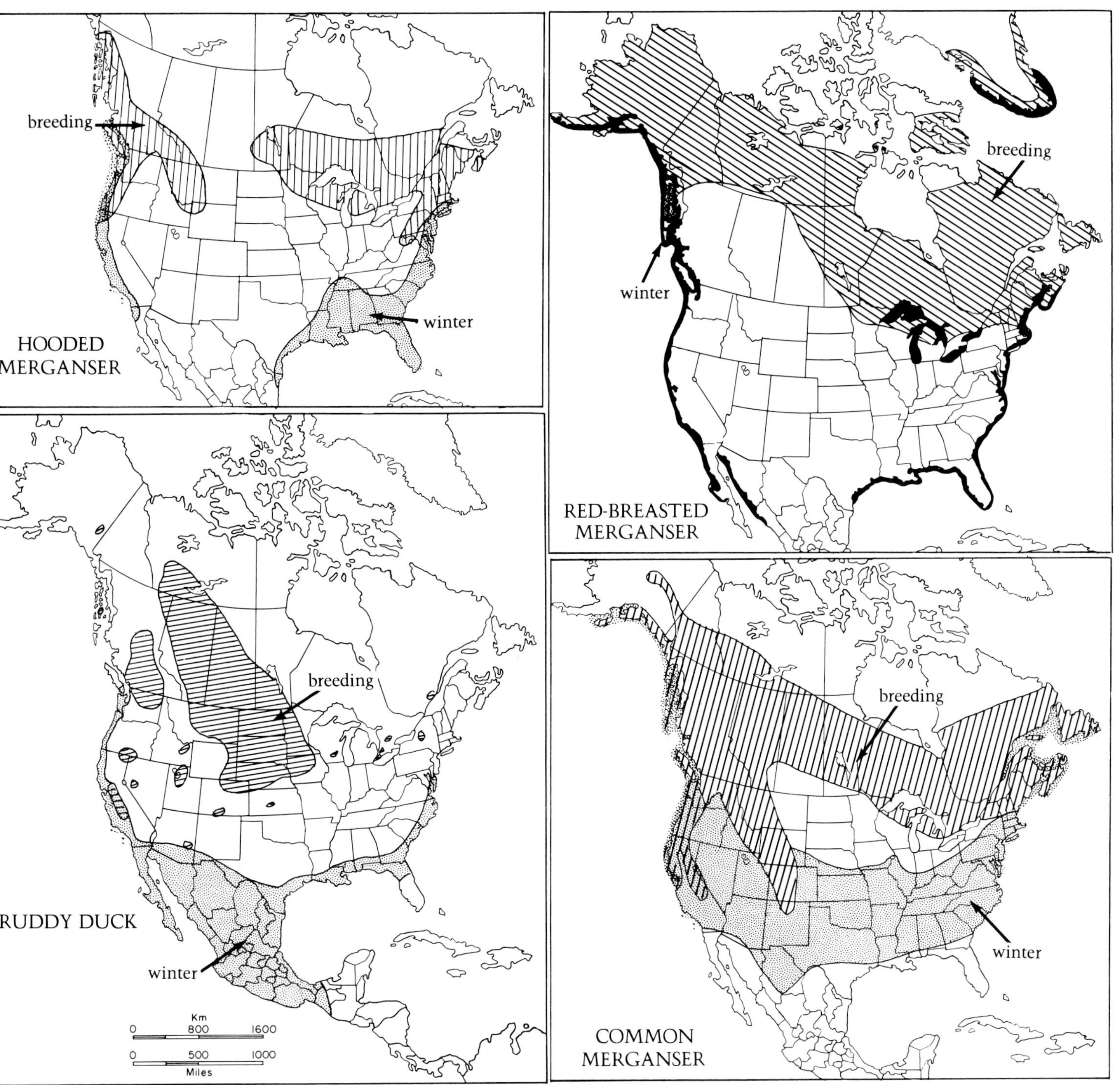

breeding
winter
HOODED MERGANSER
breeding
winter
RED-BREASTED MERGANSER
breeding
RUDDY DUCK
winter
Km
0 800 1600
0 500 1000
Miles
breeding
winter
COMMON MERGANSER

killing of these and other birds around hatcheries. Common mergansers are in no way endangered, as their continental breeding population numbers over 500,000.

Although these mergansers prefer to nest in tree cavities, they will nest on the ground if no trees are available. Nesting is similar to that of the red-breasted merganser except that common mergansers lay larger clutches (9 to 12).

These mergansers are about the last migrants to leave the ice-bound mountains and northland in fall, frequenting open holes in swift rivers or large lakes not yet frozen. They are strong flyers and adept at dodging through timber or narrow canyons.

Tribe Oxyurini (STIFF-TAILED DUCKS)

RUDDY DUCK *(Oxyura jamaicensis)*

See also pages 102–3.

RANGE: Breeds primarily in prairie pothole country, Canadian parklands, and boreal forests, but also in scattered marshes through the western United States. Winters along both coasts and in Mexico.

HABITAT: Potholes and marshes with a rank growth of emergent vegetation; will also winter on open waters, both salt and fresh.

REMARKS: The male ruddy duck in breeding plumage is deep, rusty-red, with black and white head, and sky-blue bill. This handsome plumage is lost immediately after the breeding season. The male retains his eclipse plumage (looking much like the female) through the winter, and then again in spring adopts the nuptial dress. Unlike other prairie ducks, however, ruddy drakes enter wing molt in midsummer. The hens lay an average clutch of 8 eggs (6 to 15) in a nest built over water in emergent vegetation. The eggs are very large in relation to the one-pound female. A clutch of 14 weighs three times as much as the hen that produced them—a feat of legerdemain. Although most studies have shown that ruddies are successful nesters (approximately 70 percent nest success), a high proportion of dead embryos come from additional eggs dumped in the nest by other females. In some areas, the male may attend the hen and brood for a short period.

Habitat interspersion is important in determining the spacing of the nests. The highest breeding densities recorded (4 pairs per square mile; 2.6 pairs per square kilometer) were found in the diverse prairie pothole-parklands of Manitoba. Ruddy ducks eat the seeds and vegetative parts of aquatic plants, particularly pondweeds, bulrushes, and sedges. But they also eat almost 28 percent animal matter, particularly midge larvae.

In winter, ruddy ducks usually are scattered widely over the southern half of North America; concentrations are rare. Yet in 1952, one of us found an aggregation of 107,700 in a small coastal lagoon of Guerrero (Leopold 1959: 137).

A close relative of the ruddy duck, called the masked duck *(Oxyura dominica)*, occurs sparingly in Texas and the Gulf States. It is generally resident in the West Indies and along the Gulf coast of Mexico.

Part Two

MAMMALS

Game mammals of North America range from some of the larger rodents, which generally have maintained or increased their numbers under man's influence, to wolves and bighorn sheep, whose jeopardized status reflects the progressive disappearance of wild places.

Of the herbivorous mammals discussed here, the Artiodactyla, or even-toed ungulates, are the largest in body size. Because they make their living foraging on grasses and shrubs, which often are nutritionally poor, they have large stomachs and feed during much of the day (or night) to keep them full. These animals have specialized digestive systems to derive necessary nourishment. An intestinal flora of bacteria and protozoa helps by reducing cellulose to simpler, digestible carbohydrates. The even-toed ungulates achieve some protection from predators by being fleet of foot or by complex social-warning systems.

The order Carnivora includes the mammalian predators and most of the fur bearers. A few of the largest carnivores, like wolves and pumas, are primary predators of wild ungulates but may cause trouble by killing domestic livestock. The medium-sized cats, foxes, weasels, and such prey mostly on rodents and rabbits. All members of this order have pelts of some commercial value. An additional fur bearer of minor importance is the opossum, of the order Marsupialia.

Of the many species of marine mammals in the order Pinnipedia, we discuss only the walrus, which in Alaska is classified as a game animal. It supplies some sport hunting but is much more important to Eskimos for its meat, hide, and ivory.

Rodents of the order Rodentia are herbivorous like the ungulates but utilize a wider variety of habitats and plant parts. Some live in the trees, as, for example, the squirrels, feeding on mast (acorns, beechnuts) or fungi dug from the ground. Others dwell in ground burrows or in the water. The rodents, collectively, are the "staff of life" for predators, both carnivorous mammals and the hawks and owls.

Rabbits and hares of the order Lagomorpha are ecologically similar to rodents and are also prime fare for predators. But they are entirely unrelated to the rodents. The cottontail rabbits supply much of the sport hunting in the United States.

Identification of mammal specimens is based on three sets of criteria: (1) skins, (2) skulls, and (3) body measurements. Mammal skulls have characters whose variations are useful in distinguishing species, genera, families, and orders. Numbers and kinds of teeth are especially diagnostic. A scientific specimen of a mammal consists, therefore, of both the skin and skull, along with a label on which standard measurements are recorded — total length, lengths of tail, hind foot, and ear from notch to tip. Body weight is another useful statistic.

The "tooth formula" of a typical carnivore like the coyote is expressed as follows:

$$\frac{\text{3 upper incisors}}{\text{3 lower incisors}} \quad \frac{\text{1 upper canine}}{\text{1 lower canine}} \quad \frac{\text{4 upper premolars}}{\text{4 lower premolars}} \quad \frac{\text{2 upper molars}}{\text{3 lower molars}}$$

These numbers, totaling 21, refer to the teeth on *one side* of the skull. The full dentition then is 42 teeth. All except the molars sprout first as "milk teeth" and are later replaced by permanent teeth as the animal matures. Molars emerge as permanent teeth and are not replaced.

The accompanying drawings show the dentition of a coyote and illustrate how standard body measurements are taken.

Our authority for scientific names of mammals is the checklist published in 1975 by Jones, Carter, and Genoways. Range maps were derived from many sources, but we especially acknowledge the comprehensive publication of Hall and Kelson (1959).

THE "TOOTH FORMULA" OF A COYOTE

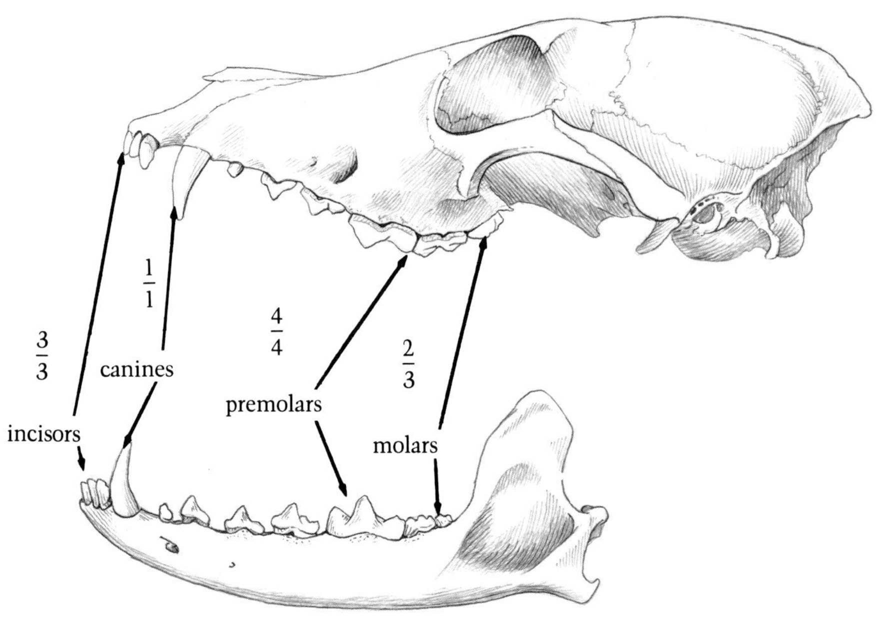

Order Marsupialia

The world's marsupial mammals, which carry their young in a ventral pouch, are primarily distributed in Australia and South America. Several species occur in Mexico. Only one species ranges north of the U.S.–Mexican border, occurring naturally in the southern and eastern United States.

Family Didelphidae (Opossums)

VIRGINIA OPOSSUM *(Didelphis virginiana)*

RANGE: Central and eastern United States, Mexico southward into South America; introduced from the eastern United States into agricultural valleys of the Pacific states.

HABITAT: Riverbottoms, woodlands, chaparral, farmland, suburban areas

REMARKS: The primitive and small-brained opossum is numerically the fourth-ranking fur bearer in the United States (behind the muskrat, nutria, and raccoon). Opossums are enormously prolific and sustain a high kill rate without becoming scarce. The fur is of low value, however, used mostly for trimming inexpensive coats.

The opossum's diet is mostly insects but also includes all manner of fruits, nuts, seeds, carrion, garbage, and invertebrates. Occasionally, the opossum robs eggs from bird nests or hen houses, and even more rarely the animal may kill a small bird or mammal.

Adults are solitary, denning in ground holes or hollow trees. The young are born only 13 days after mating, when they are one centimeter long and at an early stage of embryogenesis. The newborn opossums crawl into the marsupium (pouch) where each takes a nipple in its mouth and remains so attached for two months. Although there are thirteen nipples, usually seven or fewer young survive to weaning at three months of age. The mother abandons her offspring at weaning and may mate a second time that year. Many of the newly independent young starve or fall to predators, but a good proportion grow to maturity and breed when less than one year old. As adults, they weigh 2 to 6 kilograms.

Opossum meat is eaten in the southeastern United States and Mexico but is fatty and not very tasty.

The dental formula, unique among North American mammals, is $\frac{5\text{-}1\text{-}3\text{-}4}{4\text{-}1\text{-}3\text{-}4}$, a total of fifty teeth!

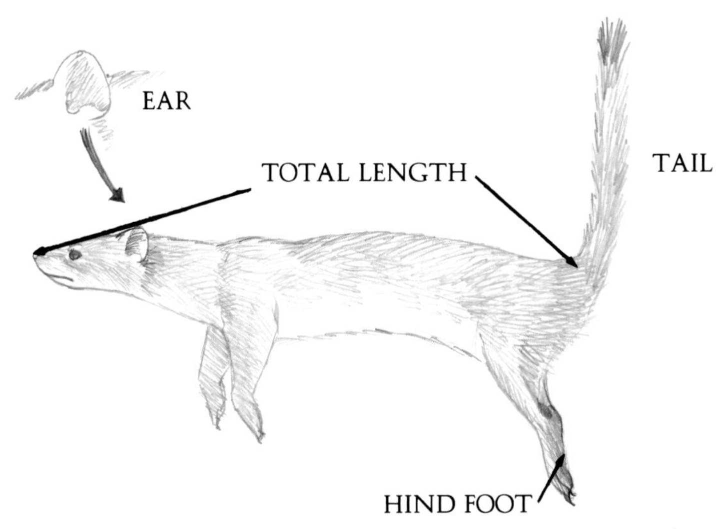

STANDARD MEASUREMENTS
OF A MAMMAL

Order Carnivora

Carnivores are valuable as sources of fur, as objects of sport hunting, and as animals of great beauty and interest to enlightened outdoorsmen. The carnivores serve a crucial role in ecosystem stabilization by preying on the more abundant herbivores. Some carnivores, however, also kill livestock or poultry, causing substantial economic loss; others transmit rabies. A few of the largest species (bears primarily) threaten human safety. From frontier days until fairly recently, carnivores collectively have been persecuted, as sources of fur or for one or another of the reasons mentioned. Many species became scarce or, locally, extinct. Today the positive values of carnivores are recognized through many protective regulations. Bounties and government-sponsored eradication campaigns are largely terminated. Only a few of the more persistent and abundant predators, such as the coyote, are still controlled on a systematic basis. Most species are legally protected, although provision is made for regulated fur harvest or for removal of individual animals when demonstrable damage is occurring.

Family Canidae (Wolves, coyotes, foxes)

GRAY WOLF *(Canis lupus)*

See also pages 112–13.

RANGE: Originally ranged over most of North America except the southeast and extreme southwest (California, Baja California). Largely eliminated from Mexico and the conterminous United States, except for local populations in Minnesota and Michigan. Wolves are still widespread in Canada and Alaska.

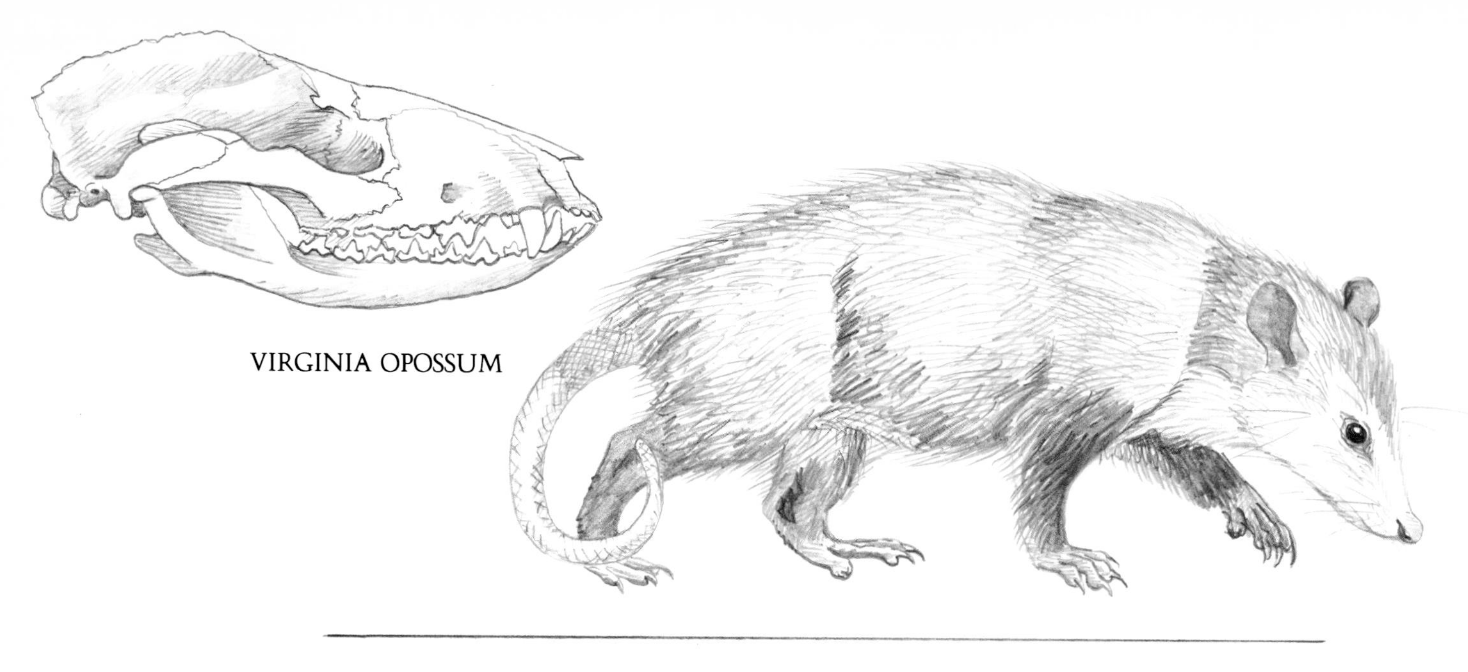
VIRGINIA OPOSSUM

GRAY WOLF

RED WOLF

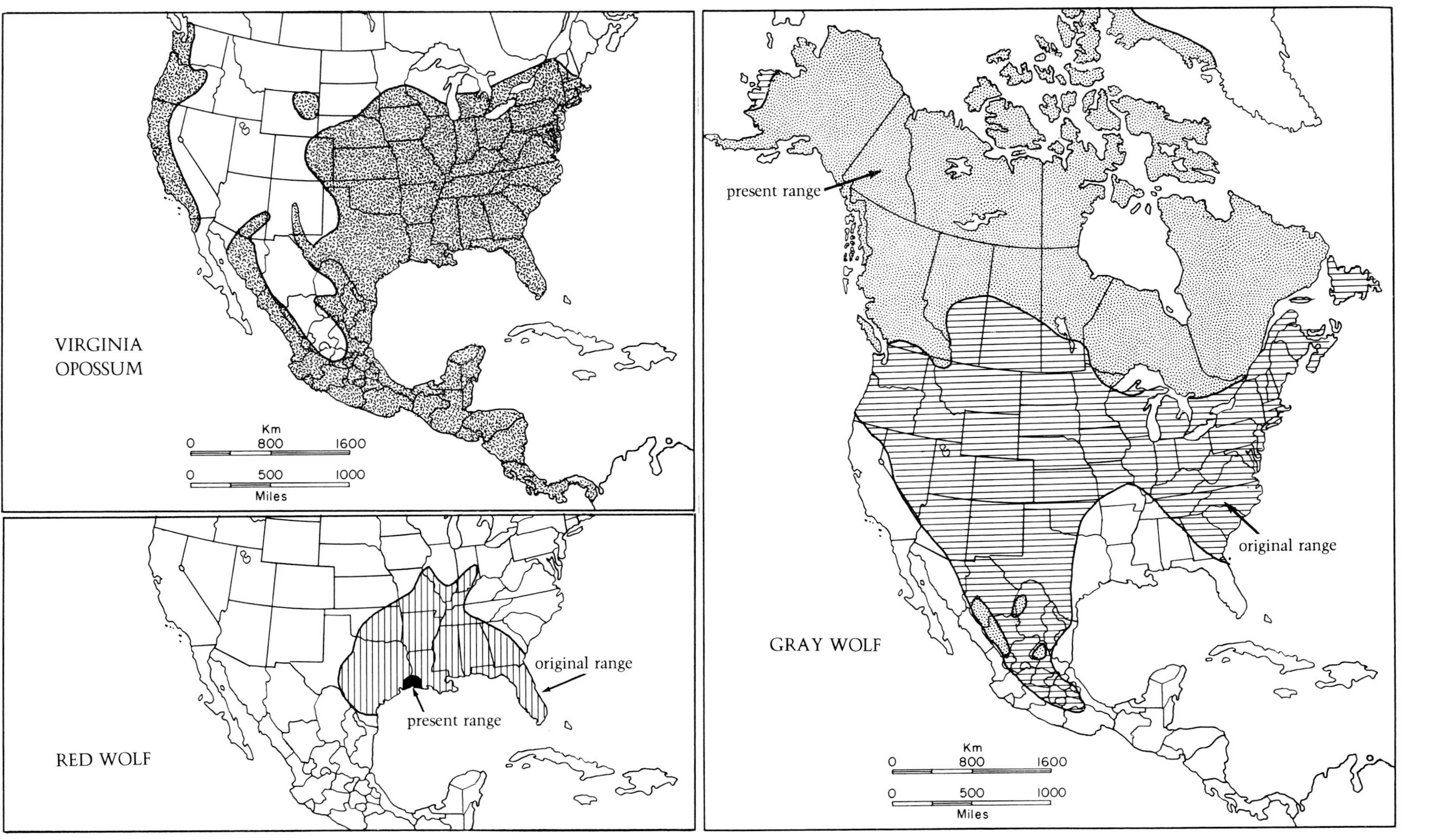
VIRGINIA
OPOSSUM
Km
0
800
1600
0
500
1000
Miles
RED WOLF
original range
present range
GRAY WOLF
present range
original range
Km
0
800
1600
0
500
1000
Miles

HABITAT: Prairies, brushlands, forests, and tundra; never abundant on the desert

REMARKS: Wolves are among the most social of animals, living in organized packs that are advantageous in their hunting of large prey animals. A pack usually consists of 4 to 20 related individuals of both sexes and all ages, organized in a dominance hierarchy. Pack order is maintained by complex communications and strong social bonds. There is an Alpha male and an Alpha female in each pack, who are social dominants as well as leaders. Ordinarily, only the Alpha pair mate and produce young. Litters average 4 to 6 pups, born after 9 weeks of gestation. Other members of the pack help feed and rear the pups. When the young wolves reach a stage of development that permits them to travel with the pack, the den site is abandoned and the pack becomes mobile to follow game wherever it may migrate. The young grow rapidly and reach adult size (30 to 50 kilograms) in two to three years. Physical attributes include a heavy gray or black pelage, and a full complement of teeth, $\frac{3\,1\,4\,2}{3\,1\,4\,3}$, set in powerful jaws.

The wolf diet is almost entirely animal flesh. In various parts of the range, the principal prey species may be bison, moose, caribou, wild sheep, or deer. When large prey is temporarily unavailable, wolves subsist on hares, rodents (like beaver), or birds. Domestic livestock is highly vulnerable to wolf predation, and the war between cattlemen or sheepherders and wolves has been incessant—in Europe as well as North America. Wolves tend to kill the individual prey animals that are most easily caught and subdued, meaning particularly the young, the old, and the infirm. Mech (1970) and Allen (1979) document the complex interrelationships between wolves and moose on Isle Royale, Michigan. A pack will "test" an individual moose. If it is so strong and active as to be dangerous to attack, the wolves move on, seeking an animal that can be killed with less risk. In attacking a caribou, there is little danger to the wolves, but most caribou are too fast to be caught. There is a tendency, then, for wolf predation among wild ungulates to be hygienic, culling the weak, the sick, and the slow. There is no such beneficial selection, however, when wolves prey on domestic livestock, all of which are susceptible.

RED WOLF *(Canis rufus)*

See also pages 112–13.

RANGE: Southeastern United States from Texas and southern Illinois to Florida

HABITAT: Southern forests of hardwood and pine, riparian thickets, coastal marshlands

REMARKS: The red wolf is intermediate in size between the gray wolf and the coyote. The weights of two males captured in Missouri by one of us were 35 and 46 pounds, or 16 and 21 kilograms (Leopold and Hall 1945). In appearance, the red wolf closely resembles the coyote, although some individuals are black rather than tawny. With settlement of the southeastern United States, the red wolf came into conflict with domestic livestock husbandry and was heavily persecuted to the point of near extinction. Concurrently, its former range was invaded by the much-more-adaptable coyote. The coyote not only outcompeted the wolf but also crossbred with it, leading to extermination by miscegenation. Today, there are only a few genetically pure red wolves left in the wild (east Texas, Louisiana) and a small captive population in zoos. The species may not survive (Riley and McBride 1972).

COYOTE *(Canis latrans)*

See also pages 116–17.

RANGE: Originally from 55 degrees latitude in central Canada southward to Costa Rica, west of the Mississippi River; now expanded as far as western Alaska, Quebec, and New England.

HABITAT: All terrestrial habitat types, except dense forest and high-arctic tundra

REMARKS: The coyote, both physically and behaviorally, is a generalized member of the dog family, principally occupying open grassland and foothills but quite at home in the mountains and on the desert. Coyotes mate in February or March and may pair for several consecutive breeding seasons, although they do not usually associate outside of the reproductive season. After a 7-week gestation, the pups are born, averaging 5 per litter. They are cared for by both parents. The young disperse in the autumn, and those that survive the heavy toll of poison, traps, predation, and starvation, reach sexual maturity at one year of age if food is plentiful (Nellis and Keith 1976). At 1½ years of age, the average coyote may have moved 30 to 40 kilometers from its place of birth and produced its first litter.

Adult coyotes weigh 9 to 13 kilograms (20 to 30 pounds), depending on the region. Their dental formula is $\frac{3\,1\,4\,2}{3\,1\,4\,3}$. This is the same as all other Canidae and Ursidae.

Coyotes are popularly believed to prey heavily on deer. In fact, they do kill a good many, especially fawns. Yet healthy adult deer in ordinary circumstances seem more or less immune. In deep, crusted snow, however, or when deer are weakened by starvation, the tables are turned in favor of the coyote. Domestic sheep are another matter; they are helpless against an attacking coyote and may suffer heavily if not well guarded. Local control of coyotes on sheep range is often necessary. Elsewhere coyotes are mainly beneficial because of their never-ending predation on small animal pests. The majority of the coyote's diet is rabbits, hares, mice, and carrion (Murie 1940). Coyotes have little effect on healthy populations of ungulate species.

The coyote is one of the most persecuted carnivores in North America. Yet it has proven so flexible in its habits, so adroit in escaping the trap and gun, and so prolific that it persists in good numbers even today. With the elimination of wolves and the clearing of timber, the coyote has even spread into the northern forest belt, where it was unknown before 1920. It has recently colonized Alaska and northern New England. Although coyotes have continued to occupy a tremendous range, their numbers locally were greatly reduced by the use of modern poisons such as thallium, a compound called "1080" (sodium fluoroacetate), and sodium cyanide. By executive order in 1971, use of 1080 to kill predators was banned in the United States. But trapping, shooting, and restricted use of sodium cyanide still continue.

As more and more Americans turn to the countryside for outdoor recreation, the coyote has assumed an important role as a symbol of wildness and natural beauty (Leydet 1977). A western sunset is enhanced by the vocal chorus of coyotes, calling to one another before setting out on their night's hunt.

COYOTE
ARCTIC FOX
RED FOX
GRAY FOX
KIT FOX

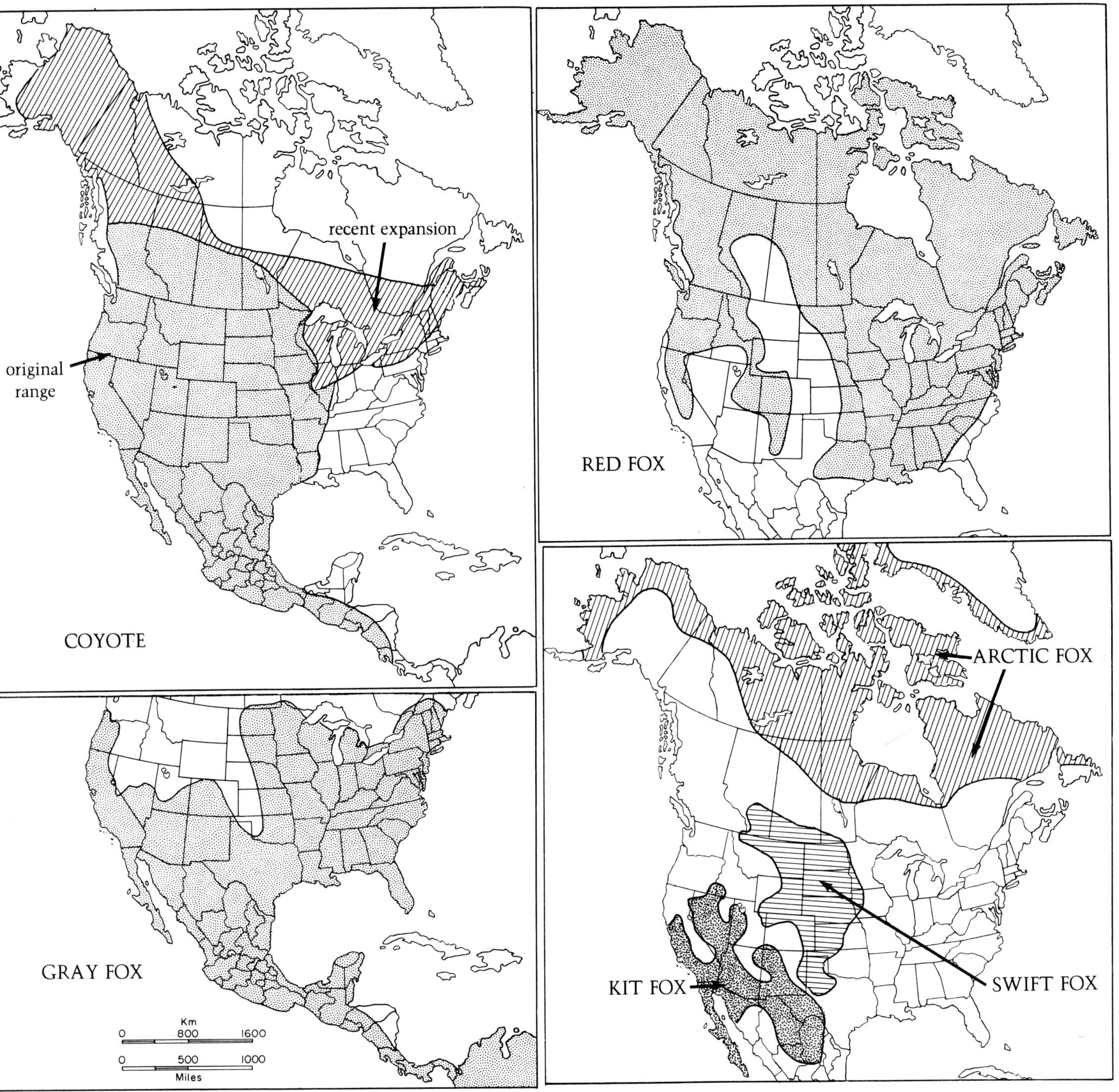
recent expansion
original range
COYOTE
RED FOX
GRAY FOX
Km
0
800
1600
0
500
1000
Miles
ARCTIC FOX
SWIFT FOX
KIT FOX

ARCTIC FOX *(Alopex lagopus)*

See also pages 116–17.

RANGE: Arctic, including northern Canada and northern and western Alaska; introduced on some of the Aleutian Islands.

HABITAT: Tundra, sea cliffs, and sea ice

REMARKS: The arctic fox is a small (1.5 to 3 kilograms) but economically important fur bearer of the far north. Many Native North Americans in Canada and Alaska trap arctic foxes as their primary source of income, selling a total of tens of thousands of pelts annually.

For food, arctic foxes depend on lemmings, carrion, and in summer the eggs and nestlings of birds. In years of low rodent numbers, arctic foxes, especially the pups, suffer heavy mortality.

In late winter, mated pairs seek established dens for the birth and rearing of their pups. Many females first breed at one year of age and wean litters of 4 to 10 offspring per year if food supplies are favorable. In years of food scarcity (meaning low years in the lemming cycle), no pups are raised.

In the 1920s, arctic foxes were introduced on some of the Aleutian Islands to add to the fur harvest. Native bird populations on these islands were decimated, one victim being the Aleutian Canada goose.

RED FOX *(Vulpes vulpes)*

See also pages 116–17.

RANGE: Most of the United States and Canada except deserts, plains, and lowlands of the Pacific and south Atlantic coasts

HABITAT: Woodlands, from boreal forests and tundra to southern prairies and pine forests

REMARKS: Mated pairs of red foxes defend a territory from others of the species (Storm *et al.* 1976). Within this area of exclusive use, they produce in an excavated burrow system a litter of 4 or 5 kits in the spring. Both parents care for the young until fall, when the family breaks up. The young first reproduce the next spring at one year of age.

Red foxes consume a variety of small animal and plant foods, including mammals and birds, eggs, invertebrates, carrion, and berries. In the north, fox populations fluctuate with changes in the numbers of lemmings, mice, and hares.

In the eastern and northern parts of the continent, large numbers of red foxes are killed each year by fur trappers, farmers, and sport hunters. In suitable habitat, however, the populations maintain their numbers well.

The species occurs in four color phases—red, cross, silver, and black. Silver foxes were rare in nature and brought up to $1000 until some enterprising trapper acquired a live pair and started breeding them. Now silver-fox farms are common in the Lakes States and New England, and the price per pelt, while still high, is materially reduced. The genetics of color breeding in foxes has been thoroughly worked out by commercial breeders.

Red foxes are hunted with hounds in the eastern and midwestern United States. The chase takes many forms, from red-jacketed riders in Maryland to a group of Ozark farmers squatting around a fire listening to "Old Blue" or "Lazy Bell" run the fox around and around the hill. In both examples, the real objective is not to kill the fox but rather to follow the hounds or merely listen to them.

KIT FOX *(Vulpes macrotis)*

See also pages 116–17.

RANGE: Northern Nevada and California's San Joaquin Valley south and east to Baja California and Durango

HABITAT: Southwestern arid plains and deserts

REMARKS: The graceful little kit fox (about two kilograms) is limited to open, sandy, arid country. It does not penetrate brushlands or even lush prairie, although on the desert it may inhabit hills and canyons.

The kit fox dens underground, coming out to hunt only at night. Four young are an average litter. After the pups are grown in the summer, the family breaks up. Individual home ranges vary from 2½ to 5 square kilometers and they overlap; no territorial defense is apparent.

Small rodents, particularly kangaroo rats of the genus *Dipodomys*, are the standard fare. Some insects, birds, rabbits, fruits, and carrion are taken, but all food habits studies stress the predominance of kangaroo rats in the diet. The ranges of the kit fox and kangaroo rats collectively (there are several species) are almost coincident in many regions.

The species is classified as rare by the U.S. Department of the Interior. Permanent elimination of the kit fox from large parts of its range is occurring with the conversion of its natural.habitat into irrigated farmland.

SWIFT FOX *(Vulpes velox)*

See also pages 116–17.

RANGE: Formerly, the Great Plains of Canada and the United States south to central Texas

HABITAT: Shortgrass plains

REMARKS: A few swift foxes may still remain, scattered over the dry plains of the United States and southern Canada (Moore and Martin 1980). This close relative of the kit fox is near extinction, however, because of its susceptibility to traps and poison meant for other predators.

Although little known, its biology is apparently similar to that of the kit fox. In fact, the two populations are considered one species by some biologists.

GRAY FOX *(Urocyon cinereoargenteus)*

See also pages 116–17.

RANGE: Canadian border to South America, and coast to coast except interior northwestern United States; related dwarf forms occur on the Channel Islands of California.

HABITAT: Mainly brushy woodland in rough terrain

REMARKS: The gray fox is the most abundant and widespread fox in North America. It is active day and night in search for food. Small mammals, birds, and carrion are primary items of diet, but fruits of many plants are taken when available. Home ranges are several square kilometers in size. There is no direct evidence of territorial defense, but gray foxes generally avoid each other and mark their home ranges with urine and feces, as do most other carnivores.

Females produce their first litter at one year of age, and bear about 4 pups per litter. Natural mortality is great, affecting young in their first winter most heavily.

The fur is coarse and of much less value than that of the red fox, yet large numbers of gray foxes are pelted because of their abundance. Gray foxes are not popular for hunting with hounds because of their propensity to take shelter in dens instead of leading the dogs. Not infrequently, gray foxes climb trees to escape pursuit.

Family Ursidae (Bears)

BLACK BEAR *(Ursus americanus)*

See also pages 122–23.

RANGE: Formerly ranged throughout wooded North America and south to central Mexico. Now limited to mountain areas of the eastern United States (Appalachians, Adirondacks, Ozarks), southeastern lowlands and swamps, and western mountains, north through Canada to Alaska. Exterminated in most of the eastern and midwestern United States.

HABITAT: Forested areas, brushlands, and timbered swamps

REMARKS: Black bears are omnivorous, utilizing a tremendous variety of fruits, nuts, seeds, roots, grass, insects, rodents, fish, and carrion. Some black bears learn to hunt fawns in early summer, and, occasionally, a lamb, pig, or calf will be taken. Others may rob bee hives, fruit orchards, or stored food of summer campers to feed their 150-kilogram bulk. In some areas, bears are causing distress to foresters by girdling hundreds of redwoods and Douglas firs in order to eat the cambium layer under the bark. Careless visitors in many national parks too often make food available to bears. Bears habituated to such easy pickings have little fear of people and frequently wreak havoc on property or may even injure people. Most individual bears, however, keep out of trouble by eating only wild foods of no commercial value.

In the cold parts of their range, black bears retire to dens and become dormant in winter, living on accumulated fat. They do not truly "hibernate," however, for the metabolic rate is not materially lowered.

Males are shunned by the females except during a brief honeymoon when the female is receptive. Young are produced every second year, or less frequently, in the winter den after a gestation of about seven months. The average litter size is 1 to 3 young, depending on the location. Cubs remain with their mother for 1½ years, or until she is ready to mate again. Between 1½ and 2½ years of age the cubs disperse and encounter heavy mortality. Although young females frequently come into estrus at three or four years of age, in some areas litters may not be produced until age six.

The general status of black bears appears stable (Herrero 1979; Pelton *et al.* 1976). Under regulated hunting, populations are maintaining themselves. In fact in some areas, bear densities are as high as one per square mile (2.5 square kilometers).

The tooth formula for all bears is $\frac{3\,1\,4\,2}{3\,1\,4\,3} = 42$. Some individuals, however, do not develop all premolars.

GRIZZLY BEAR *(Ursus arctos)*

See also pages 122–23.

RANGE: Formerly ranged throughout western North America from Alaska to central Mexico; now present only in Alaska, northern and western Canada, and parts of Montana, Wyoming, and Idaho. Remnant populations in Colorado, Chihuahua, and Sonora have been exterminated in recent years.

HABITAT: Conifer forests, brushlands, and arctic-alpine taiga and tundra

REMARKS: This largest of American carnivores thrives on a largely vegetarian diet. Grass is the most important dietary item. But when circumstances permit, the big bear eats salmon, caribou or moose calves, carrion, ground squirrels, assorted berries, fruits, nuts, and bulbs. It is a matter of wonder that so great a beast can live and actually get fat on such hard-won morsels of food as a ground squirrel painstakingly dug from its burrow, ants obtained by knocking apart rotten logs, or berries picked one by one.

The species *Ursus arctos* has an enormous range within which it varies considerably in size. The largest bears (up to 550 kilograms) are the so-called brown bears of coastal Alaska, which seasonally feast on salmon. European brown bears are somewhat smaller, and small populations still occur in the Cantabricas of Spain, in the Alps, and over much of the central and northern Soviet Union. The barren-ground grizzly of northern Alaska and the Mexican grizzly are smaller subspecies (up to 300 kilograms).

Females produce their first litter at four years of age or older. Litters (usually one or two) are nursed and cared for through two seasons before the female again comes in heat and drives the young out on their own. The late age of maturity, and small and infrequent litters, give the grizzly one of the lowest population growth rates (Hensel *et al.* 1969).

The bears dig their own dens and sleep the winter away. It is during this time that the blastocysts in females, which conceived in early summer, finally implant in the uterine wall and begin to develop. A few months later in midwinter, the diminutive and helpless cubs are born. By spring, they have become large enough and strong enough to follow their mother from the den.

Grizzly bears were exterminated from the settled areas of the western United States because of their danger to people and their occasional forays on livestock. Healthy populations remain only in the vicinity of Yellowstone and Glacier National Parks, and northward. Trophy hunting for grizzlies is still permitted in the wilder regions of Canada and Alaska. In the national parks of southern Canada and the northwestern United States, grizzly bears are becoming increasingly troublesome by harassing tourists and their camps in search of food. The bears have lost their fear of people and have become bolder when no longer hunted.

BLACK BEAR
GRIZZLY BEAR
POLAR BEAR

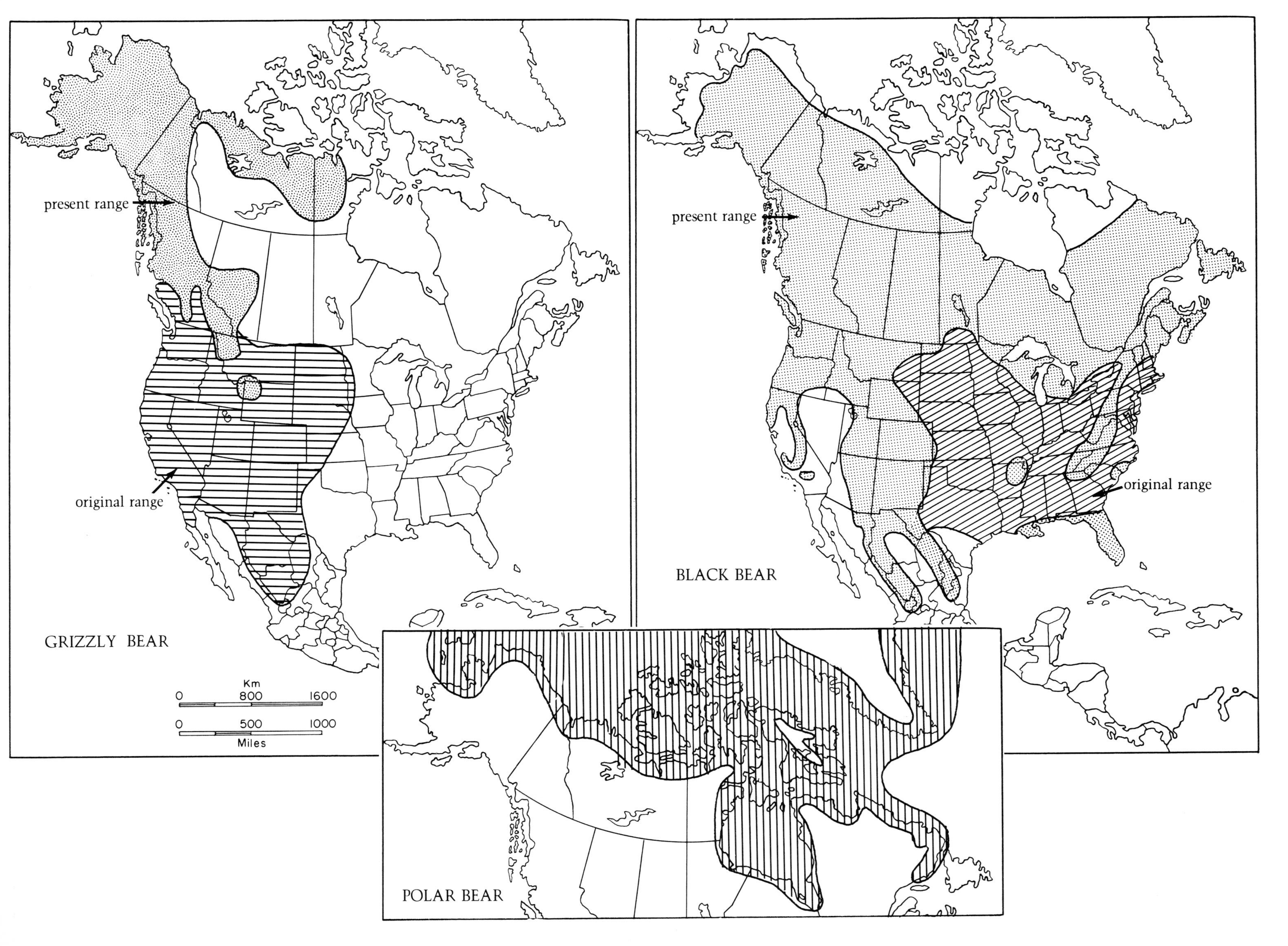
present range
original range
GRIZZLY BEAR
Km
0
800
1600
0
500
1000
Miles
present range
original range
BLACK BEAR
POLAR BEAR

POLAR BEAR *(Ursus maritimus)*

See also pages 122–23.

RANGE: Arctic Ocean and its coasts and islands

HABITAT: Coastal tundra and sea ice

REMARKS: The polar bear, second largest land carnivore, makes its living from seals in the Arctic. The bears search for ringed, bearded, harp, and bladder-nose seals at breathing holes and hauling-out areas.

As with most large mammals, the reproductive rate is low. At the onset of winter, the female bears seek out dens, especially on islands. Mating occurs in early spring, but it is December when one or two young are born in the den. The cubs stay with their mother until they are about 28 months old. Sexual maturity is reached at four or five years of age. Thereafter, a female may produce cubs every third year. Once full grown, females weigh 200 to 300 kilograms and males weigh 300 to 600 kilograms.

The world polar bear population, after a decline in the first half of the century, seems to be maintaining itself. Between 10,000 and 20,000 polar bears, including 5500 in Alaska, roam the sea ice. The species is totally or partially protected from hunting in the territories of the five countries in which it occurs. Controlled harvesting removes about 900 animals per year. Native North Americans report taking 100 to 200 of these in Alaska, as provided by the Marine Mammal Protection Act of 1972, but many more kills undoubtedly go uncounted. Some 500 to 600 are taken annually in Canada. The greatest threat to polar bears may come from development of gas and oil extraction. Exploration and drilling could preempt coastal habitat that the bears favor as denning sites. Oil spills on sea ice could kill bears by destroying the insulating quality of their fur.

Family Felidae (Cats)

The three cats here discussed—namely the puma, lynx, and bobcat—are widely distributed in North America. In southern Mexico, there are additional tropical species that extend their ranges northward up both coasts to the United States border, with individuals occasionally crossing. They are the jaguar *(Felis onca)*, ocelot *(Felis pardalis)*, margay *(Felis wiedii)*, and jaguarundi *(Felis jagouaroundi)*. For accounts of these four species, see Leopold (1959).

PUMA *(Felis concolor)*

See also pages 126–27.

RANGE: Formerly throughout North America from southern Canada to South America; now mainly in the western mountains, the wilder parts of Mexico, and in scattered locations in the eastern United States, Canada, and Mexico

HABITAT: Forests and brushlands wherever there are deer to prey upon

REMARKS: The puma, alternately called mountain lion or cougar, is a primary predator of deer. The big cat in some areas preys also on elk, bighorn sheep, javelina, and many smaller mammals, but deer constitute the major source of sustenance. Sheep, burros, and young horses are attacked occasionally. In areas where deer are abundant, pumas may reach a breeding density of one per 50 square kilometers. Home areas of males are larger than those of females and overlap very little. Female home areas overlap substantially with those of other females and with home areas of males (Seidensticker *et al.* 1973). Fighting over range jurisdiction is minimized by mutual avoidance, but males do fight occasionally. Breeding occurs mostly in winter.

After a 3-month gestation, 1 to 4 young are born. Cubs are attended by their mother until 20 months old, with the result that a female breeds only every second year, if that often. Emancipated young wander widely, seeking a home range not already preempted (Hornocker 1970).

Adult male pumas weigh about 55 kilograms (120 pounds); females and yearlings weigh about 28 kilograms (80 pounds). The tooth formula is $\frac{3\,1\,3\,1}{3\,1\,2\,1}$.

Persecution of pumas because of their predation on livestock and game has led to extermination in many developed areas and decline in numbers even in wilderness situations. Where deer are still abundant and pumas are not hunted, the big cats may sustain good populations even on the outskirts of urban areas (i.e., the San Francisco Bay Area). In most states and provinces, pumas are protected by game regulations. Only in Texas are there no legal restrictions on killing them. The puma is given "endangered" status in Florida. According to Nowak (1974), the general trend in the puma population of Canada and the United States is slightly upward (estimated at 16,000). In Mexico, the species is still decreasing.

LYNX *(Felis lynx)*

See also pages 126–27.

RANGE: Forested zones of Alaska, Canada, and the northeastern and northwestern United States, south in the Rocky Mountains to Colorado

HABITAT: Boreal forests

REMARKS: The lynx and the bobcat are two short-tailed cats that between them occupy virtually all of North America except the tundra. The lynx has longer legs and thicker pelage, and is at home in the northern forest zones where snow is deep and temperatures are low. The bobcat is more southern in distribution and has shorter legs and pelage. Weights of the two cats are much the same—averaging 10 to 15 kilograms for males and 5 to 10 kilograms for females.

The primary food of the lynx is the snowshoe hare, which undergoes violent fluctuations in abundance at 10-year intervals. During the high period of the hare cycle, the lynx flourishes. Young lynxes breed at one year of age, litters are large (up to 4), and survival is good. When the hare population crashes, most of the lynxes starve and no young are produced. The few survivors eke a living from such mice and birds as they can catch (Nellis *et al.* 1968; Nellis *et al.* 1972). Pelts of the lynx have long been a staple in the northern fur trade. Seton (1923) notes the fluctuations in numbers of pelts exported by Hudson Bay Company, varying from 4000 to 75,000 depending on the stage of the hare cycle.

For northern fur trappers, the lynx is still a valuable source of pelts. Because lynxes range generally in remote forest regions, they are not a threat to livestock or poultry.

PUMA
LYNX
BOBCAT

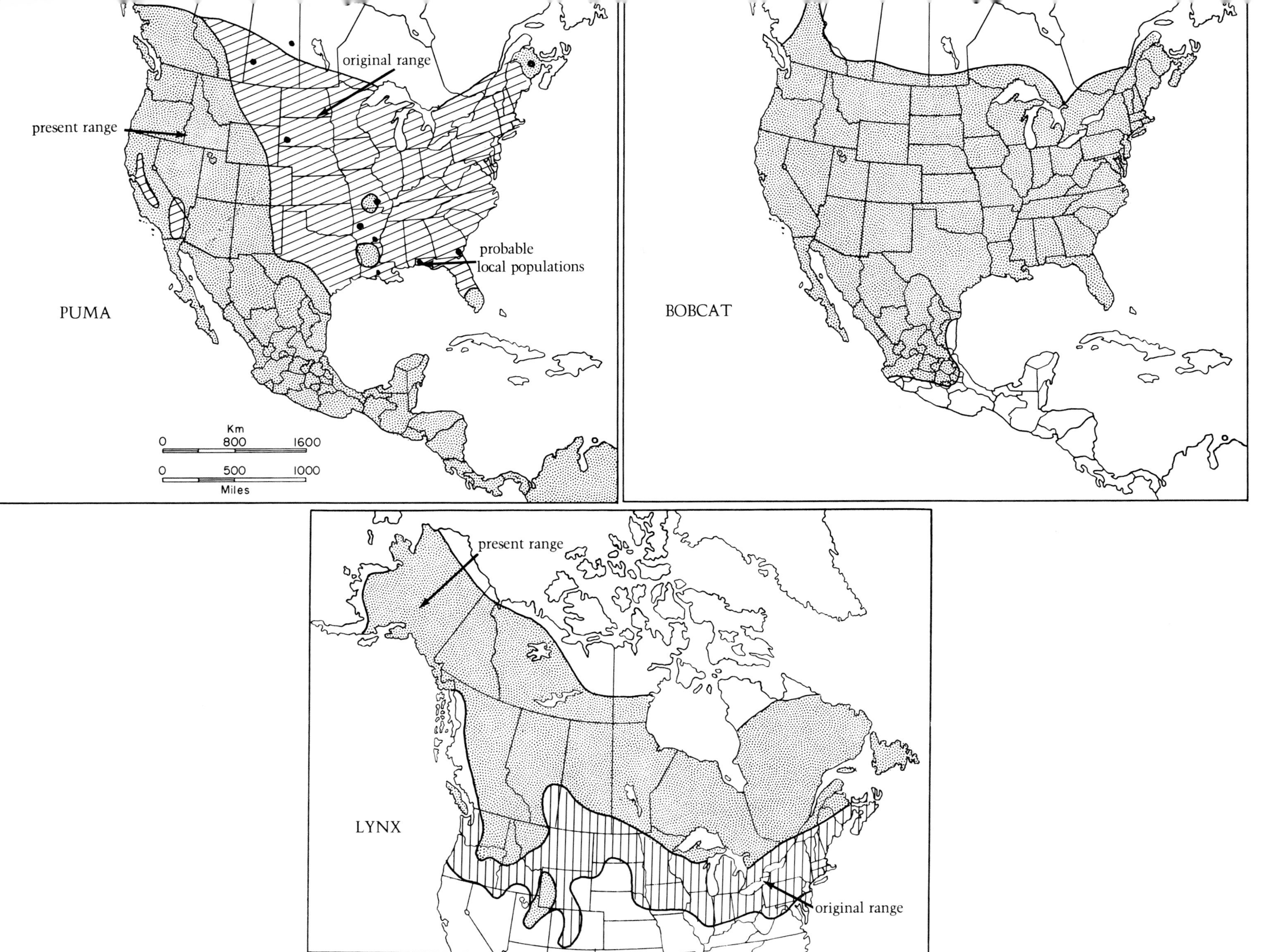

PUMA
original range
present range
probable
local populations
Km
0
800
1600
0
500
1000
Miles
BOBCAT
LYNX
present range
original range

BOBCAT *(Felis rufus)*

See also pages 126–27.

RANGE: From the Canadian border southward through all of the contiguous United States to the Mexican highlands

HABITAT: Prefers brushy woodlands but occurs sparingly from high mountains to desert.

REMARKS: The common and adaptable bobcat, or wildcat, has a varied diet, dominated by rabbits and rodents but including birds, and, occasionally, a lamb or young deer. Sporadic depredations on poultry and livestock have put the bobcat on the "vermin" list in some areas. There are local situations where control may be warranted, but generally the damage done by bobcats is minimal. Although the fur is not of best quality, it is much sought by trappers when women's fashions provide high prices, as, for example, in the 1970s. There is no evidence, however, that trapping has in any way endangered the population.

The female bobcat dens in a cave, hollow log, or stump and has an annual litter of 2 or 3 young. Gestation is 70 days (in the puma it is about 3 months). The male is with the female only during mating; he takes no part in bringing up the young. The female bears her first litter at one year of age, but the male does not reproduce until two years (Crowe 1975). At that time, males weigh 11 to 12 kilograms, compared to the females' average 8 kilograms. A few bobcats may live eight years or more.

Like other North American cats, bobcats lead solitary lives. Each individual has a home range in which it lives and hunts alone, avoiding contact with other bobcats, though not defending the home area. Established adults make their presence known by marking their ranges with urine and feces. Young become independent late in their first year and then seek vacant areas in which to establish their homes. Other large carnivores such as coyotes, wolves, and particularly pumas may prey on bobcats, especially young ones.

Cats have a reduced number of rather specialized teeth, adapted for piercing and crushing the necks of their prey. The dental formula for most members of the genus Felis is $\frac{3\,1\,2\,1}{3\,1\,2\,1}$, totalling 28 teeth. The puma has one additional upper premolar, or 30 teeth in all.

Family Mustelidae (Weasels and Relatives)

PINE MARTEN *(Martes americana)*

See also pages 130–31.

RANGE: Most of Alaska and Canada; mountains of western United States and New England and Lake States

HABITAT: Coniferous forests and boreal meadows and brushlands

REMARKS: The pine marten, sometimes called American sable, is a mink-sized mustelid that produces a high grade, rich brown fur, much sought by fur trappers. Martens live primarily in conifer forest. But in the northern reaches of their range, they are found in rocky mountain sites with scant vegetation. They forage in trees as well as on the ground and are remarkably agile in running down prey. Squirrels, hares, rabbits, pikas, chipmunks, mice, and even birds (including grouse) are regular fare. Reptiles and insects are taken on occasion.

All members of the family Mustelidae have paired anal glands that emit a strong musk odor. Only skunks can "shoot" this scent. The marten has an additional musk gland on its abdomen.

Several members of the family Mustelidae, including the marten, have delayed implantation after copulation. That is, there is a period in which the embryos do not develop. Female martens are bred in midsummer, but not until midwinter do the two or three fetuses begin to grow rapidly in the uterus, to be born in April or May. The interval between mating and birth is thus 8 to 9 months. The young are reared in a tree or rock den by the female.

Pine marten populations, once depressed by persistent trapping, have substantially recovered under protective regulation. In many areas, the species—though yielding an annual crop of furs—is again abundant.

The dental formula of the marten, and likewise of the fisher and wolverine, is $\frac{3141}{3142} = 38$ teeth.

FISHER *(Martes pennanti)*

See also pages 130–31.

RANGE: Forested parts of southern Canada, the western mountains, and the northeastern United States

HABITAT: Coniferous and mixed conifer-hardwood forests

REMARKS: The fisher produces a fine, rich fur of great value in the commercial market. The fisher is substantially larger than the marten (males up to 6 kilograms, females 2 kilograms) and is capable of capturing somewhat larger prey mammals, up to and including marmots and porcupines. The fisher, in fact, is something of a specialist in killing a porcupine by flipping it over and attacking its unprotected belly. Foresters welcome the assistance of the fisher in controlling porcupines that are damaging young pine trees. Despite the animal's name, fish are rarely if ever taken, since the fisher hunts in the forest and not in water. In northern New England, people widely but erroneously believe that fishers prey regularly on deer—a physical impossibility.

Females two years of age or older produce annual litters of 2 or 3 young, after a period of delayed implantation (Wright and Coulter 1967). Dens are usually situated in hollow trees but may be in rock caves.

Fishers were exterminated over substantial parts of their original range by overtrapping, but populations are now increasing and spreading as a result of better regulation of the trapping take. And in a number of forested areas, the fisher is being reintroduced, primarily to control porcupines but also in recognition of its value as a wild predator and a fur bearer.

PINE MARTEN
FISHER
WOLVERINE
MINK

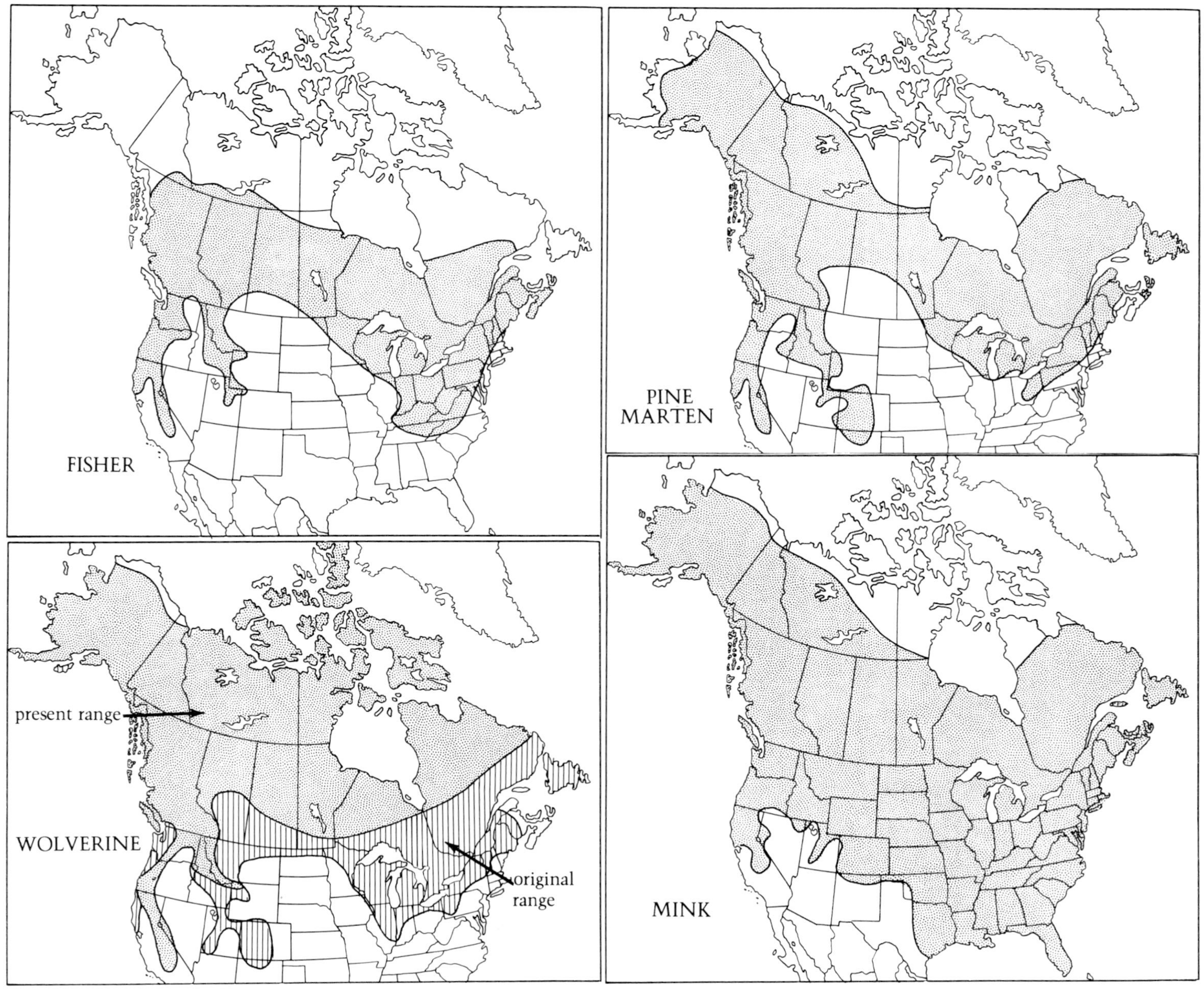
FISHER
PINE
MARTEN
WOLVERINE
present range
original
range
MINK

WOLVERINE *(Gulo gulo)*

See also pages 130–31.

RANGE: Originally ranged throughout Alaska and Canada southward through the northern tier of United States and the western mountains; now eliminated from much of its southern range.

HABITAT: Conifer forests and treeless arctic and alpine areas

REMARKS: The wolverine is the largest, rarest, and least known of the terrestrial mustelids; among all mustelids, only the sea otter is larger. The strong and constantly moving wolverines weigh 10 to 14 kilograms. The skull and teeth, $\frac{3141}{3142}$, are massive and adapted for crushing frozen meat and large bones of scavenged carcasses. Wolverines have enormous home ranges—up to 400 square kilometers in males. One marked male was known to wander nearly 100 kilometers in a day. Female home ranges are smaller—86 square kilometers in one instance.

The wolverine is notoriously fearless and aggressive. It has been known to drive coyotes, bears, and even pumas from food. Occasionally wolverines kill caribou, deer, and mountain sheep, but the normal fare is carrion and smaller animals of all kinds, including small carnivores (Seton 1937).

Some female wolverines bear young at one year of age, but most delay their first reproduction until two years. Mating occurs in summer, and the births in mid- to late winter follow delayed implantation. The average uterine litter is 3½ young, and the average den litter is 2½.

In most of the lower 48 states, wolverines are now protected. They are steadily increasing in the Pacific mountains, although they remain rare (Nowak 1973). In the far north, the apparently stable population of wolverines is hunted and trapped as fur bearers and predators. In Alaska, the annual catch totals about 1000 pelts annually (Rausch and Pearson 1972). Wolverine fur is in constant demand by Eskimos for trimming parkas because it resists deposition of frost.

WEASELS { LONG-TAILED WEASEL *(Mustela frenata)*, SHORT-TAILED WEASEL *(Mustela erminea)*, LEAST WEASEL *(Mustela nivalis)*

See also pages 134–35.

RANGE: Long-tailed weasel—from southern Canada to Panama

Short-tailed weasel—Alaska and Canada, south through western mountains, Lakes States, and New England

Least weasel—Alaska and subarctic Canada, south through northern midwest United States and Appalachians

HABITAT: Short-tailed and least weasels prefer meadows, grasslands, tundra, or brushlands with dense ground cover. Long-tailed weasels occupy a wider range of habitats including forests.

REMARKS: Weasels come in three sizes, but all are fierce little predators of small mammals and occasional birds. Slender bodies and short legs permit weasels to enter burrow systems and narrow crevices where rodents take refuge (Fitzgerald 1977). The weasel grapples with its victim and kills it with a bite at the back of the skull. In this manner, fairly large prey animals, such as rabbits, squirrels, and rats, can be subdued by a small but active and determined weasel.

Where snow covers the ground in winter, weasels molt into a white pelage in the autumn and resume their brown color by another molt in spring. The white pelts are called "ermine" in the fur trade and are more valuable than brown pelts. Because of their small size, however, many pelts are required to make an ermine wrap.

Litters average 5 or 6 young (3 to 10). Long-tailed and short-tailed weasels, after a summer mating and delayed implantation of the embryos during the winter, bear a single annual litter in spring. Least weasels mate in late winter, and the embryos are implanted and develop without delay. It is reported that females of this species may occasionally produce more than one litter in a year.

The dental formula for the genus Mustela is $\frac{3131}{3132}$ = 34 teeth.

BLACK-FOOTED FERRET *(Mustela nigripes)*

See also pages 134–35.

RANGE: Formerly the Great Plains from southern Canada to northern Texas; now reduced to scattered remnants in Wyoming and South Dakota.

HABITAT: Prairie-dog towns on the shortgrass prairie

REMARKS: The black-footed ferret is a medium-sized mustelid highly specialized to prey on prairie dogs *(Cynomys)* and to live in their burrow systems. The ferret will take other types of prey when occasion permits—including ground squirrels, rabbits, mice, and birds—but prairie dogs are the staple diet. Extensive poisoning of prairie dogs to rid the grasslands of this native rodent has all but eliminated the ferret as well. Today, this species is one of the rarest mammals in North America (Clark 1978). A few known remnant populations are given full governmental protection, but not one of these has so far shown a noticeable increase. Attempts by the U.S. Fish and Wildlife Service to breed the ferrets in captivity have not been successful.

The black-footed ferret, like the least weasel, mates in spring. The young implant and develop without delay. Litters averaging 4 young are born in early summer in a den converted from a prairie-dog burrow. When weaned, they scatter and lead a solitary life like their parents.

MINK *(Mustela vison)*

See also pages 130–31.

RANGE: All of Canada south of the tundra, and the United States except the southwestern deserts

HABITAT: Chiefly near rivers, streams, marshes, and along protected seacoasts

REMARKS: The mink is more aquatic in habit than most mustelids, though less so than otters. In fact, mink possess webbed hind feet. Muskrats and fish are favorite dietary items, but mink also prey on a wide variety of mammals, birds, young waterfowl, and frogs (Eberhardt and Sargeant 1977).

Some classical studies of predator-prey relations have centered on the depredations of mink on muskrats. Paul Errington (1962), working in Iowa, demonstrated that mink catch largely the vulnerable "surplus" muskrats that do not have a secure home area.

LONG-TAILED WEASEL
LEAST WEASEL
SHORT-TAILED WEASEL
BLACK-FOOTED FERRET
BADGER

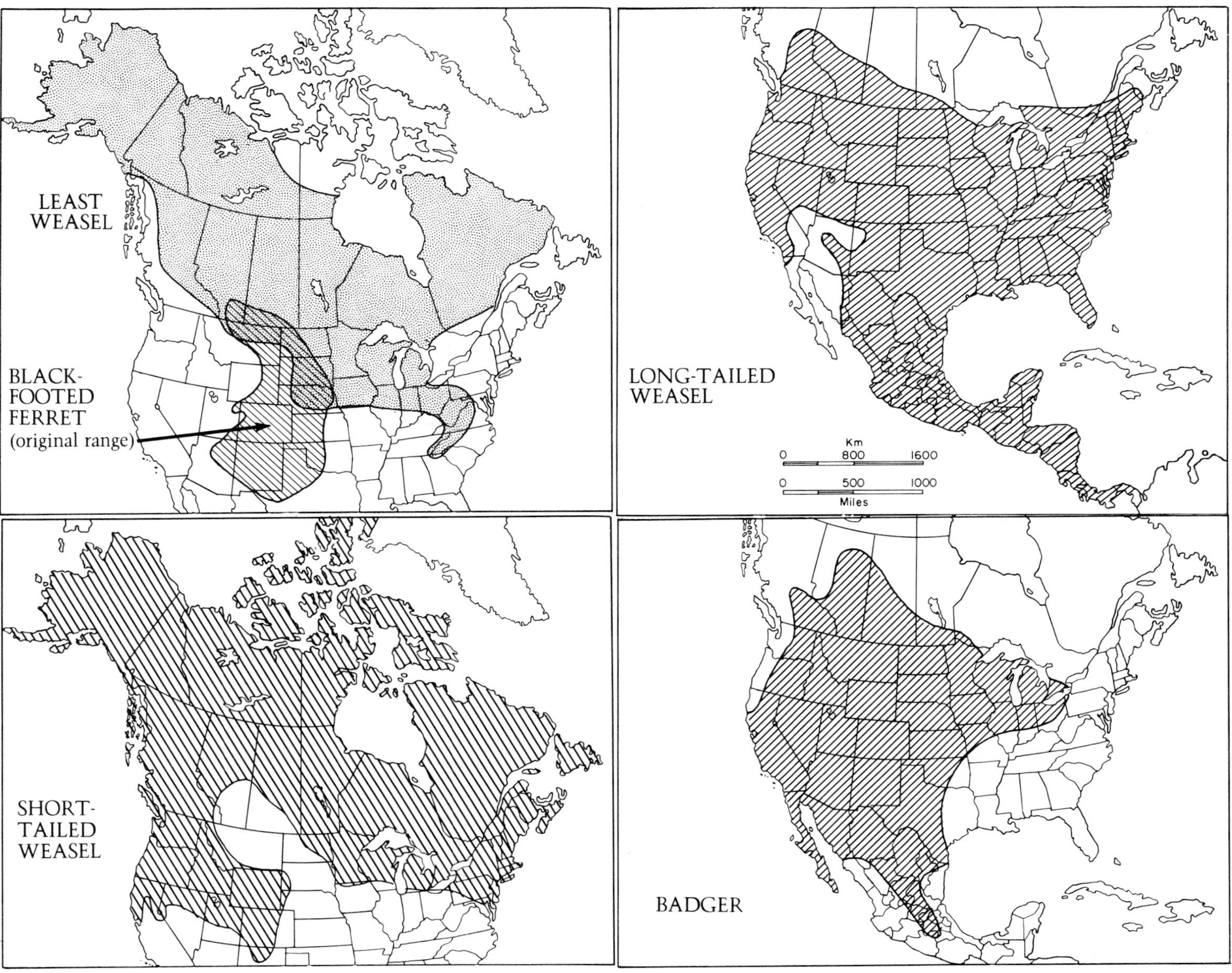
LEAST
WEASEL
BLACK-
FOOTED
FERRET
(original range)
LONG-TAILED
WEASEL
Km
0
800
1600
0
500
1000
Miles
SHORT-
TAILED
WEASEL
BADGER

In a fully stocked muskrat marsh, the young (especially males) are driven out by adults and become mink food. Where muskrats are not crowded, mink do not catch them. The effort involved is apparently not worthwhile. Thus the law of diminishing returns seems to guide the predatory activities of mink, a principle that applies to many other predators. Largely for this reason, predators rarely exterminate prey species under natural conditions.

Wild mink are still important as producers of high-quality fur, even though about forty percent of the marketed pelts are produced on mink ranches. Mink may cause local damage in poultry yards, but this rarely warrants control measures.

Mink differ from pine martens in behavioral and morphological adaptations for swimming, the absence of a yellow chest patch, slightly lower weight, and a tooth formula of $\frac{3\,1\,3\,1}{3\,1\,3\,2}$ = 34 teeth.

As in other small carnivores, females produce their first litter at one year of age. They bear annually a single litter of 5 to 8 young after a period of delayed implantation.

A closely related animal, the sea mink *(Mustela macrodon)* occurred originally along the Atlantic coast from Connecticut to the Bay of Fundy. It was trapped to extinction for its fur by the 1860s (Godin 1977). Virtually nothing is known of its natural history.

BADGER *(Taxidea taxus)*

See also pages 134–35.

RANGE: Western North America from the Prairie Provinces of Canada to central Mexico

HABITAT: Prairies, deserts, and open woodlands with friable soils and abundant burrowing rodents

REMARKS: The squat, powerful badger is designed to make a living by digging. With its strong forearms and long claws, it can dig with astonishing speed. Burrowing mammals are the primary foods, particularly ground squirrels, prairie dogs, pocket gophers, and kangaroo rats. The badger can dig faster than any of these and easily will follow one of them to the last recess of an underground tunnel. Its own den is usually situated at the end of a deep burrow, which can be up to ten meters long.

Females bear litters of 2 to 5 young (average 3) after a pregnancy that includes delayed implantation. The mother brings food to the young in the den as they are being weaned. Adult badgers are large (up to 10 kilograms), and consequently have few predators.

On the plains, badgers have been severely reduced in number by traps and poison baits put out for coyotes. Badgers have been less persecuted in mountains, which are not, however, the best habitat. Although the fur is coarse and of modest value, badgers are still trapped for their pelts.

The dental formula is $\frac{3131}{3132}$ = 34 teeth.

Skunks

STRIPED SKUNK *(Mephitis mephitis)*
SPOTTED SKUNK *(Spilogale putorius)*

See also pages 138–39.

RANGE: The striped skunk occurs throughout the United States, southern Canada, and northern Mexico. The spotted skunk has a more southern range in the United States, south through Central America.

HABITAT: Both species have a wide tolerance of habitats, favoring open areas of woodland, grassland, brush, or farmland. The striped skunk is generally more adaptable than its small cousin and considerably more abundant.

REMARKS: Skunks are best known for their unique and effective defense weapon. Glands inside the anus can be turned outward (everted) and the nozzles aimed with considerable accuracy. Sphincter muscles force out a fine stream of the acrid scent as far as eight meters. With this biological artillery available, skunks have developed a sense of invincibility that is rare in wild animals. They go about their business without sign of fear and seem to defy the world around them. The distinctive black and white pelage is a warning to predators. Yet eagles and some large hawks, horned owls, coyotes, and bobcats still prey on skunks, accepting the consequences of an acrid dousing.

Striped skunks are true omnivores (Verts 1967). They feed on insects, small mammals, carrion, and fruits in season, with occasional forays on birds' nests, poultry yards, and bee hives. Striped skunks become fat and less active in winter but do not truly hibernate. They range in weight from 1.5 to 6 kilograms.

The little spotted skunk (0.3 to 1 kilogram) or "civet cat" is much more agile than the plodding *Mephitis*. It feeds on insects, mice, reptiles, amphibians, birds' eggs, and some fruits. In the bottom of the Grand Canyon, spotted skunks live very well on food scraps left on the banks by river runners. Spotted skunks have annual litters of 4 to 5 young; striped skunks have larger litters, averaging about 6. Both breed in spring and give birth in about 8 weeks, without delayed implantation.

In years past, skunks collectively were among the most important farm fur bearers, supplying many a farm boy with pocket money. In the 1970s, however, prices for many other small furs greatly exceeded the price for skunks, and skunk trapping has decreased.

Two other species of skunks, which are widespread in Mexico, enter the United States in Arizona and New Mexico. They are the hooded skunk *(Mephitis macroura)* and the hog-nosed skunk *(Conepatus mesoleucus)*. Both are uncommon.

RIVER OTTER *(Lutra canadensis)*

See also pages 138–39.

RANGE: All of the United States and Canada except the tundra and parts of the arid southwestern United States

HABITAT: Streams, rivers, lakes, estuaries, and salt- and freshwater marshes

REMARKS: Otters live primarily in water, denning in bank holes. Normally 2 to 3 pups are born in April. The young are raised by the mother, the family staying

STRIPED SKUNK
SPOTTED SKUNK
RIVER OTTER
SEA OTTER

SPOTTED SKUNK
Km
0
800
1600
0
500
1000
Miles
present range
SEA OTTER
original range
RIVER OTTER
STRIPED SKUNK

together until the young are about a year old. Both sexes apparently reach sexual maturity at two years.

Principal foods are fish (including some game fish), crayfish, clams, snails, and an occasional muskrat or duck. Because otters prey most easily on fish that are slow and lethargic, much of the diet consists of "rough" fish like carp, suckers, catfish, and sculpins.

Otters are playful and often build slides on mud banks for sliding into the water. Whole families have been observed taking turns going down, like children on a playground. Population densities are low, even in the best habitat.

Although otter fur is not considered as fine as mink, individual pelts are worth more because of the larger size. Over 30,000 pelts are sold annually in the United States and Canada.

The dental formula is $\frac{3141}{3132} = 36$.

SEA OTTER *(Enhydra lutris)*

See also pages 138–39.

RANGE: Originally ranged along the north Pacific coastline from Japan and Siberia to Cedros Island off Baja California; currently, Kurile and Aleutian Islands, southern Alaskan coast, and central California near Monterey. Reintroduced along the coasts of Oregon, Washington, southern Alaska, and British Columbia.

HABITAT: Coastal kelp beds and isolated rocky shores

REMARKS: Sea otters live almost entirely in the ocean, taking refuge in beds of kelp. They feed on shellfish and other invertebrate animals gleaned from the ocean floor. Rocks sometimes are brought to the surface and used to crack hard-shelled invertebrates like sea urchins. The sea otter places the rock on its chest and cracks the food against it. In California, sea otters rarely go ashore, as they did originally. In Alaska and along the Siberian coast, sea otters still haul out on rocky shorelines. Females probably start bearing pups at three years of age. The majority of births occur in the spring. A single young is produced every second year and cradled in the kelp while its mother dives for food. Females average 20 kilograms in weight, while males may reach 35 kilograms.

Sea otter fur is the finest in the world. Because the otter has no blubber layer, it relies on the insulation of air trapped within the sealed pelage to withstand the frigid ocean temperatures. If the fur gets soiled or matted, the animal dies quickly of hypothermia.

High prices in China and Europe brought on severe exploitation in the past. Vulnerability to hunting by rifle, club, and spear led to the otters' near extinction. The Monterey herd was discovered in 1938 after the species was long believed extinct in California. Under international protection, sea otters are gradually expanding their range. Falling abalone harvests in California, along with increases in numbers of sea otters (up to about 1600), have resulted in political pressure to control the sea otters' range expansion in that state. In Alaska, complete protection has permitted populations to increase to a level over 100,000 animals (Kenyon 1969).

The tooth formula is unique: $\frac{3131}{2132}$.

Family Procyonidae (Raccoon and Relatives)

RACCOON *(Procyon lotor)*

See also pages 142–43.

RANGE: Southern Canada and all of the United States and Mexico, except for some mountain ranges

HABITAT: Marshes, streams, and timberlands near water; wooded residential areas; like mink, raccoons may frequent sea beaches.

REMARKS: The raccoon is perhaps the most versatile and adaptive of North American carnivores. It lives with equal facility along wild rivers or in densely settled residential areas. In wild situations, raccoons follow rivers and streams as main highways. In the city, they have learned to use the network of storm sewers for safe travel. Raccoons are omnivorous, foraging at night for crayfish, frogs, fish, insects, fruits, grains, and, on occasion, birds and their eggs. In the city, they raid garbage cans and backyard goldfish ponds.

Mating is promiscuous, the litters of 2 to 7 young (average 4) being raised by the mother alone. Dens for the young are situated in tree hollows 3 meters or more above the ground, in areas where such sites are available. Where hollow trees are not available, rock dens or caves serve. Many females, but not all, produce their first litter as yearlings. Males rarely breed until two years of age. Gestation is 63 days.

The raccoon is the most valuable American fur bearer, being second only to muskrats in number of pelts marketed and greatly exceeding it in value. In 1975–76, for example, over 3.25 million raccoon hides were sold in the United States for an income of $60.4 million. Raccoons are trapped or may be hunted with hounds. The flesh is highly edible.

As adults, raccoons weigh 4 to 13 kilograms. The dental formula is $\frac{3\,1\,4\,2}{3\,1\,4\,2} = 40$ teeth, as in related procyonids.

RINGTAIL *(Bassariscus astutus)*

See also pages 142–43.

RANGE: Southwestern United States, southward to the Isthmus of Tehuantepec

HABITAT: Arid mountains, desert canyons, and timbered river bottoms

REMARKS: The agile, lively little ringtail is strictly nocturnal, feeding largely on woodrats and other small rodents, but supplementing the diet with various fruits, nuts, lizards, birds, and invertebrates. It often makes its home in loosely constructed buildings where it is an extremely effective mouser. Early settlers welcomed this assistance, and the name "miners' cat" was widely applied to the ringtail. Ringtails are an insignificant fur species because of their low population densities and the small value of their pelts.

The annual litter, usually 2 to 4 young, is born in a den in the rocks or occasionally in a hollow tree. The father, unlike the male raccoon, helps rear and train the young. An average family of ringtails, like most other mammals, has a limited and prescribed

RACCOON
COATI
RINGTAIL

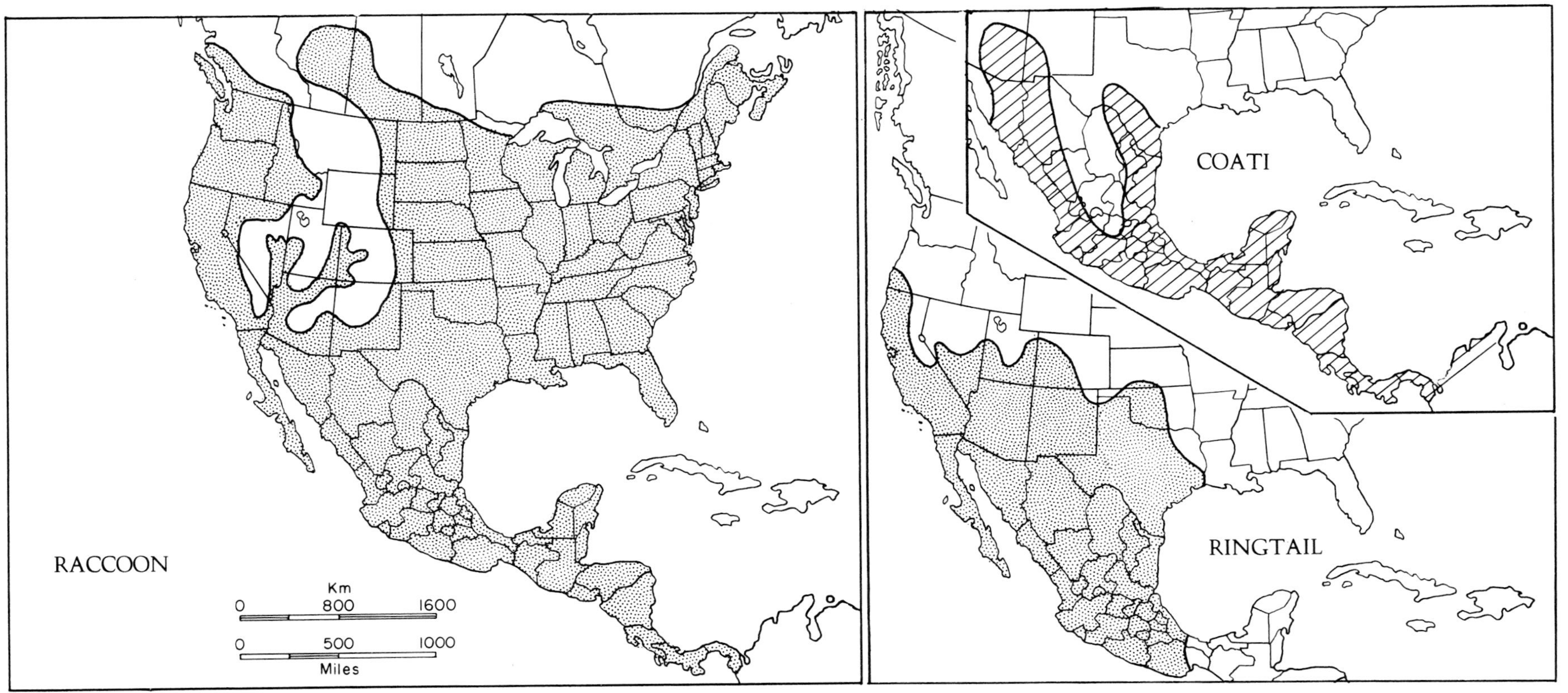
RACCOON
Km
0
800
1600
0
500
1000
Miles
COATI
RINGTAIL

home range within which it travels. When the young leave the home den, they disperse for several miles.

Body weights average about one kilogram (0.7 to 1.4). The tooth formula is identical to that of the raccoon.

COATI *(Nasua nasua)*

See also pages 142–43.

RANGE: Southern Arizona, southwestern New Mexico, and southern Texas; southward throughout Mexico excepting the central desert

HABITAT: Forested mountains, river valleys, and coastal plains

REMARKS: The coati (or "coatimundi") is a social carnivore, associating in bands of 15 or 20. Some old males travel alone and in Mexico are called *solitarios*. But females and young are usually found in groups. Like their close relatives, coatis are omnivorous, eating fruits, nuts, tender green shoots, insects, reptiles, amphibians, small mammals, and carrion. They forage mostly in morning and evening hours, unlike raccoons and ringtails, which are nocturnal. Most coati foraging is on the ground, although the animals go into trees when fruits are available. If alarmed, coatis tend to flee by running away rather than climbing trees.

The breeding habits are similar to other procyonids.

Coatis are rarely hunted, and their fur is too poor to have much commercial value.

Order Pinnipedia

Family Otariidae (Walrus and eared seals)

WALRUS *(Odobenus rosmarus)*

See also page 147.

RANGE: Circumpolar at the edge of the arctic ice cap

HABITAT: Sea ice in shallow seas

REMARKS: Walruses are restricted to sea ice. They follow the edge of the pack ice as it retreats northward in summer and advances southward in winter. Because of their dependence on clam beds as their food source, however, walruses are also confined to areas of shallow water.

The Pacific walrus population, currently of more than 100,000 animals, moves south each fall to spend the winter in the Bering Sea. In summer, the animals move with the melting ice through the Bering Straits into the Chukchi Sea. From there, some swim westward to Siberia and others eastward along Alaska's north coast. On the Walrus Islands in Bristol Bay, Alaska, a few thousand males remain behind each summer and constitute an attraction for tourists. The subspecies inhabiting the Canadian archipelago and Greenland does not make long migrations.

It is on the sea ice that mothers bear their single calves in late April and early May. Females in late pregnancy gather in herds apart from the males and nonreproductive females. Mothers bear young only every second year and nurse them for one and a half to two years. Young females reach sexual maturity between four and ten years of age and males between five and eight years. Mature males often attain weights of more than one ton.

Copulation is carried on promiscuously from December through May, with a peak of activity in February and March. Fertilization is followed by delayed implantation of the early embryo, as in many other pinnipeds and carnivores. Walruses' low birth rate accounts for their slow recovery from the depressed population after overharvesting in the nineteenth century.

In addition to their large upper canine teeth in the form of tusks, walruses have on each side four upper cheek teeth, three lower cheek teeth, and no incisors. Walruses sometimes use their tusks to climb onto ice pans by jamming them into the ice and hoisting themselves forward.

For centuries, walruses have been hunted for their ivory tusks, hides, flesh, and oil. During this century, under close legal protection, walrus numbers have increased steadily. As a consequence, the Pacific walrus population has recently approached the limit of the mollusk beds to feed them. Many thousands of walruses are harvested annually by American and Soviet natives. Hunting is wasteful, for only about half of the walruses shot remain afloat long enough to be retrieved. Additionally, some mature bulls are taken by sport hunters. Yet the population is still increasing. Depletion of the food supply may lead to high mortality in the future.

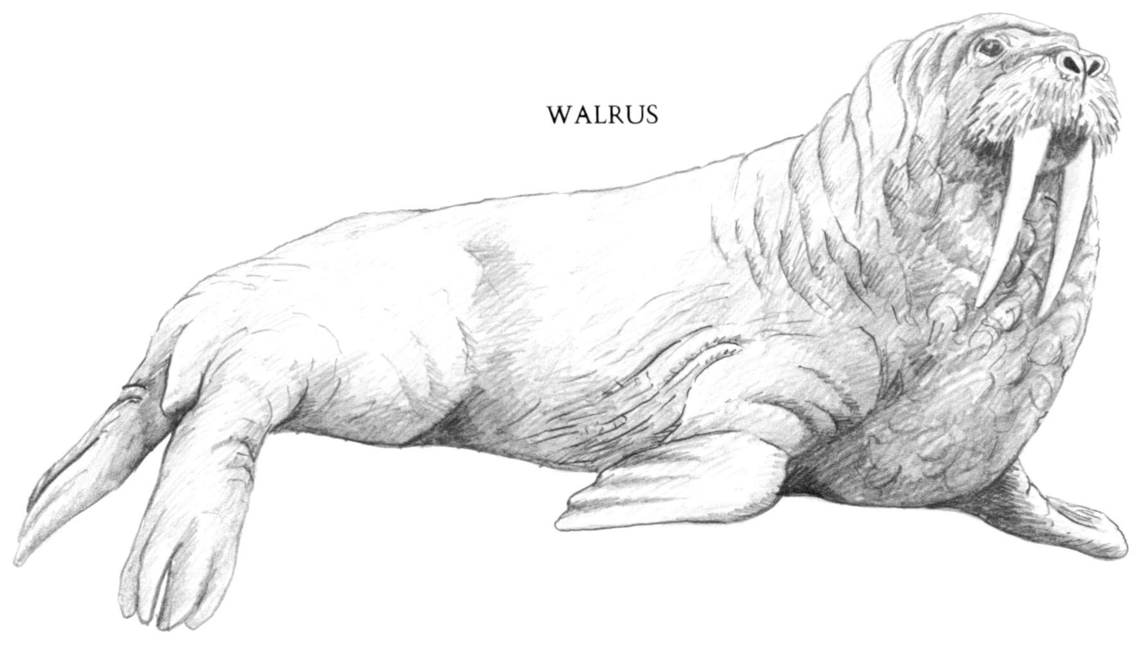
WALRUS

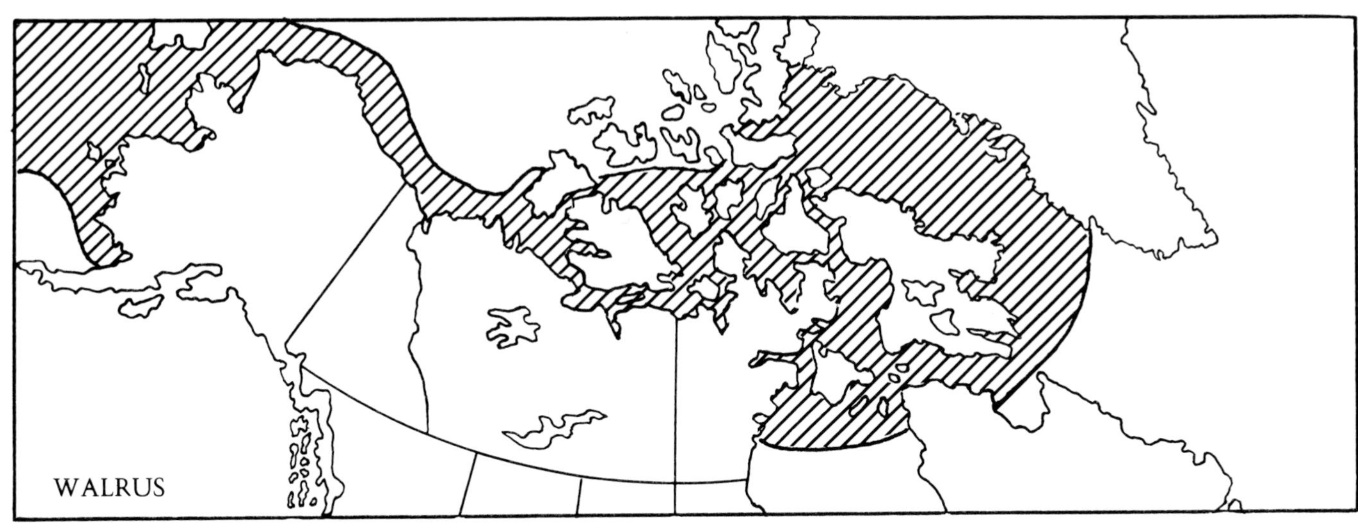
WALRUS

Order Artiodactyla

The artiodactyls (cloven-hoofed mammals) include most of the so-called big game species of North America. These are the animals that mainly supported the Native American aborigines and in turn provided food for the fur brigades and later pioneers who explored and ultimately colonized the continent. Some species, like the bison and muskox, were exploited almost to extinction. But under the protection of modern conservation laws, all native artiodactyls have recovered to the point where not one is on the endangered list.

Nearly all species are locally abundant enough to furnish some sport hunting. Four species—white-tailed deer, mule deer, elk, and moose—supply most of the big-game hunting in North America and at the same time put millions of pounds of good meat on dining tables. These four species are particularly abundant because they thrive in brushfields and scrub growth that develops after logging or other disturbance of forest lands. On the other extreme are species like bison, muskox, caribou, bighorn sheep, mountain goats, and pronghorn antelope, which are best adapted to live in undisturbed virgin vegetation (prairie, tundra, alpine), areas that generally have suffered modification by human activities. These "climax species" are now reduced in range and abundance, more as a result of adverse changes in habitat than by hunting or direct removal.

All artiodactyls here listed, except the peccaries, are classed as "ruminants." They share the following characteristics (Schmidt and Gilbert 1978):

1. Four-chambered, complex stomach;
2. Cud chewed and regurgitated once to several times before the final swallowing;
3. Metacarpals and metatarsals fused into a cannon bone;

4. Horns or antlers usually present, at least in one sex;
5. Incisors and canines usually absent in upper jaw;
6. Thirty-two or 34 teeth, depending on presence or absence of upper canines; and
7. Brittle and hollow hair, shed twice annually.

The peccaries and pigs are quite different from the ungulates in having relatively simple stomachs, which do not permit rumination or regurgitation of food for rechewing. They have more teeth, including upper incisors and canines, and differ in other anatomical details.

Family Tayassuidae (Peccaries)

COLLARED PECCARY, OR JAVELINA *(Dicotyles tajacu)*

See also pages 150–51.

RANGE: Desert mountain ranges of southern Arizona, New Mexico, and Texas south into Mexico

HABITAT: Pine forest, juniper-oak association, and mesquite-cactus brushland of mountains and plains; rock and cave cover used when available.

REMARKS: The collared peccary is a highly social ungulate of semiarid lands, extending in range only a short distance northward into the United States from the main part of its range in Mexico. Herds, varying in size up to 30 individuals, are composed of all ages and sexes. The herds are organized as dominance hierarchies, social rank being determined by size (Sowls 1974). Females mate with several dominant males during estrus. Males seldom fight over mating privileges. Herd territories of several hundred hectares are defended by adults of both sexes. Communication by sound, musk scent, and bodily contact is well developed.

The diet consists of prickly pear, mast, mesquite beans, century plant, green plants, and tubers and roots. Variation in the temporal pattern and amount of rainfall results in changes in food abundance. Food availability in turn strongly influences ovulation rate and survivorship and is the primary natural controlling factor of population size. Water is taken when available, but in desert situations the animals often subsist on succulent vegetation. Peccaries afford little or no competition to livestock.

Mating is carried out all year, with a peak in January, February, and March. Most young are born in June, July, or August after a 20- to 21-week gestation. Females first become pregnant at 1½ years of age, and they bear 2 young (rarely 3 or 4) in their annual litter. Peccaries may live to be as old as 9 years in the wild.

Peccaries differ from their relatives the pigs in several obvious morphological characters. The dental formula of the collared peccary is $\frac{2\,1\,3\,3}{3\,1\,3\,3}$ = 38 teeth. The canine teeth are long and continuously sharpened as in pigs, but remain straight and do not protrude beyond the closed lips. Peccaries possess a large musk-secreting gland on the back, which functions in communication and marking of territory.

Under careful regulation of hunting, peccaries are reoccupying range from which they were extirpated. Their numerical status is such that legal hunting is permitted in

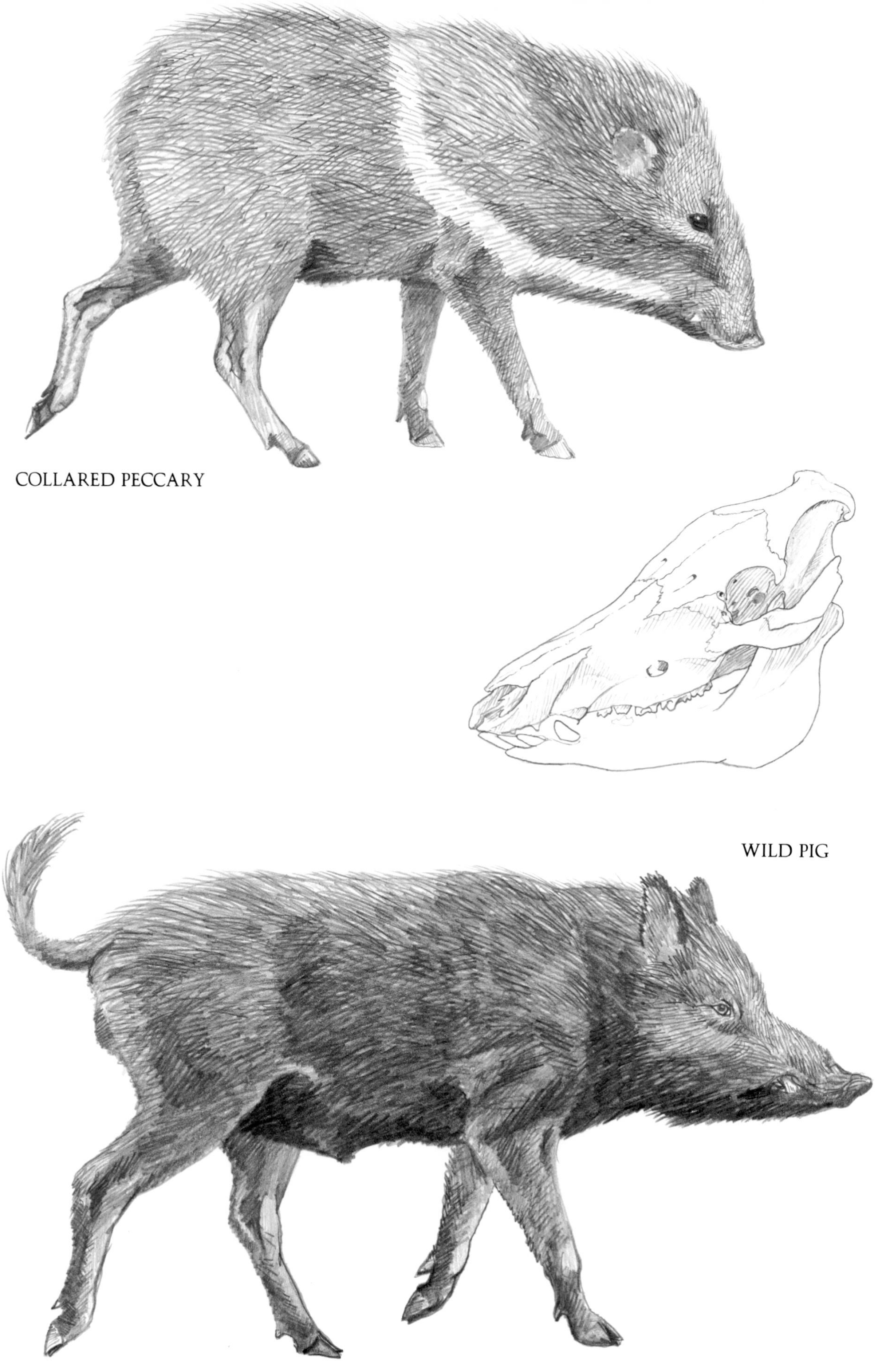
COLLARED PECCARY
WILD PIG

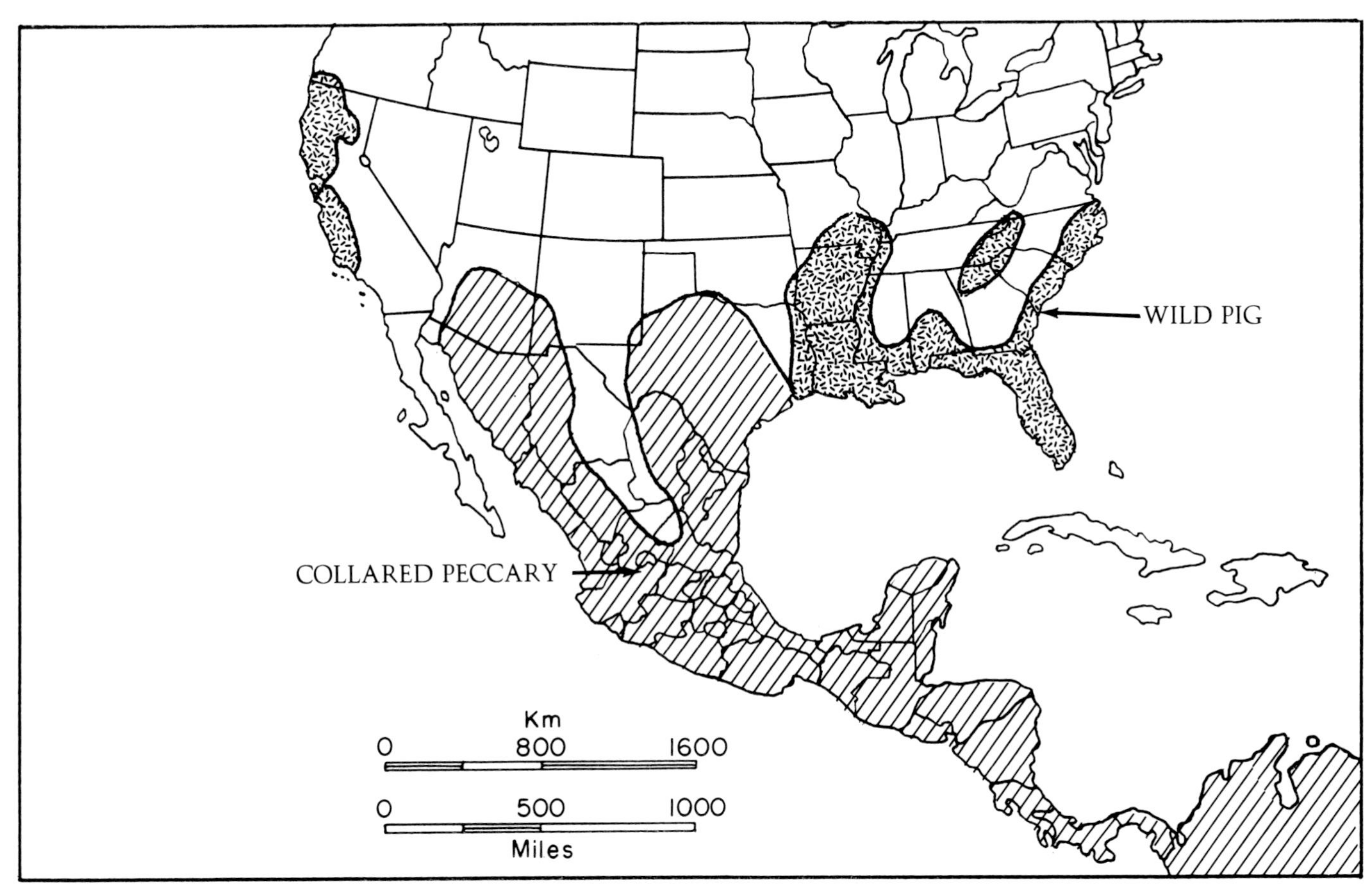
WILD PIG
COLLARED PECCARY
Km
0
800
1600
0
500
1000
Miles

all three states where they occur. The annual kill in Arizona has fluctuated recently from 2200 to 6600 and in New Mexico from 50 to 75. Kill statistics from Texas are not available, but most of the U.S. peccary population is in that state, and the kill probably exceeds that of Arizona.

Family Suidae (Pigs)

WILD PIG *(Sus scrofa)*

See also pages 150–51.

RANGE: Atlantic coastal plain from North Carolina to east Texas; Mississippi Valley and Ozark Mountains to central Missouri; Great Smoky Mountains; Coast ranges of California and foothills of Sierra Nevada; Hawaiian Islands

HABITAT: Coastal forests and marshes; mountains with mast-producing trees such as oak and beech; chaparral and other brushlands

REMARKS: Two varieties of pigs have been introduced in North America. Domestic pigs have strayed from the barnyard and adopted an independent or "feral" way of life; these are the most widespread and abundant. The European wild boar, introduced into North Carolina from Germany in 1912, has been transplanted to sites in Tennessee, Texas, and California. Both strains are still increasing and extending their ranges.

The wild boar and the domestic hog interbreed freely, and hybrids are common in areas where the two occur together. They share many characters of behavior and anatomy, such as the tooth formula: $\frac{3\,1\,4\,3}{3\,1\,4\,3} = 44$ teeth. They differ, however, in chromosome count (36 for wild boar, 38 for the pig) and in coat color. Young boars are striped brown and black, and adults are blackish agouti color; pigs come in a wide variety of colors. Wild-boar females, after they are a year old, produce one litter of 2 to 4 young each spring, but pigs may breed as young as 6 months and at frequent intervals produce litters averaging 6 young. Gestation is 4 months and lactation 3 to 4 months in both varieties (Sweeney *et al.* 1979). Females and young associate in well-organized groups, or "sounders." Adult males are solitary.

Pigs are omnivorous. Grass, forbs, mast, underground roots and tubers, invertebrates, and small vertebrate animals are eaten in approximately that order of importance. Carrion and garbage are taken freely when available. Rates of ovulation and weaning are directly related to the abundance and nutritive value of the diet: a big crop of acorns or beechnuts is followed by a big crop of piglets.

Feral pigs and wild boars are widely hunted for sport. In California, for example, a recent postcard survey of hunters indicates an annual pig kill approaching that of deer. Local densities of up to 40 animals per square kilometer and a high breeding potential permit a high harvest without reducing population level. High populations, however, create serious management problems by transmitting tuberculosis and other diseases to domestic livestock and by uprooting vegetation and accelerating soil erosion, by consuming agricultural crops and pasturage, and by disrupting natural ecosystems (Bratton 1975). In Hawaii, hogs are a primary menace to native vegetation and to associated endemic birds.

Family Cervidae (Deer and Relatives)

WAPITI, OR AMERICAN ELK *(Cervus elaphus)*

See also pages 154–55.

RANGE: Formerly southern Canada and most of the conterminous United States to extreme northern Mexico; now confined largely to mountainous areas in western North America.

HABITAT: Forest, woodland, and grasslands, from the highest Rockies in summer to low foothills and river valleys in winter

REMARKS: As regards habitat relations, elk are the most versatile and adaptable of all North American ungulates. They graze the prairies where they compete with bison and pronghorn; they are completely at home in forests and brushlands competing with deer (and locally with moose) for browse; and in summer they may invade the alpine realm of the bighorn and partake of the scant ground cover existing there. In pioneer times, the elk was a major " . . . source of meat and was one of the most widely distributed members of the deer family in North America" (Boyd 1978:11). Yet with the advance of civilization, the elk disappeared more rapidly than most other big-game mammals. At the end of the nineteenth century, it was virtually extinct. Though tolerant of a wide range of environments, the elk was nonadaptive to changes that came with settlement, including unregulated hunting. With the development of effective conservation programs, the elk has recovered in the wilder reaches of western mountains, where it is once again an important game animal.

Elk populations are socially structured, the cows and calves forming well-organized bands, each under the leadership of an old female (McCullough 1969). This matriarchal system is interrupted only during the brief period in spring when the cows separate to have their calves. Bulls associate with other bulls in loose groups, which break up in late summer when the males vie for dominance. During the rut in September, older bulls take over the cow bands as harems and herd them day and night. When a bull tires, he is driven out by a fresh bull who takes over the function of tending the harem and servicing the cows. Females first breed as two-year-olds, bearing the calf when they are three. Thereafter, they produce one calf a year (Murie 1951).

American elk were once named *Cervus canadensis*, but they are now considered conspecific with the European red deer, *Cervus elaphus*. Most elk in western mountains are Rocky Mountain Elk *(Cervus elaphus nelsoni)*. Many local herds were reestablished by transplanting breeding stock from Yellowstone National Park. In the Pacific northwest, the dominant form is Roosevelt elk *(C. e. roosevelti)*. These two races supply most of the elk hunting. In California, a very small race persists—the Tule elk *(C. e. nanodes)*—in a few scattered bands. Several races originally present in the eastern and southwestern United States are now extinct.

Elk dentition differs from that of deer by including the upper canines, which are the teeth worn on watch fobs by members of the Elks Lodge. The formula is $\frac{0\,1\,3\,3}{3\,1\,3\,3} = 34$ teeth. Male elk of the larger varieties weigh 300 to 400 kilograms; cows are somewhat smaller.

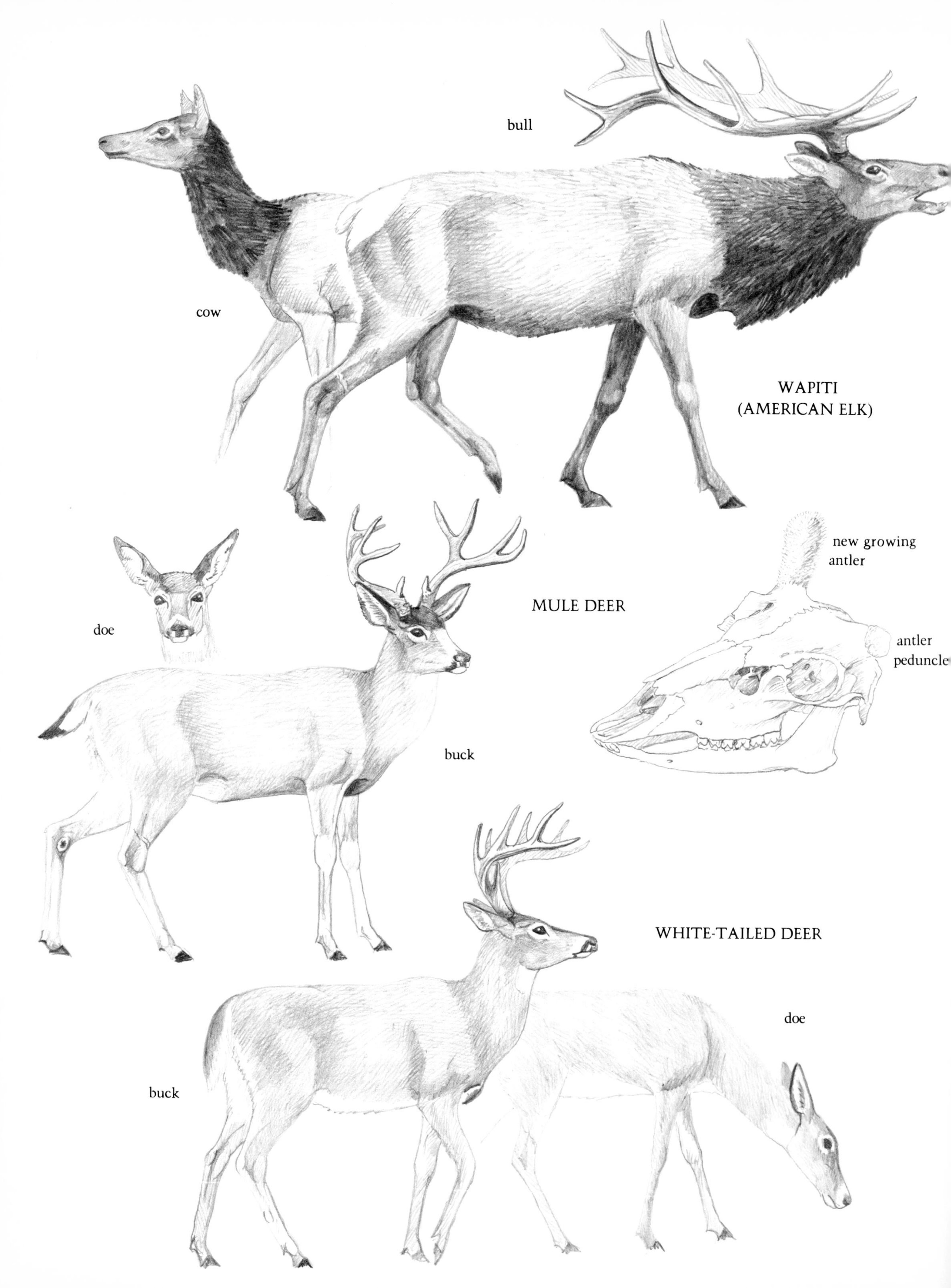
bull
cow
WAPITI
(AMERICAN ELK)
new growing
antler
MULE DEER
doe
antler
peduncle
buck
WHITE-TAILED DEER
doe
buck

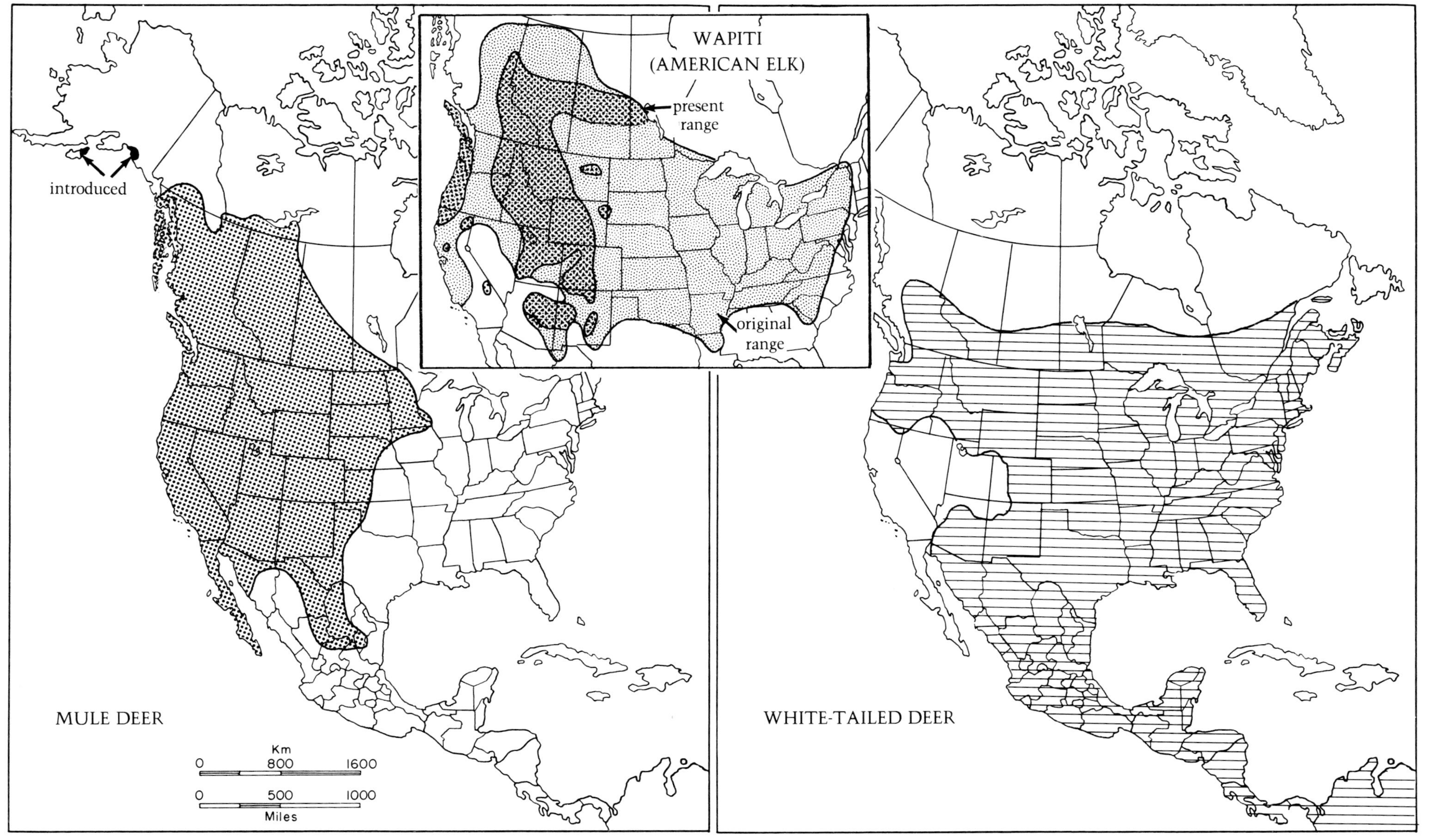
introduced
WAPITI
(AMERICAN ELK)
present
range
original
range
MULE DEER
WHITE-TAILED DEER
Km
0
800
1600
0
500
1000
Miles

MULE DEER *(Odocoileus hemionus)*

See also pages 154–55.

RANGE: Western Canada and the United States southward into Mexico; the range in the midwestern United States is steadily progressing eastward into Minnesota, Iowa, and Wisconsin.

HABITAT: Mountains, forests, brushlands, and wooded riverbottoms

REMARKS: The mule deer has evolved into several well-defined subspecies or races, adapted to different local habitats and climates. The smallest of these races, called the black-tailed deer *(O. h. columbianus)*, is so distinct that in California it was long classed as a separate species, until it was proven to hybridize freely with contiguous populations. The largest race, the Rocky Mountain mule deer *(O. h. hemionus)*, frequents the Canadian and United States Rockies, west to the Sierra Nevada and south to New Mexico. Different authorities recognize from 5 to 9 other races, but all are members of the mule deer species.

During the period of active plant growth, mule deer eat forbs and green grass, along with fresh sprouts of some shrubs and trees. In the dormant season (winter, or summer drought) they eat primarily browse, or the past year's growth of certain shrub species. The woody plants that supply this crucial part of the seasonal diet vary from place to place, but some of the prominent genera of "browse plants" are *Ceanothus, Purshia, Prunus, Salix, Artemisia,* and *Juniperus.* The more palatable and nutritious browse plants are high in protein and soluble carbohydrates. Good browse plants must also be low in volatile oils that inhibit the digestive action of rumen microbes. The microbial flora plays an essential role in deer nutrition by breaking down cellulose to digestible carbohydrates. Even plants of one species may vary in nutritive value according to growth stage, the youngest sprouts usually being the most palatable and digestible. A mature stand of chamise *(Adenostoma)* supports few deer. But if the area burns, the new chamise sprouts are highly nutritious and the population of deer increases rapidly (partly by influx, of course, but partly by higher birth and survival rates among the resident deer). Population levels of deer are largely determined by the quality of diet available to the individual doe.

The mating season, or "rut," in California blacktails occurs in October. Fawns appear 7 months later, in May, when the spring foliage is at peak growth. In the Rocky Mountains, mating occurs in November–December and fawning in June–July, after the snow has melted and the does have migrated back up to mountain meadows. Each local population has evolved a mating cycle that optimizes habitat conditions for the lactating doe and the new fawn. Among female mule deer, only animals 18 months or older breed. A few old bucks do most of the breeding as they move about the range seeking receptive does. Mule deer do not form harems like elk. The bucks are opportunistic breeders.

The tooth formula of mule deer, and of most of their relatives, is $\frac{0\,0\,3\,3}{3\,1\,3\,3}$ = 32 teeth. Shortly after birth, the deciduous "milk teeth" erupt (3 lower incisors, 1 incisiform canine, and 3 upper and 3 lower premolars). These teeth serve the fawn during the period of weaning, with most of the chewing being accomplished by the opposing third premolars. The molars emerge slowly, becoming functional as the animal approaches one year of age. In the second year, the milk teeth are shed, and new permanent teeth take their places. During this process, a deer's age can be judged by the stage of tooth molt. The age of older deer can be estimated by the amount of tooth wear.

The mule deer is the most numerous big-game mammal in western North America. The precise population is unknown, but must number in the millions. In recent years, two million hunters annually harvest more than 500,000 mule deer, with an estimated yield of 22.5 million kilograms (50 million pounds) of good meat. Additionally, the species contributes significantly to the enjoyment of people who hunt the deer and to the many more whose pleasure derives from seeing this graceful animal.

WHITE-TAILED DEER *(Odocoileus virginianus)*

See also pages 154–55.

RANGE: Throughout southern Canada, most of the United States except the southwest, and all of Mexico except Baja California

HABITAT: Forests, woodlands, and brushlands, from the boreal zone to the low tropics

REMARKS: The white-tailed deer is the most adaptable, most widely distributed, most numerous, and most important big-game mammal in North America. It thrives in a wide range of habitats and withstands a substantial hunting harvest. When range conditions are favorable, it has a high rate of reproduction—much higher than the mule deer, since well-fed whitetail fawns readily mate and give birth to young as yearlings. One or two fawns are born after the 7-month period of gestation. The 30 recognized subspecies of whitetails vary enormously in size, from 200 pounds (91 kilograms) in Canada to 70 pounds (32 kilograms) in Chihuahua. Local populations have breeding cycles adjusted to climatic conditions; peak of fawning may be as early as May in midcontinent to as late as August in Chihuahua.

White-tailed deer eat almost exclusively browse in winter, supplemented by fruit, acorns, and other mast when available. In farming country, the deer make good use of crop residues such as corn, wheat, or soybeans. Forbs are consumed in summer, but grass is much less important to this animal than to western mule deer. Removal of forest or mature brush may stimulate second-growth of shrubs and tree reproduction, which provides ideal forage for whitetails. So logging or fire can lead to increase in deer populations. Good management dictates that deer numbers should be regulated in balance with available forage, since too many deer can severely damage their own range. To reduce excess populations, it is often necessary to shoot some of the does as well as bucks—a situation that provokes sentimental opposition from uninformed citizens.

MOOSE *(Alces alces)*

See also pages 158–59.

RANGE: Most of Canada, Alaska, and forested areas in northern United States (i.e., northern New England and the Lake States, Montana, and Wyoming)

HABITAT: Moist forests, swamps, and muskegs, particularly in areas of willow

REMARKS: This largest member of the deer family seems to be maintaining a stable continental population. Although moose numbers are lower than in primitive times, due to overhunting and to removal of forests, especially in the southern parts of

MOOSE
bull
cow
CARIBOU
cow
bull
bone core
new horn
PRONGHORN
doe
buck

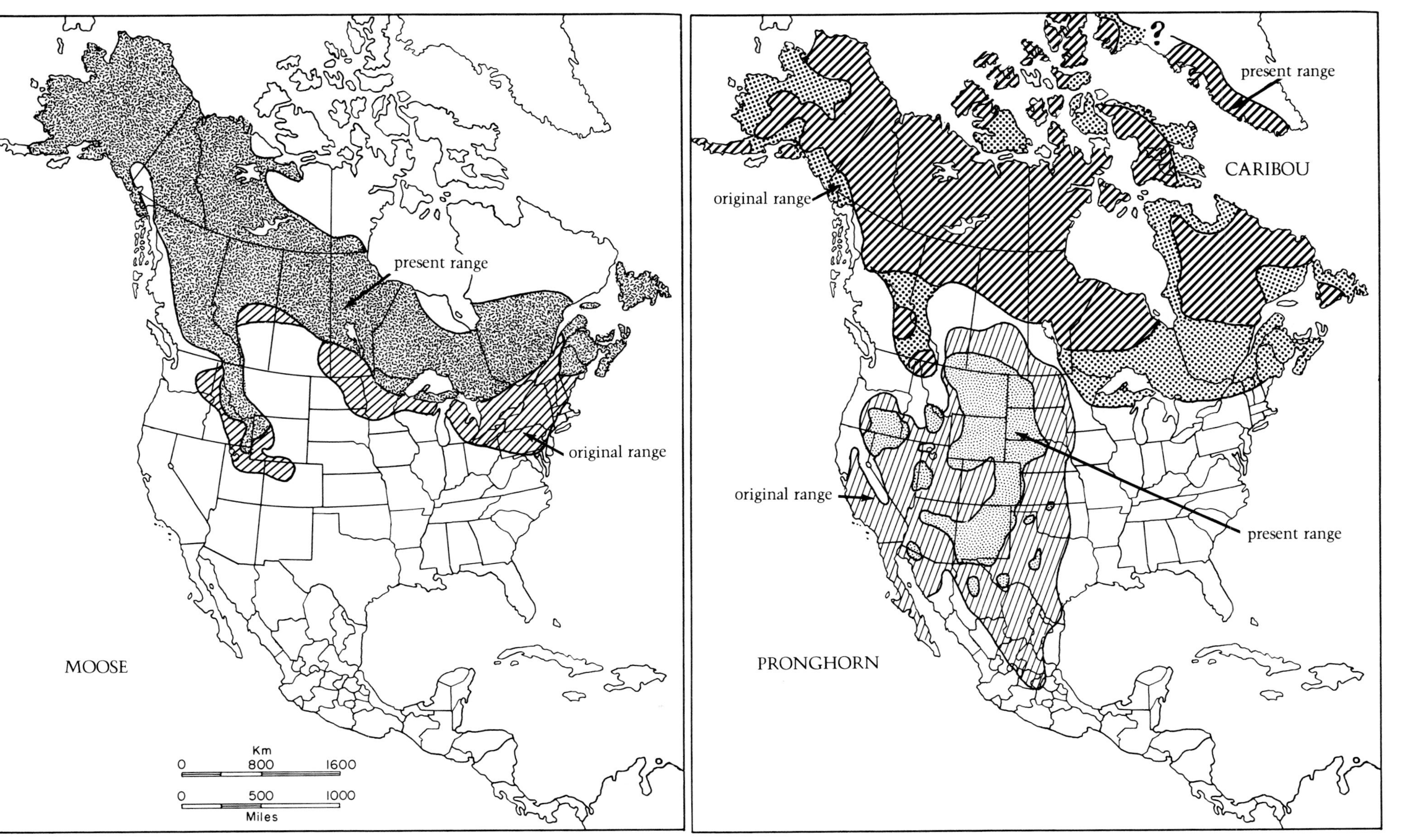
MOOSE
present range
original range
Km
0
800
1600
0
500
1000
Miles
CARIBOU
present range
?
original range
PRONGHORN
original range
present range

the range, enforcement of modern game regulations has permitted moose to recover from previous population lows. In fact, under some circumstances in which predators have been removed and not replaced by hunter harvesting, moose have become so abundant that they have destroyed their winter food supply and starved in large numbers. Such a catastrophe occurred on Isle Royale in northern Michigan. When wolves later took up residency on Isle Royale, they adopted moose as their primary winter prey. Both wolves and moose have since maintained healthy populations, without the interference of hunters.

Moose constitute one of the most important sources of meat for "subsistence" hunters in the wilds of Alaska and Canada. A bull moose, weighing as much as 600 kilograms, may feed several families in the course of a long northern winter. In some areas, wolves compete with man for moose as prey. Where pressure from hunters is strong, as in southcentral and western Alaska, game agencies sponsor wolf-reduction programs from time to time. Further management problems ensue where trains and automobiles pass through traditional moose wintering grounds and accidental collisions with moose are frequent. The Alaska Railroad, for example, kills hundreds of moose each winter along tracks in the Matanuska-Susitna Valley.

Cows generally bear a single calf, although two are sometimes observed. Females can breed at two years of age, and usually produce an offspring annually thereafter. Except for a brief rut in the fall, adult moose are solitary and avoid each other (Peterson 1955).

Moose feed largely on browse in winter—willow, birch, and aspen being three of the most important forage plants. In summer, moose eat a variety of forbs and aquatic plants such as water lilies (Peek *et al.* 1976). Willows frequently invade new burns in the coniferous forest, and moose often are most abundant around such burns just as deer are. In fact, deer, elk, and moose can all be designated as "successional" game species—adapted to thrive on early stages of forest succession (e.g., brush). In contrast, caribou, bighorn sheep, mountain goats, and bison are "climax" species, which do best on undisturbed climax vegetation.

CARIBOU *(Rangifer tarandus)*

See also pages 158–59.

RANGE: Alaska, Canada, and Greenland; formerly also in New England, the Lake States, and southeastern Canada

HABITAT: Arctic and alpine tundra, and boreal forest

REMARKS: Originally caribou traveled about the north country in herds estimated in millions. Besides being gregarious, the barren-ground populations have always been mobile and restless, moving freely over the tundra in summer and shifting southward into the conifer forests in winter. Indians and Eskimos depended heavily on the caribou for food and hides. With the introduction of modern rifles, caribou were severely overhunted and populations declined precipitously. Equally serious to the welfare of the animals was the loss of winter range caused by man-set fires. In 1891 and 1892 the United States government imported domesticated reindeer from Finland to replace the vanishing caribou in the economy of Alaskan Eskimos. The reindeer increased and destroyed winter range for themselves and for the remaining caribou, further exacerbating the problem. The caribou have never recovered their original numbers and remain at a relatively low level in both Alaska and Canada. Hunting and wolf predation hold down current numbers and prevent reoccupation of some areas of range from which they were extirpated.

Caribou are unique among the deer family in that both sexes bear antlers. During the fall rut, males vie for dominance in the vicinity of female groups. After breeding activity subsides, the males in small groups tend to drift away from the big herds of females. Antlers are shed and new ones grown in preparation for the next breeding season. In the sterile tundra soils, calcium is often in short supply. So caribou eat their own shed antlers, or even bones of dead animals, to acquire materials needed to grow another massive rack. In summer, mosquitoes and biting flies are a major scourge of caribou, sometimes causing herds to stampede across the tundra or up a mountain slope in a vain effort to escape.

Family Antilocapridae (Pronghorn)

PRONGHORN ANTELOPE *(Antilocapra americana)*

See also pages 158–59.

RANGE: Originally in the western half of North America, including southern Canada and northern Mexico; now in scattered populations in the Great Basin and Rocky Mountain states, and marginally into Canada and Mexico

HABITAT: Open plains and desert scrub

REMARKS: Pronghorn antelope populations are currently maintaining their numbers far below pre-settlement level. Preemption of habitat by fences, grazing, highways, and agriculture has restricted recovery of numbers and ranges after drastic reductions by hunting during the settlement of the west. Restrictions on hunting, however, and redistribution of breeding stock by game agencies have been responsible for reoccupation of some ranges and modest recovery in pronghorn numbers.

Pronghorns of both sexes and all ages have complex visual, acoustic, and olfactory signals and displays, which are used in territorial and dominance relations (Kitchen 1974). Males defend territories in prime habitat for much of the year. Bucks successful in holding territories frequented by does during the fall rut accomplish most of the breeding. Males younger than three or four years of age and those unable to acquire territories gather into bachelor herds in marginal habitat. Does, accompanied by their fawns (single or twin) born in the spring, form their own groups, socially independent of the males.

The pronghorn is the only bovid- and antelopelike form in the world that sheds its horns. Males discard the horny sheath each winter, permitting the prong to grow higher on the main shaft of the horn. Females have minute horns or none at all. Pronghorn dentition is the same as that of deer and the closely related bovids: $\frac{0\,0\,3\,3}{3\,1\,3\,3} = 32$ teeth.

Pronghorns feed largely on forbs; browse constitutes a less important food. Grass is taken only in small quantities. There is considerable overlap in diet between pronghorns and domestic sheep, but relatively little between pronghorns and cattle, which are principally grass eaters.

Pronghorns are renowned for their speed and have been clocked up to 100 kilometers (60 miles) per hour, although 65 kilometers per hour is a more usual top speed.

Family Bovidae (Bison and Relatives)

BISON, OR AMERICAN BUFFALO *(Bison bison)*

See also pages 164–65.

RANGE: Originally extended from northcentral Canada to the Gulf of Mexico, and from the eastern Piedmont westward to the northwestern Great Basin. The species is currently scattered in hundreds of herds on preserves and commercial ranches in Canada and the United States.

HABITAT: Open grassland

REMARKS: From a population of about 75 million before the arrival of the Europeans, bison were reduced to approximately 800 animals in the late 1880s, mostly by commercial slaughter on the plains between 1870 and the disappearance of the herds in 1884. Now, about 30,000 bison exist, half of them in Canada and half in the United States.

Bison are gregarious. Dominance hierarchies are maintained among the herd bulls by means of fighting, especially during the mating rut in July and August (Lott 1974). Females weigh 320 to 400 kilograms and bear their first calf at three years of age. Single calves are born yearly, usually in May, on the wintering ground in the case of migratory herds. Males reach 900 kilograms (one ton) and are capable of breeding at about four years of age. Most breeding is accomplished by older bulls.

Bison graze on grass and sedges primarily. All members of the Bovidae have the dental formula $\frac{0\,0\,3\,3}{3\,1\,3\,3}$, which is the same as in deer (Cervidae).

Like other members of the Bovidae (sheep, goats, and cows), the bison has true horns that are never shed. The living bony core is covered by a permanent keratinous sheath that grows slowly and continuously. Both sexes have horns.

MOUNTAIN GOAT *(Oreamnos americanus)*

See also pages 164–65.

RANGE: Southeastern Alaska and the southern Yukon southward through British Columbia to the northernmost Rockies and Cascades in the United States; introduced in central Rockies and on several islands in Alaska.

HABITAT: Inaccessible mountains and crags, usually above timber line

REMARKS: Not a true goat, this species is closely related to the Old World mountain antelope. It is a sure-footed and skillful climber. Mountain goats live almost exclusively in the high alpine zone where slopes are so steep and winds so strong that snow does not accumulate and cover the sedges, grasses, forbs, and low shrubs on which the goat feeds. Females bear one or, rarely, two kids, first breeding at the age of two years (Banfield 1974).

Both sexes carry sharp horns. Adult males use theirs in sometimes fatal flank-to-flank fighting for dominance and mating prerogatives over groups of females. Females use their horns to acquire and maintain social position among other nannies and docile billies.

Although never abundant, mountain goats are maintaining their numbers better than bighorn sheep. The fortunate status of mountain goats is a result of their living year round in areas too rough for domestic livestock and too inaccessible for development by recreationists. As long as hunting is carefully regulated, the mountain goat is in no danger of depletion. Currently, an estimated 16,000 mountain goats live in the United States and as many more are in Canada.

MUSKOX *(Ovibos moschatus)*

See also pages 164–65.

RANGE: Current natural range is Canadian arctic mainland and islands, and the coast of northern Greenland. Former range included Alaska's North Slope to the west shore of Hudson Bay. Introduced to Iceland, Spitsbergen, Nunivak Island in Alaska, and Kargulen Islands in Antarctica.

HABITAT: Tundra

REMARKS: Muskoxen are social ungulates. Cows with their offspring up to two years of age form the nuclei of herds. Herds also contain several bulls and may range in size up to 50 animals, although 12 to 24 is the average (Tener 1965). Bulls are usually found singly or in small herds. At six years of age and older, males engage in ramming contests for possession of groups of females in the August rut. Females reach reproductive maturity at three or four years of age and bear a calf every second year. The single calves are dropped from late April to the end of May.

Herds move up to 3 kilometers per day in search of shrubs and sedges. Some grasses and forbs are also eaten. Migrations between summer and winter ranges are short, not exceeding 80 kilometers.

Muskoxen possess striking adaptations for problems encountered in the Arctic. The coat consists of an inner fleece, and an outer layer of coarse hair up to 45 to 62 centimeters long. The long, downswept horns and boss of horn across the skull in both sexes are used in defense against wolves as well as in combat among males. Muskoxen faced with attacking wolves typically turn their heads toward the predators in a tight circle, with young on the inside. Natural mortality is caused mostly by starvation in heavy winter snow and by wolf predation. Populations typically consist of only 10 to 15 percent calves, half of whom do not survive their first year. Maximum muskox age is 25 years.

Although the muskox has been protected in Canada since 1917, recovery of numbers and range has been slow because of the species' low reproductive rate. An estimated 10,000 muskoxen now roam arctic Canada. A nucleus herd was brought from Greenland to Alaska, where a substantial population has accrued on Nunivak Island. Breeding stock is now being transplanted to various points in northern Alaska. Excessive numbers of muskoxen on Nunivak are damaging the range, and there is pressure to permit limited hunting.

BISON
(AMERICAN BUFFALO)
growth rings
MOUNTAIN GOAT
MUSKOX

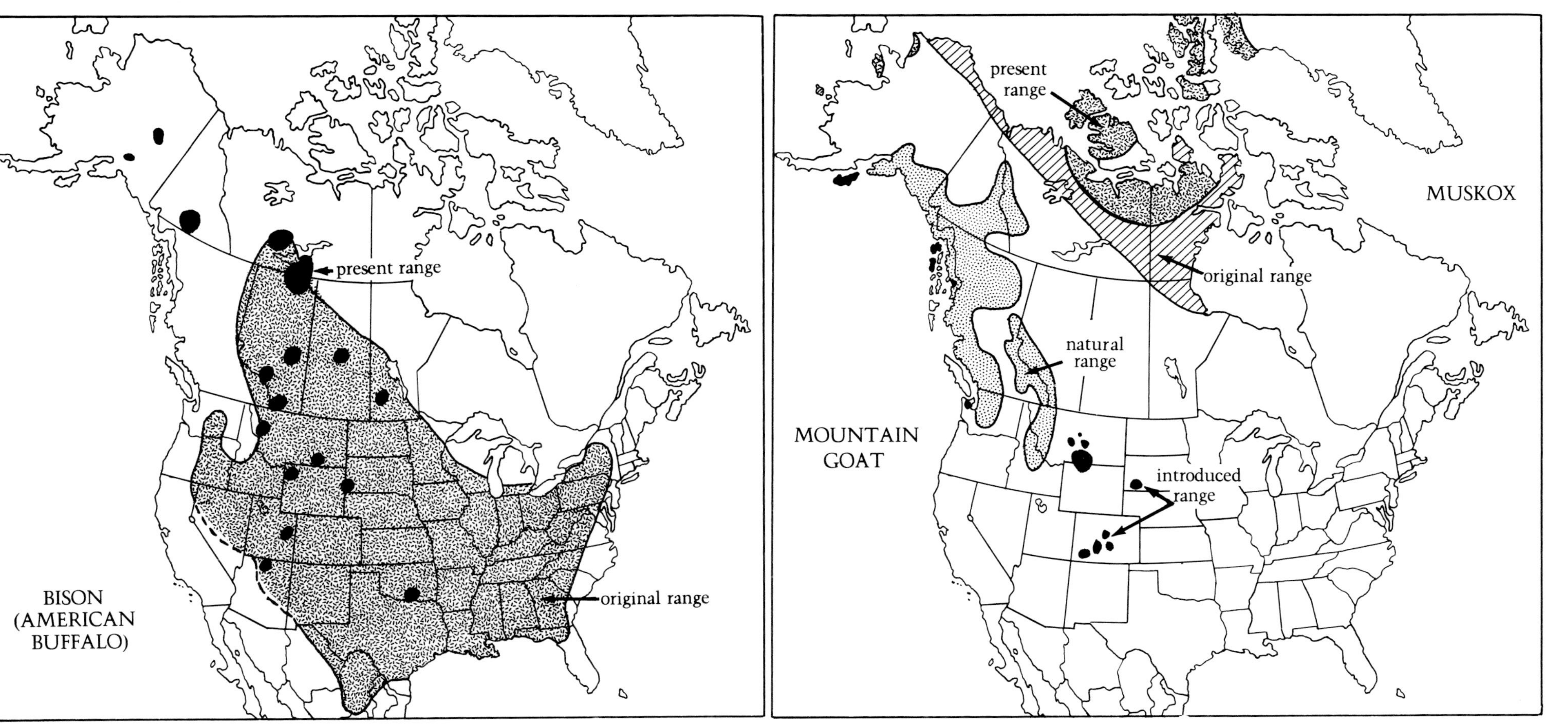
present range
original range
BISON
(AMERICAN
BUFFALO)
present
range
original range
MUSKOX
natural
range
MOUNTAIN
GOAT
introduced
range

BIGHORN SHEEP *(Ovis canadensis)*

See also pages 168–69.

RANGE: Originally, range extended from British Columbia to northern Mexico, and from the eastern slopes of the Rocky Mountains to the Cascades and Sierra Nevada; in the southern parts of its range, currently restricted to small pockets.

HABITAT: Alpine and subalpine zones of mountains; desert mountain ranges and canyons

REMARKS: The bighorn sheep is one of the most highly evolved ungulates, and yet it is among those most harmed by man's influence. Bighorns have an advanced social system in which old rams with the largest horns dominate all other sheep and maintain a social order. In this hierarchy, enforced by head-to-head-clash fights among rams, breeding is the prerogative of the dominating males. The massive horns, attaining weights of 10 kilograms, grow more in summer than in winter and show annual rings by which the animals can be aged. Females have small horns. Ewes and lambs band separately from adult rams, the two groups mingling only during the 3-week rut in autumn.

Females first mate as two- or three-year-olds and drop their single lamb after a 175-day gestation period. Under excellent conditions of weather and range, lamb-to-ewe ratios may approach 100:100, and average adult ages are low (e.g., six years). In declining populations, the ratio is as low as 30:100 (Geist 1971), and the average adult is older.

Sheep populations in the mountains are ultimately controlled by food. Bighorns eat coarse herbs and forbs of climax-plant communities. Overgrazing and preemption of low-elevation winter ranges by.livestock result in malnutrition and dispose bighorns to scabies, lungworm, and a pneumonial form of *Pasteurella* bacteria. In the desert ranges, feral burros are decimating the vegetation. As a direct result, native bighorn sheep populations are disappearing. Despite protection from hunting, the numbers of bighorn sheep are declining almost everywhere. There is cause for serious concern over the future of this interesting and beautiful mammal in the United States and Canada.

DALL SHEEP *(Ovis dalli)*

See also pages 168–69.

RANGE: Alaska, Yukon territory, northern British Columbia

HABITAT: Mountains and treeless slopes

REMARKS: The natural history and behavior of Dall sheep is much like that of their southern relatives the bighorn sheep. Dall sheep, however, are slightly smaller, carry thinner horns, and wear white coats. The Stone sheep *(Ovis dalli stonei)* of southern Yukon and northern British Columbia is actually a gray subspecies of the Dall sheep.

Dall sheep populations remain near their original abundance, despite trophy hunting of the rams. Much less of their habitat has been preempted by man than is true of the bighorn sheep ranges, although the continued construction of transportation corridors in the Arctic and sub-Arctic threatens to disturb Dall sheep in their formerly inaccessible homes. On the other hand, large new national parks created in Canada and Alaska in the 1970s will preclude some development and protect sheep populations.

Dall sheep have fairly strict habitat requirements. Necessities include steep, barren mountainsides with occasional salt licks and areas that remain snow-free all year. Sheep concentrate on small open areas in winter where strong winds keep the sedges, grasses, and browse free of snow. For this reason, winters of heavy snow accumulation are a major source of lamb and yearling mortality and are responsible for geographical variation in sheep occurrences and population declines (Nichols 1978). Less important mortality factors are wolf predation and tooth disease in older sheep. Murie (1944) in Mount McKinley National Park, Alaska, discovered that a large proportion of the sheep skulls he picked up in the field were of old animals with necrotic (rotten) abscesses in their teeth and jaws. Apparently, individuals beyond nine or ten years of age are prone to such infirmities, become weakened, and are rapidly eliminated by wolf predation or accidents.

STONE SHEEP
DALL SHEEP
BIGHORN
ewe
ram
lamb
annual growth rings

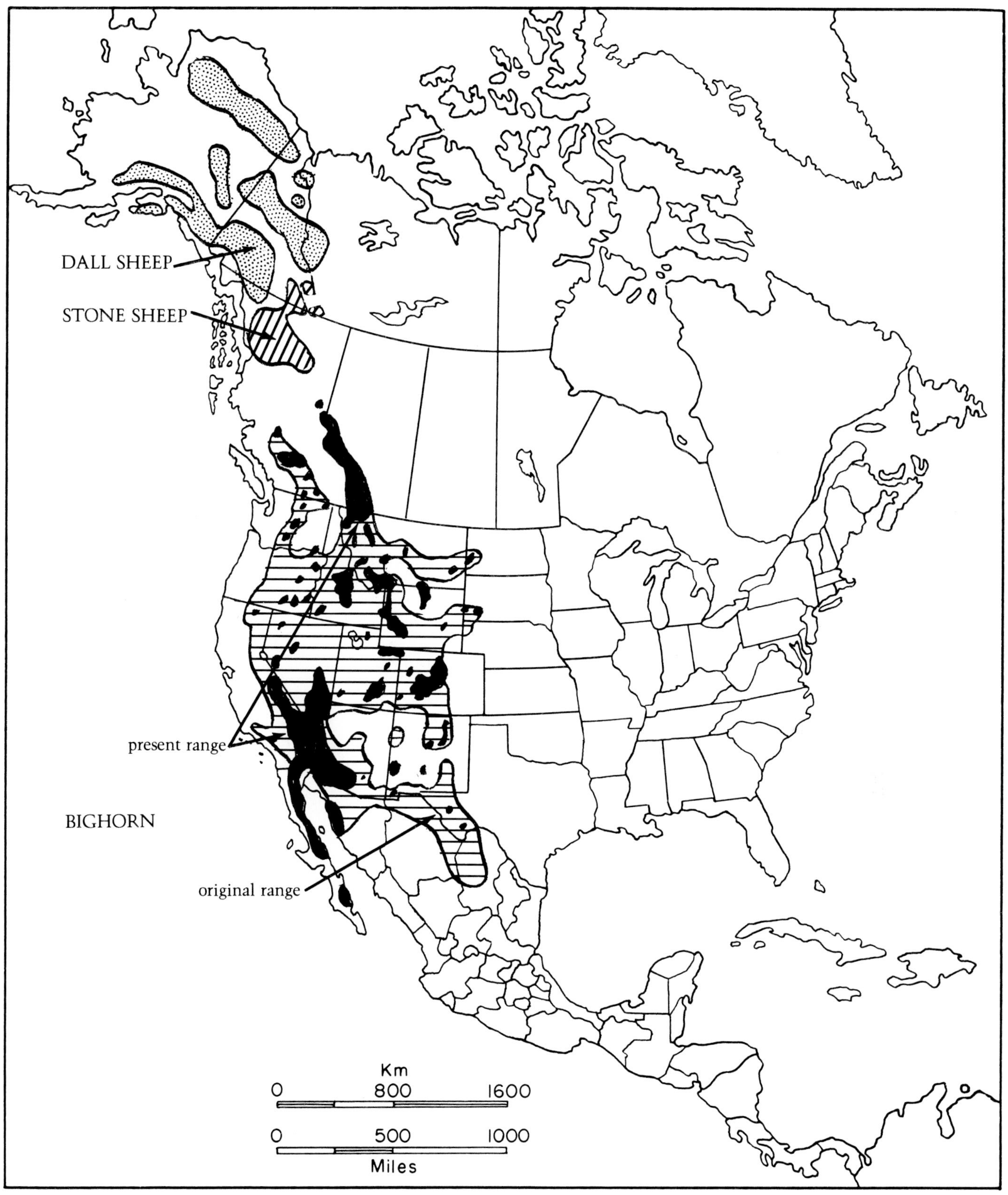
DALL SHEEP
STONE SHEEP
present range
BIGHORN
original range
Km
0
800
1600
0
500
1000
Miles

Order Rodentia

The rodents constitute a very large component of the American mammalian fauna. Though mostly small in body size, rodents occur in such variety and in such large numbers that they are the primary agents in the conversion of vegetation into protein. Only a few of the larger rodent species have significance as game species or fur bearers. The tree squirrels have been traditional fare since the days of Daniel Boone and the fabled squirrel rifle. Beavers, of course, were a primary incentive drawing the mountain men westward to capture furs for the eastern and European markets. The stovepipe hat of Lincoln's time was made of felted beaver fur. More recently, the musk-rat and the introduced nutria have become major fur species.

Family Sciuridae (Squirrels)

Gray Squirrels

EASTERN *(Sciurus carolinensis)*
WESTERN *(Sciurus griseus)*
MEXICAN (*Sciurus* sp.)

See also pages 172–73.

RANGE: Eastern half of the United States and southeastern Canada; western mountain slopes of Washington, Oregon, and California; lowland forests of Mexico and Central America

HABITAT: The eastern and western squirrels occupy hardwood forests, or mixed hardwood and conifers, containing oaks as one component. The Mexican gray squirrels are associated with tropical and subtropical forests.

REMARKS: The arboreal, secretive gray squirrels are of widespread occurrence in North America, frequenting many types of habitats. The eastern species occupies the widest range and has been most studied. Females bear two litters per year, of 2 or 3 young each, which when weaned enter a highly competitive society. Aggression and social dominance are primary controls of population size. Older squirrels with established home ranges tolerate neighboring residents but attack young dispersing weanlings (Thompson 1978). Only a few new squirrels, out of many that are weaned, find an unclaimed area and survive to enter the breeding population. The majority fall victim to predators, or to hunters who prefer young animals to adults.

The western gray squirrel suffered a catastrophic die-off in the 1920s, completely disappearing from much of its range in central California. The malady was not accurately diagnosed, but symptoms resembled scabies. In the 1950s, the population began to reoccupy its original range and is now back to pre-epidemic numbers. There is no strong tradition of squirrel hunting in the western United States, and *griseus* is little hunted.

The Mexican gray squirrels are highly variable in color, and are listed under many species names. "Not only are there striking differences in color between adjacent populations . . . but even in one locality there may be a great divergence of color patterns" (Leopold 1959:364). Squirrels are widely hunted in Mexico, where meat for the table is scarce.

Gray squirrels eat buds, fruits, seeds, and nuts of many kinds. Acorns are especially important in the more northerly ranges. In California, *griseus* is found to eat many kinds of mushrooms, truffles, and other fungi dug from the soil or gathered on the surface.

None of the tree squirrels hibernate, nor do they have cheek pouches for carrying food. They habitually bury food items in the ground for later recovery when food is scarce. Acorns in particular are thus stored for winter use.

The tooth formula of gray squirrels is $\frac{1\,0\,2\,3}{1\,0\,1\,3}$, the second upper premolar being only a tiny peg without real function.

Fox Squirrels

EASTERN *(Sciurus niger)*
ARIZONA *(Sciurus arizonensis)*
MEXICAN (*Sciurus* sp.)

See also pages 172–73.

RANGE: Eastern half of the United States; pine-oak highlands of Arizona and Mexico, south to Mexico City

HABITAT: Open hardwood forests or mixed oak and conifer forests; the eastern fox squirrel has been introduced in urban parks in California.

WESTERN GRAY SQUIRREL
EASTERN GRAY SQUIRREL
FOX SQUIRREL
RED SQUIRREL
ABERT SQUIRREL

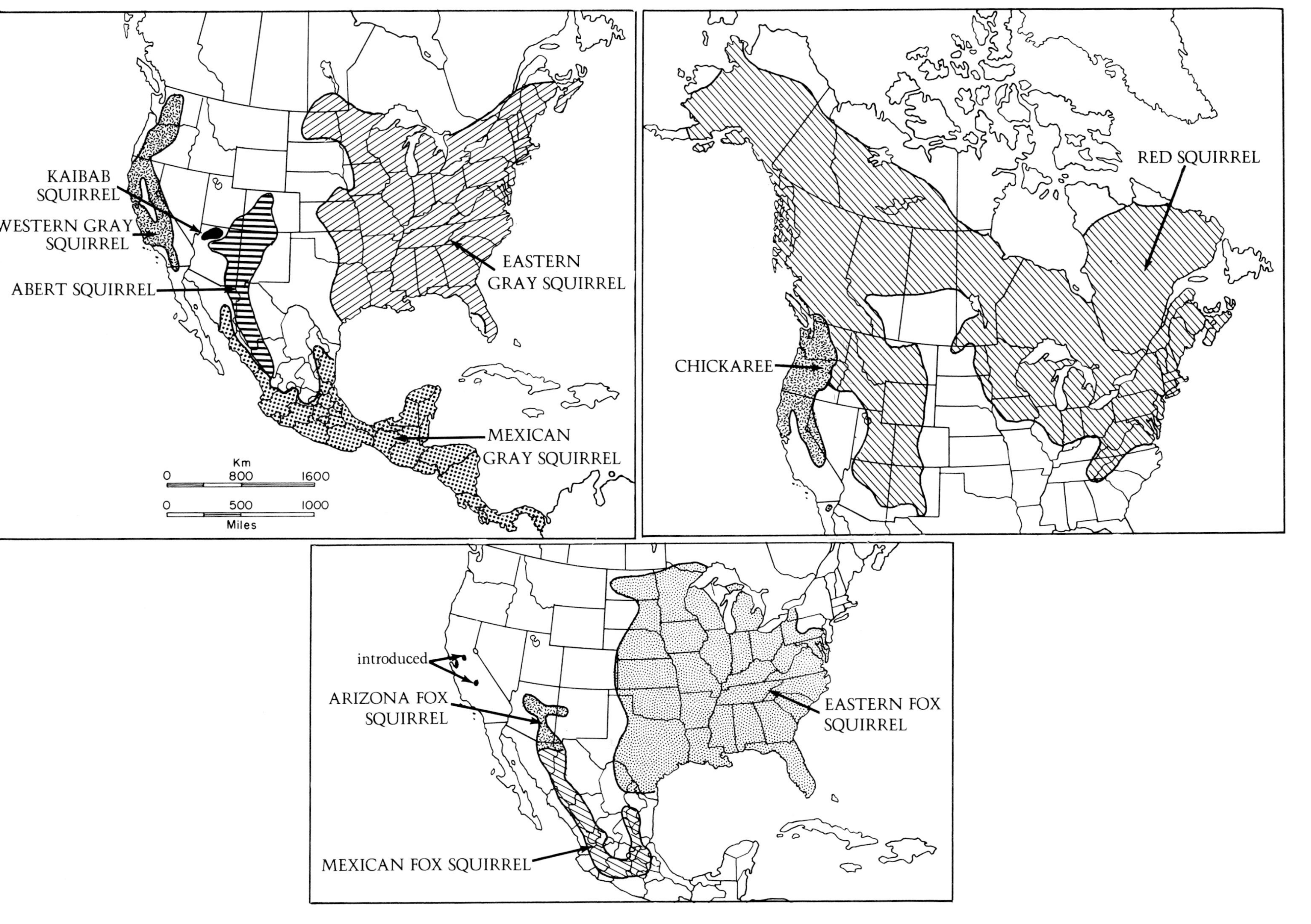
KAIBAB SQUIRREL
WESTERN GRAY SQUIRREL
ABERT SQUIRREL
EASTERN GRAY SQUIRREL
MEXICAN GRAY SQUIRREL
Km
0 800 1600
0 500 1000
Miles
RED SQUIRREL
CHICKAREE
introduced
ARIZONA FOX SQUIRREL
EASTERN FOX SQUIRREL
MEXICAN FOX SQUIRREL

REMARKS: The eastern fox squirrel is the largest of arboreal squirrels, some individuals weighing a kilogram or more. The forms occurring in Arizona and Mexico are smaller. All the fox squirrels tend to be polymorphic in pelage color, melanism being common, particularly in the southeastern United States and in the Mexican populations. Fox squirrels have two litters of young a year, and in other ways generally resemble gray squirrels in natural history. Food habits are much the same, with acorns being the most important single item. Fox squirrels are less shy than gray squirrels and adapt better to urban environments. Fox squirrels, in fact, are considered a pest when they raid backyard orchards and gardens, or bird feeders.

Fox squirrels differ from other arboreal squirrels in their dentition, lacking the second upper premolar or "peg" tooth. The formula therefore is $\frac{1\,0\,1\,3}{1\,0\,1\,3}$ = 20 teeth.

Tassel-eared Squirrels

ABERT *(Sciurus aberti)*
KAIBAB *(Sciurus kaibabensis)*

See also pages 172–73.

RANGE: Southern Rocky Mountains from Utah and Colorado south in the Sierra Madre Occidental to Durango; Kaibab squirrel is limited to the Kaibab Plateau on the north side of the Grand Canyon.

HABITAT: Yellow-pine forest

REMARKS: Abert squirrels occur sparsely in mature yellow-pine forests. Rarely are they numerous enough to offer much hunting. The Kaibab squirrel is an aberrant, isolated population of the tassel-eared tribe that has evolved a white tail, but otherwise closely resembles the typical Abert type. The Kaibab squirrel is particularly rare and is fully protected.

Tassel-eared squirrels are unique in food habits: they cut twigs of yellow-pine trees and eat the cambium layer after peeling off the rough bark. When other foods such as acorns or pine cones are available, the squirrels take them readily. But in winter or in other times of scarcity, they can make do with pine twigs. Some individual pine trees are clearly more palatable than others, but the chemical basis of preference is not understood.

Tassel-eared squirrels build bulky nests of leaves and twigs in the upper branches of tall pine trees. Cavities in hollow oaks may be used for denning. In the nests or dens, females rear their litters of 3 or 4 young, born in spring. There is some question whether tassel-eared squirrels have a second litter. The general scarcity of these squirrels suggests a low reproductive rate.

Pine Squirrels

RED SQUIRREL *(Tamiasciurus hudsonicus)*
CHICKAREE *(Tamiasciurus douglasii)*

See also pages 172–73.

RANGE: The red squirrel ranges throughout boreal and alpine forests from northern Alaska to southern New Mexico and Tennessee. The chickaree occupies similar habitat in the Pacific montane area.

HABITAT: Coniferous forest of pine, fir, or spruce, or a mixture

REMARKS: Red squirrels and chickarees are small tree-dwelling squirrels whose defended territories encompass a midden (pile) of stored green cones at the base of a tree and enough trees to provide a supply of cones and mast for a year (Smith 1970). They vigorously defend their territories, 1 to 2 hectares in size, against other members of the species or intruding gray squirrels and jays. In addition to seeds of cones, which are cut when green and then stored, these squirrels eat nuts, flowers, buds, fruit, mushrooms, catkins, sap, cambium, and small animals (such as fledgling birds).

A single litter is born annually in the north, and two are produced in the longer summers of the south. Four or 5 young are usual, but litters may be as large as 8 and as small as one. Young that are fortunate and skillful enough to acquire their own territory will reproduce at one year of age. Squirrels unable to find an undefended area with suitable resources perish.

Although pine squirrels destroy seeds and some young trees by girdling, they also aid the forest by distributing seeds, and they serve as an important source of food for avian and mammalian predators. Bears profitably rob their massive middens of stored cones, and Native American women in the north utilize their colorful pelts for decorating baskets and clothing. But perhaps most importantly, the melodious scolding voice of this busy little forest dweller, and its pert and sassy demeanor, lend color to the otherwise drab boreal landscape.

Family Castoridae (Beaver)

BEAVER *(Castor canadensis)*

See also pages 176–77.

RANGE: Throughout Canada and the United States, except tundra

HABITAT: Rivers, streams, and lakes bordered by hardwood forage plants

REMARKS: For almost two centuries, beaver pelts spurred the exploration of the American West. This largest North American rodent, originally numbering about 60 million, was exterminated over vast areas of its range. The species has since recovered somewhat and is common in the north, the western mountains, and the northeastern United States. The present population is probably between one and two million, since the annual yield of pelts is over half a million. Beavers have not been restored along the Atlantic seaboard or in much of the Ohio River basin.

BEAVER
MUSKRAT
NUTRIA

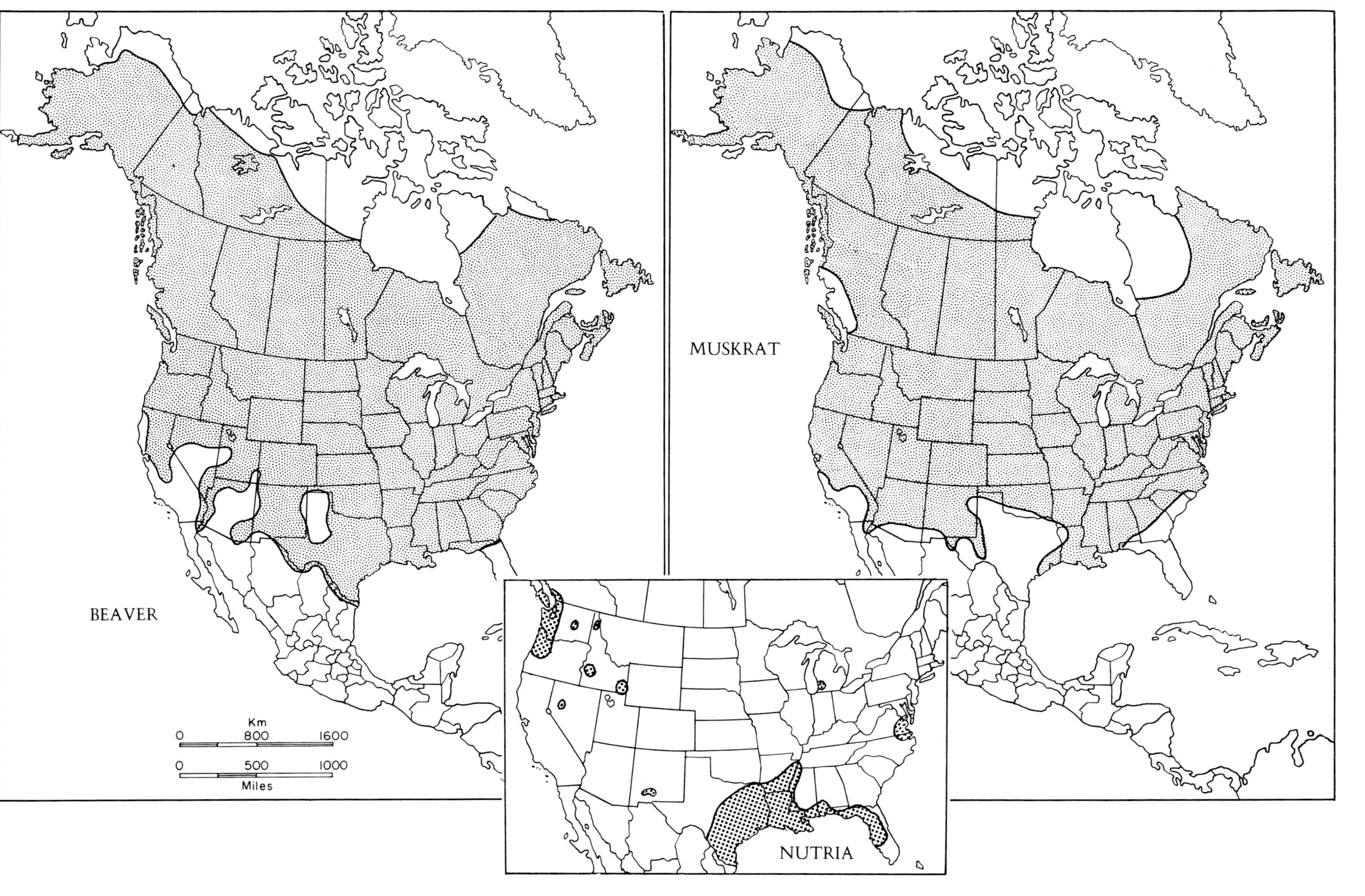
BEAVER
Km
0
800
1600
0
500
1000
Miles
MUSKRAT
NUTRIA

Beavers are aquatic but go on land to cut trees whose cambium layer they eat. Aspen and willow are primary foods, but alder and even oaks and conifers may be utilized. Upland beavers build dams on streams to impound water for storing food and for safety from predators; these animals live in lodges built of sticks and mud, or in bank burrows. Lowland beavers on large bodies of water normally live in bank burrows. One litter of 2 to 6 young is born in late winter after 4 months gestation. In their second year, the young set out to establish new colonies, leaving their parents with the new litter. Young may first breed at 21 months. The beaver is one of the two mammals that mate for life; the other is the wolf.

Grown beavers weigh up to 25 or 30 kilograms. They have webbed hind feet and a broad, flat tail for swimming and to "whack" the water as a danger warning. The tooth formula is $\frac{1\,0\,1\,3}{1\,0\,1\,3}$ = 20 teeth. The sharp, heavy incisors are effective in chiseling away wood. An intestinal flora helps the animal digest cellulose.

In addition to being valuable fur bearers, beavers store water in the high country and thereby help maintain stream flow in summer and fall. In some situations, however, beaver dams block migrating salmon and steelhead. The dams, if poorly placed, create difficulties in irrigation. Bank burrows sometimes cause breaks in levees.

Family Cricetidae (Native rats and mice)

MUSKRAT *(Ondatra zibethica)*

See also pages 176–77.

RANGE: From the northern edge of the boreal forest in the Arctic to the southern United States

HABITAT: Fresh- and saltwater marshes, sloughs, lakes, and streams

REMARKS: From a numerical standpoint, the muskrat has been the most important fur bearer in North America. Approximately six million pelts are sold annually, bringing Canadian and United States trappers $22 million each year. Highest yields come from brackish marshes along the Gulf coast of Louisiana and from interior marshes in the Lake States.

Muskrats eat aquatic vegetation such as tules, cattails, rushes, and pondweeds. Their activities help maintain open water, which is used by waterfowl. The only serious damage caused by muskrats is their undermining of levees and dikes. Like beavers, which they resemble in appearance and habit, muskrats either live in bank burrows or else build houses by piling up cut stems of emergent plants. Litters average 6 young (1 to 11) and in warm climates there may be 3 litters a year. The tooth formula of the muskrat is $\frac{1\,0\,0\,3}{1\,0\,0\,3}$ = 16 teeth. For a discussion of predation, see the account of mink. A classic book on the muskrat was written by Errington (1962).

Family Capromyidae (Nutrias)

NUTRIA *(Myocastor coypus)*

See also pages 176–77.

RANGE: Southern South America; in the United States, introduced in Louisiana, mid-Atlantic seaboard, and in scattered western mountain valleys. The range is currently expanding.

HABITAT: Freshwater and brackish marshes

REMARKS: This large, muskratlike rodent was introduced into Louisiana as a fur producer in 1938. A population became established and began rapidly to increase (Lowery 1974). Nutrias were subsequently introduced into other areas of the country; nutria fur farms were organized, and a thriving trapping industry developed around this exotic rodent. Although the pelts are worth only about five dollars apiece at this writing, millions of dollars are paid for them annually, mostly to Louisiana trappers.

Litters average between 4 and 6 (range 3 to 12). In the south, breeding is year-round, with 2 or 3 litters produced annually. Nutrias reach sexual maturity in less than a year and before they have attained their adult weight of about 5 kilograms.

Nutrias build their burrows in riverbanks, and in levees and dams. They consume large quantities of vegetation, including sugar cane and rice in some instances. Alligators are the main predators of adults. The nutria tooth formula is $\frac{1\,0\,1\,3}{1\,0\,1\,3}$.

Order Lagomorpha

Hares and rabbits are second only to rodents in importance as herbivores. One or more species occurs in every part of North America. And though not as abundant as the small rodents, hares and rabbits are individually larger animals with consequent high biomass. Most of the medium-sized carnivores and the larger birds of prey consume hares or rabbits as an important part of their diet. Multiple litters of young permit these prey animals to maintain their populations in the face of heavy predation. Most lagomorphs, in addition to having ecologic significance, are hunted either for food or for sport. The eastern cottontail rabbit, in fact, supports more hunter-days of sport than any other species of game bird or mammal in North America.

Family Leporidae (Hares and rabbits)

SNOWSHOE HARE *(Lepus americanus)*

See also pages 182–83.

RANGE: Northern half of the continent with southward extensions down the Pacific ranges, Rocky Mountains, and Appalachians

HABITAT: Coniferous forests, thickets of aspen, alder, willow, and brush

REMARKS: The snowshoe, or varying, hare is a major prey and game animal in the northern part of its range. The number of snowshoe hares in a region fluctuates on an eight- to eleven-year cycle. In peak years, the animal is enormously abundant in boreal forests, and it supports in large part the heavy populations of fur bearers that periodically build up in the north. When the snowshoe hares have destroyed their food base, they die off (Pease *et al.* 1979). The fur catch continues high for one more year and then drops to a low level as the predators' numbers fall. Fluctuations in fur take, governed by the hare cycle, are strikingly illustrated in records of the Hudson Bay Company that go back to 1821 (Seton 1923).

Snowshoe hares are brown in summer and white in winter, changing colors by complete spring and fall molts. In the winter pelage, long, stiff hairs grow on the feet, protecting the feet from cold and supporting the hare on the snow.

Two or three litters of 2 to 4 young are born in the spring and summer; the frequency and size of the litters varies regionally. Young are born fully haired and arrive with eyes open, as with all members of the genus *Lepus*. Snowshoe hares first reproduce at one year of age.

In winter, the snowshoe hare feeds on bark and twigs of alder, aspen, willow, and other deciduous trees and shrubs and on the shoots of young evergreens. Various tender green plants are taken in summer.

The tooth formula is the same for all rabbits and hares, $\frac{2\ 0\ 3\ 3}{1\ 0\ 2\ 3}$. The second upper incisors are pegs situated behind the functional central pair. All hares and rabbits have this arrangement of teeth.

ARCTIC HARE: *Lepus arcticus* AND ALASKA HARE: *Lepus othus*

See also pages 182–83.

RANGE: Extreme northern fringe of the continent, in Alaska, Canada, and Greenland

HABITAT: Tundra

REMARKS: Arctic and Alaska hares are the largest lagomorphs, weighing up to 12 pounds (5.4 kilograms) or more. Like the snowshoe hare, they change coats seasonally: white in winter, gray in summer. They feed primarily on the low-growing tundra willows, eating leaves, twigs, and roots. Seasonally, they utilize grasses, sedges, and flowering herbs as available. In the northern part of their range, these large hares sometimes gather into loose bands of up to 120. Gestation time is unknown. Litters of from 4 to 8 are born in spring, secreted in nests in the tundra. After weaning, the young strike off on their own, protected from the arctic winds by their thick, dark coats. Many are taken by foxes, snowy owls, and other predators, as well as by Eskimos.

BLACK-TAILED JACKRABBIT *(Lepus californicus)*

See also pages 182–83.

RANGE: From Oregon east through Nebraska and south to central Mexico

HABITAT: Open brushlands, grasslands, and deserts; sparse populations occur in forested areas and chaparral.

REMARKS: The black-tailed jackrabbit is the common species known to nearly everyone in the western United States. When abundant, it can be a serious agricultural and range pest, making control necessary. Some principal foods are forbs, grasses (espe-

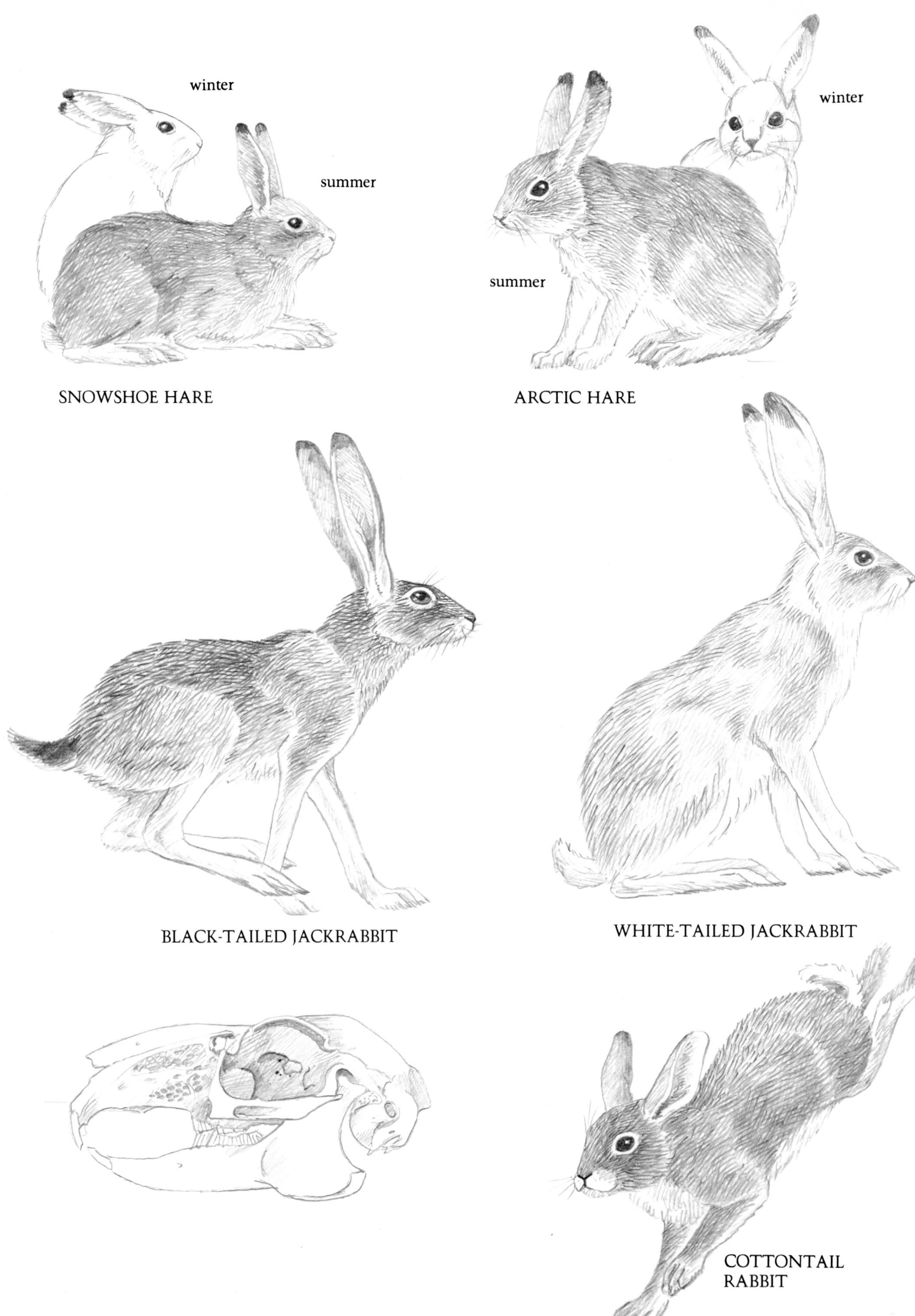
winter
summer
SNOWSHOE HARE
winter
summer
ARCTIC HARE
BLACK-TAILED JACKRABBIT
WHITE-TAILED JACKRABBIT
COTTONTAIL
RABBIT

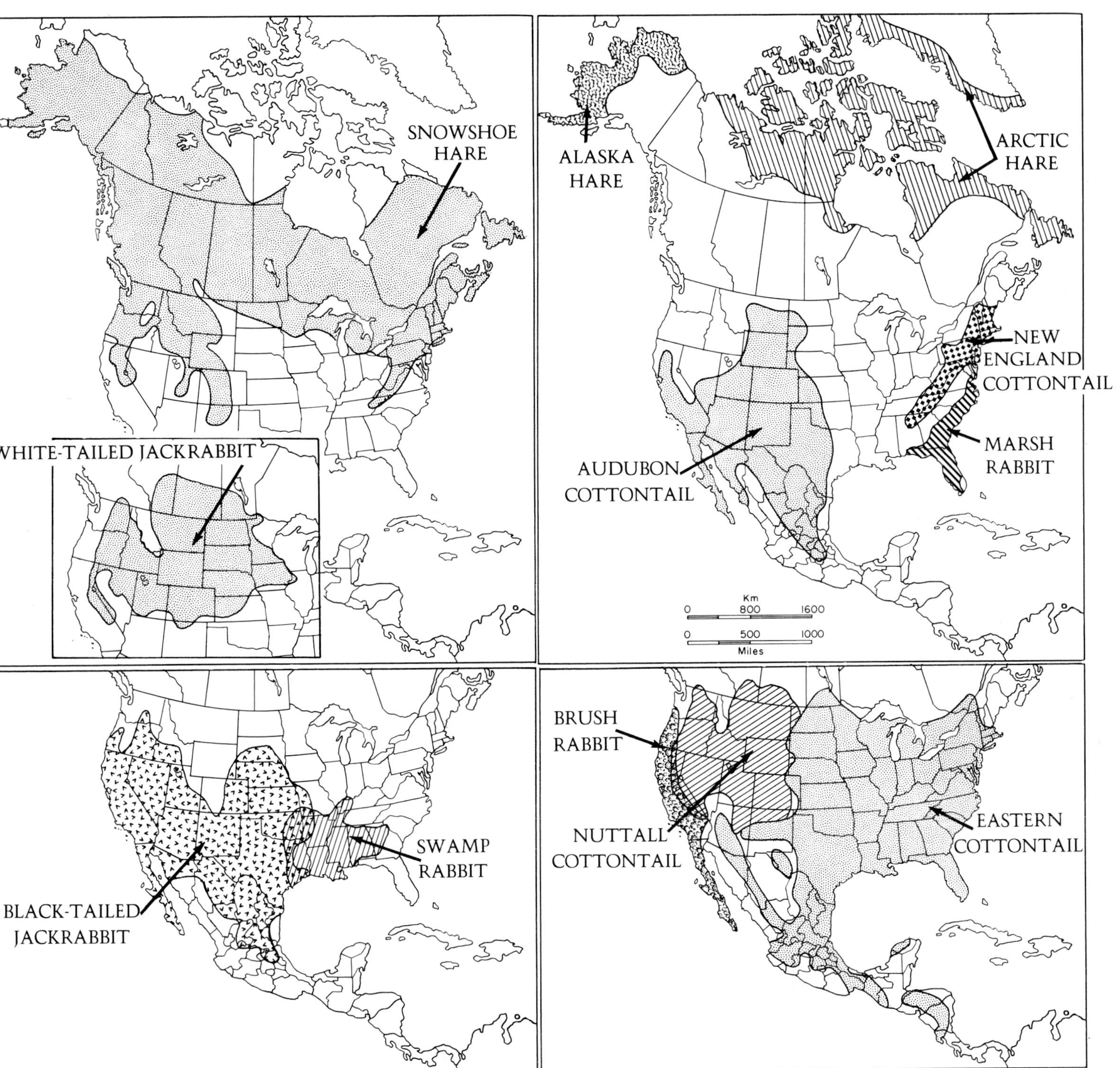
SNOWSHOE HARE
WHITE-TAILED JACKRABBIT
ALASKA HARE
ARCTIC HARE
NEW ENGLAND COTTONTAIL
MARSH RABBIT
AUDUBON COTTONTAIL
Km
0
800
1600
0
500
1000
Miles
BRUSH RABBIT
NUTTALL COTTONTAIL
EASTERN COTTONTAIL
SWAMP RABBIT
BLACK-TAILED JACKRABBIT

cially annuals), bark and twigs of many shrubs, and cultivated crops and fruit trees. Millions of jackrabbits are hunted to control damage or for target practice. In some parts of the country, jackrabbits are hunted for sport and are eaten.

Litter sizes average 3 to 4 young. They are produced when food is abundant. On irrigated land, breeding continues all year.

Jackrabbits are prey for all the large predators in their range. Half of the coyotes' diet may be jackrabbits where the hares are abundant.

WHITE-TAILED JACKRABBIT *(Lepus townsendii)*

See also pages 182–83.

RANGE: Northern plains and prairie provinces, through Rocky Mountains, Cascades, and Sierra Nevada

HABITAT: Sagebrush foothills, prairies, mountain meadows

REMARKS: The white-tailed jackrabbit prefers more open habitat than that chosen by the snowshoe hare, although in western mountains they often exist together. Whitetails are most at home in open brushlands such as the sage foothills of the Great Basin or in open alpine meadows. Black-tailed jackrabbits also share some ranges with whitetails but tend to select more arid grasslands or desert shrublands. In the northern parts of its range, the white-tailed jack turns white in winter. But in the south it remains grayish-brown.

Several litters of 3 to 6 young are produced in the warmer months of the year. Jackrabbit mothers scatter their precocial young to avoid attracting predators. The young are visited and nursed individually at night.

In southern Arizona and New Mexico, there occur some similar hares, which are called white-sided jackrabbits—*Lepus alleni* in Arizona and *Lepus gaillardi* in southwestern New Mexico. These species and several related forms extend their ranges southward through Mexico to the Isthmus of Tehuantepec.

Cottontail Rabbits

EASTERN COTTONTAIL *(Sylvilagus floridanus)*
NUTTALL COTTONTAIL *(Sylvilagus nuttallii)*
BRUSH RABBIT *(Sylvilagus bachmani)*
AUDUBON COTTONTAIL *(Sylvilagus audubonii)*
SWAMP RABBIT *(Sylvilagus aquaticus)*
MARSH RABBIT *(Sylvilagus palustris)*
NEW ENGLAND COTTONTAIL *(Sylvilagus transitionalis)*

See also pages 182–83.

RANGE: Throughout the United States and Mexico

HABITAT: Wide diversity of habitats

REMARKS: Rabbits of the genus *Sylvilagus* have evolved to occupy every sector of the continent south of the Canadian boreal-forest zone. Hall and Kelson (1959) list the seven species whose ranges are depicted in the accompanying map. Most of these species are locally abundant and highly productive. They contribute enormously to the sport and the table fare of American and Mexican hunters. The eastern cottontail alone yields an estimated annual kill of 25 million animals.

Cottontails can withstand such persecution because of their high rate of reproduction and their wide diversity in habitats. They occupy intensively cultivated croplands as well as deserts, forests, wildlands, and even suburban gardens. Four to 7 young are born 28 days after mating. The young are on their own in 3 weeks, and the mother immediately mates again. In this manner, and depending on the duration of mild weather and the availability of succulent food, 3 or more litters are weaned a year. A wide spectrum of forbs, grasses, and shrubs are acceptable cottontail fare.

Glossary

Age ratio Number of young per 100 adults

Allowable harvest Percentage of an autumn population that may safely be removed by hunting, leaving adequate breeding stock

Antlers Branched, cranial bony appendages of Cervidae that are shed and regrown annually. *See also* Horns; Pronghorn

Arthropods Invertebrate animals of the phylum Arthropoda, including insects, crustaceans, spiders, and related groups

Artiodactyla Cloven-hoofed mammals

Biomass Aggregate weight of animal bodies

Boreal Pertaining to the north; northern.

Breeding potential Maximum, unimpeded rate of increase of a species

Brood patch Defeathered, edemous area on belly of an incubating bird that facilitates warming of the eggs; feathers regrow after breeding season

Browse Twigs of woody shrubs or trees fed upon by ungulates

Bursa of Fabricius A ductless gland with a deep lumen (cavity), situated on the dorsal side of the cloaca of some young birds

Caecum Blind intestinal pouch in some birds and mammals, situated at the junction of the large and small intestines

Carnivore Meat-eating animal

Carrying capacity Habitat-imposed limit on the size of an animal population

Climax species Plants and animals characteristic of terminal stages of plant succession as dictated by local climate and soils (e.g., a mature forest, or arctic tundra)

Cloaca Posterior section of bird gut, into which the genital and urinary tracts open

Covey A flock of upland game birds that tends to remain intact

Cycle Periodic fluctuation in population density of a species

Cygnet Young swan

Delayed implantation Fertilized ovum residing for a time in the uterus of a female mammal before implanting and developing

Dimorphic Having two distinct forms in the same species (e.g., gray and brown phases of ruffed grouse)

Dump nest A bird nest to which two or more females of the same species contribute eggs

Eclipse plumage A female-like plumage assumed by male ducks in a postnuptial molt; a subsequent molt in autumn restores the characteristic male plumage

Exotic Not indigenous; from another part of the world

Feral Domestic animal reverted to wild state

Flyway Continental migratory pathway followed by birds

Gallinaceous Fowls belonging to the order Galliformes

Genetic adaptation Heritable characteristics that help a population accommodate to living in a specific environment

Guzzler Underground tank storing drinking water for wildlife

Herbivore Plant-eating animal

Herd An aggregation of hoofed mammals

Home range Area utilized by an individual animal or an organized group of animals (e.g., a pack of wolves, covey of quail)

Horns Unbranched, cranial appendages of Bovidae that are never shed. *See also* Antlers; Pronghorn

Intestinal flora Bacteria and protozoa residing in the intestinal tracts of birds and mammals that break down cellulose into simpler, digestible compounds

Invertebrates Insects, crustaceans, spiders, and other small animals without backbones. *See* Arthropods

Irruption A large, nonperiodic increase in numbers of a species

Juvenal Young, adjective

Juvenile Young animal, noun

Lagomorphs Hares and rabbits

Lek Arrangement of breeding males, each defending a small territory, to which females are attracted for mating

Mast Fruits or seeds produced by trees (e.g., acorns, beech nuts, madrone berries)

Melanism Dark pigment manifest in some animals (e.g., black wolf or black squirrel)

Mesic Moist or well-watered environment

Midden Cache of pine cones, acorns, or other tree mast assembled by a squirrel

Migratory Bird Treaty Act Congressional confirmation in 1918 of the Migratory Bird Treaty, signed with Great Britain (Canada) in 1916

Milk teeth Deciduous incisors, canines, and premolars that are replaced by permanent teeth when a mammal matures

Molar teeth Rear teeth of a mammal that are not molted or replaced

Monogamous Paired mating; having only one mate in a given breeding season

Monomorphic Sexes externally similar

Nest parasitism A female bird laying eggs in the nest of another species of bird

Omnivore Animal that eats both plants and animals

Opportunistic breeding Breeding at any season of the year when food supply and other conditions are favorable

Passerine Small birds of the order Passeriformes

Pectinate Comblike

Pelage Mammal fur

Phenology Seasonal sequence of plant development

Plumage Feather covering of a bird

Polygamous Having more than one mate in a given breeding season

Population turnover Annual rate of death and replacement in a population

Precocial Young vertebrates capable of locomotion immediately after hatching or birth (e.g., grouse chick)

Pronghorn Antelope of family Antilocapridae that sheds and regrows horn sheaths annually

Raptors Hawks and owls

Recreational hunting Hunting and killing of game for sport as well as for food

Rectrices Tail feathers of a bird

Refuge An area maintained for wildlife, usually closed to hunting. *See* Sanctuary

Remiges Flight feathers (primaries, secondaries) on the wing of a bird

Renesting A nesting attempt following an earlier failure the same season

Rut Mating season of ungulates

Sanctuary An area maintained for wildlife, closed to hunting. *See* Refuge

Sex ratio Number of males per 100 females

Species A group of animals capable of interbreeding

Speculum Area of color on secondary feathers of duck wing

Subsistence hunting Killing of game for necessary human food

Subspecies Segments of a species, recognizably different in morphologic and/or behavioral characteristics but still capable of interbreeding; also called a "race"

Successional species Plants and animals characteristic of early stages of plant succession (e.g., vegetation that springs up after a forest fire, and animals therewith associated)

Sympatric Closely related species coexisting on same area

Taxonomy Orderly classification of living organisms into related groups or taxa

Territory Area utilized by an individual animal, or group of animals, and defended from others of the same species

Wing coverts Small feathers on bird wing, covering the base of the flight feathers, sometimes differentially colored in young versus adult individuals and used to recognize age classes

Xeric Dry environment (i.e., desert)

Bibliography

ALDRICH, J. W., and DUVALL, A. J. 1955. *Distribution of American gallinaceous game birds.* U.S. Fish and Wildlife Service Circular 34. 30 pp.

ALISON, R. M. 1975. *Breeding biology and behavior of the oldsquaw* (Clangula hyemalis *L.*). Ornithological Monographs 18. 52 pp.

ALLEN, D. L. 1979. *The wolves of Minong: their vital role in a wild community.* Boston: Houghton Mifflin Co. 499 pp.

American Ornithologists' Union. 1957. *Check-list of North American birds.* Baltimore: Lord Baltimore Press. 691 pp.

AMMANN, G. A. 1957. *The prairie grouse of Michigan.* Michigan Dept. of Conservation, Technical Bulletin. 200 pp.

BANFIELD, A. W. F. 1974. *The mammals of Canada.* Toronto: Univ. of Toronto Press. 438 pp.

BELLROSE, F. C. 1976. *Ducks, geese, and swans of North America.* Harrisburg, Pa.: Stackpole Books. 543 pp.

BENGSTON, S.-A. 1966. *Field studies on the harlequin duck in Iceland.* Wildfowl Trust Annual Report 17:79–94.

BOLEN, E. G.; MCDANIEL, B.; and COTTAM, C. 1964. Natural history of the black-bellied tree duck *(Dendrocygna autumnalis)* in southern Texas. *Southwestern Naturalist* 9:78–88.

BOYD, R. J. 1978. American elk. In *Big game of North America,* eds. J. L. Schmidt and D. L. Gilbert, pp. 11–29. Harrisburg, Pa.: Stackpole Books. 494 pp.

BRATTON, S. P. 1975. The effect of the European wild boar, *Sus scrofa,* on gray beech forest in the Great Smoky Mountains. *Ecology* 56:1356–66.

BUMP, G.; DARROW, R. W.; EDMINSTER, F. C.; and CRISSEY, W. F. 1947. *The ruffed grouse: life history, propagation, management.* New York State Conservation Department. 915 pp.

CAMPBELL, H.; MARTIN, D. K.; FERKOVICH, P. E.; and HARRIS, B. K. 1973. *Effects of hunting and some other environmental factors on scaled quail in New Mexico.* Wildlife Monographs 34. 49 pp.

CLARK, T. W. 1978. Current status of the black-footed ferret in Wyoming. *Journal of Wildlife Management* 42:128–34.

CLAWSON, R. L.; HARTMAN, G. W.; and FREDRICKSON, L. H. 1979. Dump nesting in a Missouri wood duck population. *Journal of Wildlife Management* 43:347–55.

COTTAM, C. 1939. *Food habits of North American diving ducks.* U.S. Dept. of Agriculture, Technical Bulletin 643. 140 pp.

——, and TREFETHEN, J. B., eds. 1968. *Whitewings: the life history, status, and management of the white-winged dove.* Princeton: Van Nostrand Co. 348 pp.

CROWE, D. M. 1975. Aspects of aging, growth, and reproduction of bobcats from Wyoming. *Journal of Mammalogy* 56:177–98.

DEEMS, E. F., JR., and PURSLEY, D. 1978. *North American furbearers: their management, research, and harvest status in 1976.* College Park, Md.: Univ. of Maryland Press. 171 pp.

DELACOUR, J., and AMADON, D. 1973. *Curassows and related birds.* New York: American Museum of Natural History. 247 pp.

DREWIEN, R. C., and BIZEAU, E. G. 1977. Cross-fostering whooping cranes to sandhill crane foster parents. In *Endangered birds: management techniques for preserving threatened species,* ed. S. A. Temple, pp. 201–22. Madison: Univ. of Wisconsin Press. 466 pp.

EBERHARDT, L. E., and SARGEANT, A. B. 1977. Mink predation on prairie marshes during the waterfowl breeding season. In *Proceedings of 1975 Predator Symposium,* eds. R. L. Phillips and C. Jonkel, pp. 33–43. Montana Forest and Conservation Experiment Station, Univ. of Montana, Missoula. 268 pp.

EISENHAUER, D. I., and KIRKPATRICK, C. M. 1977. *Ecology of the emperor goose in Alaska.* Wildlife Monographs 57. 62 pp.

ELLISON, L. N. 1974. Population characteristics of Alaskan spruce grouse. *Journal of Wildlife Management* 38:383–95.

ERRINGTON, P. L. 1962. *Muskrat populations.* Ames, Iowa: Iowa State Univ. Press. 665 pp.

ERSKINE, A. J. 1971. *Buffleheads.* Canadian Wildlife Service Monograph Series 4. 240 pp.

FITZGERALD, B. M. 1977. Weasel predation on a cyclic population of the montane vole *(Microtus montanus)* in California. *Journal of Animal Ecology* 46:367–97.

GEIST, V. 1971. *Mountain sheep: a study in behavior and evolution.* Chicago: Univ. of Chicago Press. 383 pp.

GODIN, A. J. 1977. *Wild mammals of New England.* Baltimore: Johns Hopkins Univ. Press. 304 pp.

GULLION, G. W. 1960. The ecology of Gambel's quail in Nevada and the arid southwest. *Ecology* 41:518–36.

——. 1972. Improving your forested lands for ruffed grouse. Minnesota Agricultural Experiment Station publication 1439. 34 pp.

GUTIÉRREZ, R. J. 1980. Comparative ecology of the mountain and California quail in the Carmel Valley, California. *The Living Bird* 18:71–93.

——; BRAUN, C. E.; and ZAPATKA, T. P. 1975. Reproductive biology of the band-tailed pigeon in Colorado and New Mexico. *Auk* 92:665–77.

HALL, E. R., and KELSON, K. R. 1959. *The mammals of North America.* 2 vols. New York: Ronald Press. 1083 pp.

HENSEL, R. J.; TROYER, W. A.; and ERICKSON, A. W. 1969. Reproduction in the female brown bear. *Journal of Wildlife Management* 33:357–65.

HERRERO, S. M. 1979. Black bears: the grizzly's replacement? In *The black bear in modern North America*, pp. 179–95. New York: Boone and Crocket Club. 299 pp.

HOCHBAUM, H. A. 1944. *The canvasback on a prairie marsh.* Washington, D.C.: American Wildlife Institute. 201 pp.

HORNOCKER, M. G. 1970. *An analysis of mountain lion predation upon mule deer and elk in the Idaho Primitive Area.* Wildlife Monographs 21. 39 pp.

JEFFREY, R. G. 1977. Band-tailed pigeon *(Columba fasciata).* In *Management of migratory shore and upland game birds in North America*, ed. G. C. Sanderson, pp. 210–45. Washington, D.C.: International Assn. of Fish and Wildlife Agencies. 358 pp.

JENKINS, D.; WATSON, A.; and MILLER, G. R. 1963. Population studies on red grouse, *Lagopus lagopus scoticus* (Lath.) in north-east Scotland. *Journal of Animal Ecology* 32:317–76.

JOHNSGARD, P. A. 1973. *Grouse and quails of North America.* Lincoln: Univ. of Nebraska Press. 553 pp.

———. 1975. *Waterfowl of North America.* Bloomington: Indiana Univ. Press. 575 pp.

JONES, J. K.; CARTER, D. C.; and GENOWAYS, H. H. 1975. *Revised checklist of North American mammals north of Mexico.* Occasional Papers Museum Texas Tech. Univ. 28:1–14.

JONES, R. E., and LEOPOLD, A. S. 1967. Nesting interference in a dense population of wood ducks. *Journal of Wildlife Management* 31:221–28.

KEITH, L. B. 1963. *Wildlife's ten-year cycle.* Madison: Univ. of Wisconsin Press. 201 pp.

KENYON, K. W. 1969. *The sea otter in the eastern Pacific Ocean.* North American Fauna Series 68. New York: Dover Publications. 352 pp.

KITCHEN, D. W. 1974. *Social behavior and ecology of the pronghorn.* Wildlife Monographs 38. 96 pp.

LARSON, J. S., AND TABER, R. D. 1980. Criteria of sex and age. In *Wildlife Management Techniques Manual*, ed. S. D. Schemnity, pp. 143–202. The Wildlife Society, Washington, D.C. 686 pp.

LEHMANN, V. W. 1941. *Attwater's prairie chicken: its life history and management.* North American Fauna Series 57. 65 pp.

LEOPOLD, A. 1933. *Game management.* New York: Charles Scribner's Sons. 481 pp.

———. 1949. *A sand county almanac.* New York: Oxford Univ. Press. 226 pp.

LEOPOLD, A. S. 1959. *Wildlife of Mexico: the game birds and mammals.* Berkeley: Univ. of California Press. 568 pp.

———. 1977. *The California quail.* Berkeley: Univ. of California Press. 281 pp.

———, and HALL, E. R. 1945. Some mammals of Ozark County, Missouri. *Journal of Mammalogy* 26:142–45.

———, and MCCABE, R. A. 1957. Natural history of the Montezuma quail in Mexico. *Condor* 59:3–26.

LEWIS, J. C. 1977. Sandhill crane *(Grus canadensis).* In *Management of migratory shore and upland game birds in North America*, ed. G. C. Sanderson, pp. 4–43. Washington, D.C.: International Assn. of Fish and Wildlife Agencies. 358 pp.

LINDUSKA, J. P., ed., 1964. *Waterfowl tomorrow.* Washington, D.C.: U.S. Government Printing Office. 770 pp.

LINDUSKA, J. P. ed., 1964. *Waterfowl tomorrow.* Washington, D.C.: U.S. Government Printing Office. 770 pp.

LOTT, D. F. 1974. Sexual and aggressive behaviour of adult male American bison *(Bison bison).* In *The behaviour of ungulates and its relation to management.* Vol. 1, eds. V. Geist and F. Walther, pp. 382–94. International Union for the Conservation of Nature, New Series 24, Morges, Switzerland. 940 pp.

LOWERY, G. H., JR. 1974. *The mammals of Louisiana and its adjacent waters.* Kingsport, Tenn.: Louisiana State Univ. Press. 565 pp.

MARTIN, A. C.; ZIM, H. S.; and NELSON, A. L. 1951. *American wildlife and plants: a guide to wildlife food habits.* New York: McGraw-Hill. 500 pp.

McCULLOUGH, D. R. 1969. *The tule elk: its history, behavior, and ecology.* Berkeley: Univ. of California Publication in Zoology, vol. 88. 209 pp.

MECH, L. D. 1970. *The wolf: the ecology and behavior of an endangered species.* Garden City, N.Y.: Natural History Press. 384 pp.

MENDALL, H. L. 1958. *The ring-necked duck in the northeast.* Orono, Maine: Univ. Maine Studies, 2nd Series no. 73. 317 pp.

MOORE, R. E., and MARTIN, N. S. 1980. A recent record of the swift fox *(Vulpes velox)* in Montana. *Journal of Mammalogy* 61:161.

MURIE, A. 1940. *Ecology of the coyote in the Yellowstone.* Fauna of the National Parks 4. Washington, D.C.: U.S. Govt. Printing Office. 206 pp.

———. 1944. *The wolves of Mount McKinley.* Fauna of the National Parks 5. Washington, D.C.: U.S. Govt. Printing Office. 238 pp.

MURIE, O. J. 1951. *The elk of North America.* Harrisburg, Pa.: Stackpole Books. 376 pp.

NELLIS, C. H., and KEITH, L. B. 1968. Hunting activities and success of lynxes in Alberta. *Journal of Wildlife Management* 32:718–22.

———. 1976. Population dynamics of coyotes in central Alberta. *Journal of Wildlife Management* 40:389–99.

———; WETMORE, S. P.; and KEITH, L. B. 1972. Lynx-prey interactions in central Alberta. *Journal of Wildlife Management* 36:320–29.

NICHOLS, L. 1978. Dall sheep reproduction. *Journal of Wildlife Management* 42:570–80.

NOWAK, R. M. 1973. The return of the wolverine. *National Parks and Conservation Magazine* 47:20–23.

———. 1974. *The cougar in the United States and Canada.* Washington, D.C.: U.S. Fish and Wildlife Service, Office of Endangered Species. 190 pp.

ODOM, R. R. 1977. Sora *(Porzana carolina).* In *Management of migratory shore and upland game birds in North America,* ed. G. C. Sanderson, pp. 57–65. Washington, D.C.: International Assn. of Fish and Wildlife Agencies. 358 pp.

PALMER, R. S., ed. 1976. *Handbook of North American birds: waterfowl.* Vol. 2. New Haven: Yale Univ. Press. 521 pp.

PATTERSON, R. L. 1952. *The sage grouse in Wyoming.* Denver. Sage Books. 341 pp.

PEASE, J. L.; VOWLES, R. H.; and KEITH, L. B. 1979. Interaction of snowshoe hares and woody vegetation. *Journal of Wildlife Management* 43:43–60.

PEEK, J. M.; URICH, D. L.; and MACKIE, R. J. 1976. *Moose habitat selection and relationships to forest management in northeastern Minnesota.* Wildlife Monographs 48. 65 pp.

PELTON, M. R.; LENTFER, J. W.; and FOLK, G. E., eds. 1976. *Bears—their biology and management.* Morges, Switzerland: International Union for Conservation of Nature. 467 pp.

PETERSON, R. L. 1955. *North American moose.* Toronto: Univ. of Toronto Press. 280 pp.

RAUSCH, R. A., and PEARSON, A. M. 1972. Notes on the wolverine in Alaska and the Yukon Territory. *Journal of Wildlife Management* 36:249–68.

RILEY, G. A., and McBRIDE, R. T. 1972. A survey of the red wolf *(Canis rufus).* Washington, D.C.: U.S. Fish and Wildlife Service, *Special Scientific Report* 162. 15 pp.

ROSENE, W. 1969. *The bobwhite quail: its life and management.* New Brunswick, N.J.: Rutgers Univ. Press. 418 pp.

SANDERSON, G. C., ed. 1977. *Management of migratory shore and upland game birds in North America.* Washington, D.C.: International Assn. of Fish and Wildlife Agencies. 358 pp.

SCHMIDT, J. L., and GILBERT, D. L., eds. 1978. *Big game of North America: ecology and management.* Harrisburg, Pa.: Stackpole Books. 494 pp.

SCHORGER, A. W. 1955. *The passenger pigeon: its natural history and extinction.* Madison: Univ. of Wisconsin Press. 424 pp.

——. 1966. *The wild turkey: its history and domestication.* Norman, Okla.: Univ. of Oklahoma Press. 625 pp.

SEIDENSTICKER, J. C. IV; HORNOCKER, M. G.; WILES, M. V.; and MESSICK, J. P. 1973. *Mountain lion social organization in the Idaho Primitive Area.* Wildlife Monographs 35. 60 pp.

SETON, E. T. 1923. *Arctic prairies.* New York: Charles Scribner's Sons. 308 pp.

——. 1937. *Lives of game animals,* Vol. II. New York: Literary Guild of America. 746 pp.

SHELDON, W. G. 1967. *The book of the American woodcock.* Amherst: Univ. of Massachusetts Press. 227 pp.

SMITH, C. C. 1970. *The coevolution of pine squirrels* (Tamiasciurus) *and conifers.* Ecologic Monographs 40:349–71.

SOWLS, L. K. 1974. Social behaviour of the collared peccary, *Dicotyles tajacu* (L). In *The behaviour of ungulates and its relation to management.* Vol. 1, eds. V. Geist and F. Walther, pp. 144–165. International Union for Conservation of Nature, New Series 24. Morges, Switzerland. 940 pp.

STODDARD, H. L. 1931. *The bobwhite quail: its habits, preservation, and increase.* New York: Charles Scribner's Sons. 559 pp.

STORM, G. L.; ANDREWS, R. D.; PHILLIPS, R. L.; BISHOP, R. A.; SINIFF, D. B.; and TESTER, J. R. 1976. *Morphology, reproduction, dispersal, and mortality of midwestern red fox populations.* Wildlife Monographs 49. 82 pp.

STOUDT, J. H. 1969. Relationships between waterfowl and water areas on the Redvers Waterfowl Study Area. *Canadian Wildlife Reports* Series 6, pp. 123–31.

SWEENEY, J. M.; SWEENEY, J. R.; and PROVOST, E. E. 1979. Reproductive biology of a feral hog population. *Journal of Wildlife Management* 43:555–59.

TENER, J. S. 1965. *Muskoxen: a biological and taxonomic review.* Canadian Wildlife Service Monograph Series 2. 166 pp.

THOMPSON, D. C. 1978. Regulation of a northern grey squirrel *(Sciurus carolinensis)* population. *Ecology* 59:708–15.

TUCK, L. M. 1972. *The snipes: a study of the genus* Capella. Canadian Wildlife Service Monograph Series 5. 429 pp.

VERTS, B. J. 1967. *The biology of the striped skunk.* Chicago: Univ. of Illinois Press. 218 pp.

WALKINSHAW, L. H. 1949. *The sandhill cranes.* Bloomfield Hills, Mich.: Cranbrook Institute of Science Bulletin 29. 202 pp.

WEIGAND, J. P. 1980. *Ecology of the Hungarian partridge in north-central Montana.* Wildlife Monographs 74. 106 pp.

WRIGHT, P. L., and COULTER, M. W. 1967. Reproduction and growth in Maine fishers. *Journal of Wildlife Management* 31:70–87.

YOUNG, S. P. 1958. *The bobcat of North America.* Harrisburg, Pa.: Stackpole Books. 193 pp.

Index